P9-CFJ-189

H. G. Wells

Revised Edition

Twayne's English Authors Series

Kinley E. Roby, Editor

Northeastern University

TEAS 43

H. G. Wells

Revised Edition

By Richard Hauer Costa

Texas A & M University

Twayne Publishers • *Boston*

H. G. Wells, Revised Edition

Richard Hauer Costa

Book production by Elizabeth Todesco

Book design by Barbara Anderson

Printed on permanent/durable acid-free
paper and bound in the United States of
America.

Library of Congress Cataloging in Publication Data

Costa, Richard Hauer.
   H.G. Wells, Revised Edition.

   (Twayne's English authors series; TEAS 43)
   Bibliography: p. 164
   Includes index.
   1. Wells, H. G. (Herbert George), 1866–1946—
Criticism and interpretation.   I. Title.   II. Series.
PR5776.C6   1985   823'.912   84-25305
ISBN 0-8057-6887-4

For Jo

Contents

About the Author

Richard Hauer Costa is professor of English at Texas A&M University, where he has taught since 1970. He received the B.S. and M.A. degrees from West Chester (Pennsylvania) University and Syracuse University, respectively, and the Ph.D. from Purdue University. He served in the infantry in World War II with the 99th Division in Germany, France, Belgium, and Holland. After a fourteen-year career in newspaper journalism and public relations in upstate New York, he began teaching at Utica College of Syracuse University in 1961.

He teaches modern British fiction, the Edwardians, and literary analysis. He is also the author of a biographical memoir, *Edmund Wilson: Our Neighbor from Talcottville* (1980), of which James Atlas, writing in 1983 in the *Atlantic,* observed: "Costa's memoir is so vivid that it acquires an independent life." He also wrote a Twayne critical biography of Malcolm Lowry (1972). A biographical monograph on Graham Greene has just been published in the *Dictionary of Literary Biography.* His interviews with W. Somerset Maugham, Conrad Aiken, and Morley Callaghan have been published recently.

Professor Costa, a native of Philadelphia, has published articles on such writers as Samuel Richardson, Fyodor Dostoevski, Leo Tolstoy, James Joyce, and Joseph Heller.

He has twice—in 1976 and 1984—won university-wide awards for distinguished teaching at Texas A&M. He is currently doing research for a biography of Irwin Shaw.

Preface

Walter Allen records in his recent memoirs[1] the strongest of pluses for H. G. Wells but with an implicit, if familiar, disclaimer: "I came on Wells, who I still think had the largest natural talent of any English novelist of the century. He did not, as we all know, always use it well, but he was a positive cornucopia of ideas, which he poured out in a ceaseless stream. And he had, too, an enormous capacity for fun. Almost certainly, he will look much greater in the future than he does now." That future is now. During the twenty years since I completed my research for the original edition of this book a massive salvage operation—"reassessment" is the polite term—has been under way. The solid Wells revival alone not only justifies but requires this revised edition.

For anyone writing in the early sixties, it was easy to accept the prevailing view that serious literary interest in H. G. Wells had long since ebbed. Formalism, generally, and the New Criticism, specifically, appeared to have buried him. Mark Schorer had had what seemed to be the last word. Demolishing *Tono-Bungay*, Wells's best novel, by forming a hangman's noose of words a desperate H. G. W. had tossed back as a defensive lob against Henry James, Schorer damned Wells by his exclusive syllogism: no accepted technique(s), no achieved content. It did not matter that if read with an open mind, *Tono-Bungay* is as compelling for literature students today as it was when Arnold Bennett reviewed it as an "epic . . . which display[s] an unsurpassable dexterity of hand," and D. H. Lawrence was so impressed that he despaired of ever being able to match it.

I wrote the original version in the shadow of an assumed discreditation, and I could not jump over it. This revision seeks, if not to reverse, at least to qualify that verdict. I shall demonstrate, in chapter 7, that in novels like *Mr. Britling Sees It Through* Wells lavished, in degree if not in kind, a concern for narrative honesty and fidelity of viewpoint equal to that shown by James in *The Ambassadors*. David Lodge[2] has demonstrated best the "other ways" by which Wells, in *Tono-Bungay*, has engaged the imagination (chapter 5).

The rescue of Wells from what Schorer devastatingly called "the annals of an era" is a combined enterprise, since the late 1960s, of literary historians, textual critics, and science-fiction scholars. In England, reappraisals of Wells's novels of social realism by Lodge, Bernard Bergonzi, Lucille Herbert, William Bellamy, Samuel Hynes, and John Batchelor have joined those in the United States by Kenneth B. Newell, Robert Bloom, John R. Reed, and William Scheick. More than merely according him the unofficial diadem as the father of science fiction, a brilliant group of science-fiction scholars has revised Wells *in toto*. Their scrutiny has both extended the old terms by which Wells had been written off or erected new markers in his behalf. The books and papers of Mark Hillegas, Robert Y. Hughes, R. D. Mullen, Patrick Parrinder, Robert Philmus, Darko Suvin, and J. P. Vernier have been of inestimable value in helping me to crystallize my own ideas. At the start, W. Warren Wagar[3] taught me much about the grain of Wells's thinking. Within the last year, the grasp of Wells's scientific thinking as developed in their books[4] by Roslynn Haynes and John Huntington has benefited me substantively.

"Wells and the Critics" (chapter 10) attempts to summarize early and contemporary criticism and to place old and new directions in perspective. "Wells and Science" (chapter 8) deals with science fiction—a term never used by Wells or even mentioned in my original book—but tries to do so in the larger context of science.

The second thrust of this revision is to reflect, albeit inadequately, the influence of Wells. Mark Hillegas[5] was the first to expand into a book the notion expressed by many writers from George Orwell to E. F. Bleiler that Wells was himself, in terms of futurist extrapolations, the shape of things to come. Hillegas, the first teacher of science fiction at an American university, proved that professed anti-Wellsians from Aldous Huxley and George Orwell to Kurt Vonnegut and William Golding have drawn on the Wellsian imagination—its mythopoeic figurations—to contest the Wellsian faith in the future. I seek to show in chapter 10 and elsewhere that what is important is that Wells's influence as a fabulist—that is, as a writer of fables carrying moral lessons—continues to be felt by modern writers.

The third thrust is to give fuller attention to the crusade on which at least one commentator[6] believes Wells had most influence: the emancipation of women. My chapter 6 ("New Women for Old: Wells and Feminism") addresses something easily misunderstood, namely, Wells's involvement in women's causes. Here—and elsewhere—I am indebted to Norman and Jeanne MacKenzie's major biography[7]—a comprehensive work that was published seven years after my book.

Finally, although necessarily extending into extraliterary regions that were undreamed of when I was writing two decades ago, this revision remains unchanged in at least one respect. It resists any tendency to treat Wells as other than a literary figure of almost the first order.

Richard Hauer Costa
Sylvan Beach, N.Y.

Texas A&M University

Acknowledgments

For permission to quote from some fifty of the works of H. G. Wells I am indebted to the executors of his estate, his sons, Dr. G. P. Wells of the University College of London and the late Frank Wells.

I can merely record, though never adequately express, my gratitude to the late Edmund Wilson, who, through an accident of geography, made his summer home (Talcottville, New York) and his presence available to me for a number of fruitful discussions.

I should like to acknowledge three cases of special indebtedness: to Mark R. Hillegas (recently retired from the University of Southern Illinois) who through another accident of geography—Colgate University and Utica College are within an hour's drive of each other—made his profound knowledge of the scientific romances accessible to me; to novelist John F. Hopkins who, as head of the Fiction Department, Free Library of Philadelphia, and a personal friend now for over forty years, guided me into many a Wellsian path I might never have found; and to William J. Scheick of the University of Texas at Austin, principal editor of the forthcoming comprehensive bibliography of Wells, who kept me abreast of new material I should not have known about otherwise.

To Gordon N. Ray, now director general of the Guggenheim Foundation, and Royal Gettmann my special thanks for permission to use the valuable holdings of the H. G. Wells Archive, University of Illinois, Champaign-Urbana, Illinois, in the summer of 1962, and, during the summer of 1983, to Frederick Nash and Mary Ceibert for their assistance during a second visit twenty-one years later. I am also indebted to Mary Dudley and her staff at the Utica College library for painstaking efforts to obtain materials on microfilm and interlibrary loan; to the library staffs, in the case of the original edition, of Hamilton College, Colgate University, and Syracuse University; and, for this revision, to the staffs at Hamilton as well as at Texas A&M University.

I am indebted to the late Thomas F. O'Donnell and to Raymond Simon, chairmen of Languages and Business Administration, respectively, at Utica College for their forebearance over the long haul; to two of my teachers, Mary Elizabeth Clark of Lock Haven, Pennsylvania, who made H. G. Wells required reading in her modern novel class at West Chester (Pennsylvania) University, and Roland E. Wolseley of Syracuse University, who first encouraged me to apply my interest in Wells to a book.

I should like to thank Utica College for two summer grants in the early 1960s which helped to free me to work on the book. Most recently, I should like to thank the Office of University Research, Texas A&M University, for a minigrant which enabled me to revisit the Wells Archive at Champaign-Urbana, Illinois.

I should like to thank Dorothy Judd Sickels, the then chairperson of publications at Utica College, for her generous assistance in preparing the galley and page proofs. And I should like to acknowledge my indebtedness to Sylvia E. Bowman and Robert J. Milch, general editor and copy editor for the first edition, and to Emily McKeigue, Kinley E. Roby, and Webb Dordick, editor, TEAS field editor, and copyeditor, respectively, for this revised edition, for their intelligent and conscientious editorial supervision. The photograph opposite the title page is reproduced through courtesy of the H. G. Wells Archive, the University of Illinois at Champaign-Urbana. I acknowledge the cooperation of the editors of *English Literature in Transition: 1880–1920*, *Journal of Modern Literature*, and *Modern Fiction Studies*.

Chronology

1905   *A Modern Utopia* and *Kipps*. Mother dies.

1906   *In the Days of the Comet*.

1907   *First and Last Things*.

1908   *New Worlds for Old* and *The War in the Air*.

1909   *Tono-Bungay* and *Ann Veronica*.

1910   *The History of Mr. Polly*. Father dies.

1911   *The New Machiavelli* and *The Country of the Blind, and Other Stories*, including all stories he thought to have merit, published.

1912   *Marriage*.

1913   *The Passionate Friends*.

1914   First visit to Russia. *The World Set Free*, containing forecast of atomic warfare. Also publishes *The War That Will End War*, an optimistic forecast of the outcome of the great war, and *The Wife of Sir Isaac Harman*. Son, Anthony West, born to Cicily Fairfield (Rebecca West) and Wells.

1915   *Boon* published, touching off bitter exchange of letters with Henry James.

1916   *Mr. Britling Sees It Through*. Visits Italian, French, and German fronts.

1917   *God the Invisible King* and *The Soul of a Bishop*.

1918   Advocates League of Free Nations as requisite to gaining permanent peace. *In the Fourth Year* and *Joan and Peter*. Collaborates with others in preparing propaganda literature against Germany.

1919   Resigns from the League of Nations Union. *The Undying Fire*.

1920   Second visit to Russia; talks to Lenin. *Russia in the Shadows* and *The Outline of History*.

1921   Modernized dramatic version of *The Wonderful Visit* performed in London. Accepts invitation of the *New York World* to cover Washington peace conference as special correspondent. *The Salvaging of Civilization*.

1922   Becomes member of Labor party; accepts Labor candidacy for the lord rectorship of Glasgow University but is defeated; defeated in bid for Parliament. *The Secret Places of the Heart*.

1923   *Men Like Gods*.

1924   Atlantic Edition of his works published in twenty-eight volumes. *The Story of a Great Schoolmaster* and *The Dream*.

1925   *Christina Alberta's Father*.

1926   *The World of William Clissold*.

1927   Wife, Amy Catherine Wells, dies. *Meanwhile*. Begins collaboration with Julian Huxley and his son, G. P. Wells, on a major outline of biology.

1928   *Mr. Blettsworthy on Rampole Island*.

1929   *The King Who Was a King*.

1930   *The Autocracy of Mr. Parham* and *The Science of Life*.

1932   *The Work, Wealth and Happiness of Mankind*.

1933   *The Shape of Things to Come*.

1934   Third visit to Russia for talk with Stalin. Public controversy with Shaw over the Kremlin interview. Visits the United States for talk with President Franklin D. Roosevelt. *Experiment in Autobiography*.

1935   Films scenarios for *Things to Come* and *The Man Who Could Work Miracles*.

1936   *The Anatomy of Frustration* and *The Croquet Player*. Banquet celebrating seventieth birthday attended by hundreds.

1937   *Brynhild* and *Star-Begotten*.

1938   *Apropos of Dolores*. Orson Welles's radio broadcast, based on *War of the Worlds*, frightens much of the United States.

1939   *The Fate of Homo Sapiens* and *The Holy Terror*.

1940   *Babes in the Darkling Wood*. Visits United States on lecture tour.

1941   *You Can't Be Too Careful*.

1945   *Mind at the End of Its Tether*.

1946   Wells dies 13 August in eightieth year.

1969   Posthumous publication of *The Wealth of Mr. Waddy*.

Of the vast and diversified library he left us, nothing has pleased me more than his narration of some atrocious miracles: *The Time Machine, The Island of Dr. Moreau, The First Men in the Moon*. They are the first books I read; perhaps they will be the last. I think they will be incorporated, like the fables of Theseus or Ahasuerus, into the general memory of the species and even transcend the fame of their creator or the extinction of the language in which they were written.

Jorge Luis Borges

Chapter One

H. G. Wells:
Life, Career, and Times

Cosmic Player

In the autumn of 1936, many British members of the fraternity of writers known as P.E.N. gathered at London's Savoy to celebrate the seventieth birthday of the organization's international president. Their guest of honor carried a name—H. G. Wells—that was known to virtually every household in the civilized world where books were read and authors discussed. After J. B. Priestley as master of ceremonies had called on distinguished writers for tributes, Wells rose and, in that reedy cockney accent that seemed anticlimactic after Bernard Shaw's mellifluous essay, declared that he felt like "a little boy at a lovely party, who has been given quite a lot of jolly toys and who has spread his play about on the floor. Then comes his Nurse. 'Now Master Bertie,' she says, 'it's getting late. Time you began to put away your toys.' . . . I hate the thought of leaving. . . . Few of my games are nearly finished and some I feel have hardly begun."[1] Later, as Somerset Maugham reported, the tone changed as player tried again to be seer. Yet his opening metaphor dies hard, for its imagery is drawn from the games-playing Bertie Wells treasured as a child and H. G. made standard procedure at any of the houses where he and Jane played willing hosts to every literary star—rising, falling, stationary—he encountered. For one dismissed longtime lover, the games-playing was the man. Once he had served notice as a savior but only the player remained. The game was the thing.

But what a game it was. No imaginative writer, before or since, had claimed so much of the planet—of the cosmos, really—for a literary playing field. Surely I am not alone in regretting, after the American moon shot and landing in the summer of 1969, that the lunar dawn brought nothing like the miracle of exfoliation with which Wells had endowed it fictionally in 1901. To my generation of faithful readers of the scientific romances, all those glimpses, via television, of astronauts striding on Gulliverian stilts suggested nothing so much as the cosmic playground of

H. G. Wells. And who can say that the vogue of UFO sightings is not a response to the human urge for wonderment in an age of computers?

For wonderment it was that his "atrocious miracles" lent to readers who will always seek the literary intoxicant. And afterward, when he deemed that no other kind of writing but the novel of social realism could earn him a living, what a surprise for devourers of his fin-de-siècle myths to find that the same writer would weave another kind of wonderment in the tapestry of down-to-earth characters like Mr. Polly—rhymes with "jolly," a favorite word of Wells—who would prove that the unlikeliest of persons can change their lives.

When, after his stirring apostrophe to change near the end of *The History of Mr. Polly,* Wells presents "these things as facts and information, and with no moral intimations," it is not Alfred Polly who is speaking but the authorial voice of command—Wells's. Polly simply determines he will leave his oppressive wife—"clear out." But his creator came finally to take change, not as Polly did as "something you got to work out and take the consequences," but as an imperative whose consequences were a series of utopian blueprints—Fabian, fictional, always frenetic—which sought to recruit mankind under systems that never took persons like Mr. Polly into consideration at all.

Vincent Brome is right when, after assessing Wells's many incarnations one by one—novelist, partyless politician, dragon-slayer, educator—he finds that "at heart it seems Herbert George Wells believed in his Utopia, was prepared to give all the rest to see it realized in his lifetime and had an obsessive desire to be a great scientist in it. . . . [But] Wells had mistaken his vocation. . . . He was a music-maker, a dreamer of sociological dreams. He belonged to the world of Plato and mistook it for the world of Pythagoras."[2]

Yet, for a time Orwell pinpoints as between the publication of *The Time Machine* (1895) and *The Outline of History* (1920), the dreams were starbegotten. J. Middleton Murry, despite deep differences with him, could see the passing of Wells as a crucial watershed: "He was the prophet of the future in which science was the key to liberty. . . . the last manifestation of a united Europe . . . the last intellectual effort of a common culture, a common belief in a common emancipation."[3]

Wells has continued to infect alike major novelists who prophesy doom and minor science-fiction writers and film scenarists who exploit that prophecy. If the best of them—Huxley, Orwell, Forster, C. S. Lewis, and Golding—have declined to believe in that side of Wells that was messianic about inevitable progressive evolution, all of them imbibed the fabulist in him and accepted his visions even while they reversed his later themes. And none of them could be more foreboding than the earliest Wells.

Pip Without Great Expectations

What is perhaps the most amply self-documented life in the annals of English literature began on 21 September 1866 when to Sarah Neal Wells, a lady's maid, and to Joseph Wells, an unsuccessful tradesman though accomplished cricket-player, was born the last of three sons, Herbert George Wells. The infant first "squinted and bubbled at the universe" in a shabby bedroom over a china shop in Bromley, Kent, that was called "Atlas House." Wells, in the retrospect provided by his massive *Experiment in Autobiography* (1934), appears to have retained a devotion to his parents tempered by his rebel's view of them as victims of the inflexible society into which they were born.

Sarah Wells, viewed almost clinically in the autobiography, committed the one unpardonable sin in her son's cosmology: she had a "set" mind about religion, respectability, and her "place." She took for granted her Victorian world, the one her Bertie was to spend a lifetime exorcising from his soul. Not even her desperate single-handed battle to keep the family afloat made her sense for a moment that "her God in his Heaven was under notice to quit." But from this little black figure of a woman "curiously suggestive (in later years) of Her Majesty Queen Victoria," Wells inherited an awareness of the impact of a God-figure. If he could not adhere to the furious deity to whom he was compelled to pray as a child, he sensed his need for something to fill the void, a God substitute, which in his books was to take many names. This need he took from his mother, along with a stoicism that stood him well during a lifetime of bodily ills and during a shattering period when he nursed his devoted wife, Jane, in what both knew was a futile effort to stave off a fatal disease.

Undistinguished as he was, Joseph Wells evokes poignant recollections from his son in the matchless early pages of the autobiography. Principally, however, Wells views him in the context of a social system he despised: as a not-quite-willing victim of eighteenth-century determinism in which, for such as he, only a chance legacy might offer passage out of the humdrum from cradle to grave. Wells's portrait of Mr. Polly (1910) is a tribute to the man his father might have been, but where Mr.Polly broke out in true Wellsian style from the bondage of circumstance Herbert George's father reserved his dreams for stargazing, a practice that only affirmed his enslavement. Wells was to write twenty-five years after his father's death that if Joseph Wells "could look out of this planet and wonder about the stars, it may be he could also look out of his immediate circumstances and apprehend their triviality by stellar standards."[4]

If stargazing provided an imaginative springboard which in Bertie Wells would culminate in several of literature's best cosmic voyages, it probably contributed to his father's undoing. At any rate, Joseph Wells was as deficient at shopkeeping as Mr. Polly, and the household in Bromley trembled constantly on the verge of financial collapse. Wells never forgot the shadows of insolvency that threatened Atlas House. At the end of his autobiographical novel, *Tono-Bungay,* published when Wells was forty-three, the enterprising Teddy Ponderevo dies after an over-extended, rags-to-riches venture with a fake patent medicine. Writing in 1915, Van Wyck Brooks, himself a typical new-worlds-for-old Wellsian, saw *Tono-Bungay* as "an epic of irresponsible capitalism from the socialist point of view."[5] But the book and its preposterous (for 1908) Ponderevo are, in a more human sense, a projection from the Victorian point of view by Wells of the doom that awaited solo upstart adventurers.

The student of Victorian life as seen through novels finds Wells, no less than Dickens, intent on portraying an economic and social system that is fast degenerating. A significant parallel between Dickens and Wells is the portrayal of the confusion that exists in people's minds between money and class, developed through the characterizations of Estella and Beatrice with whom Pip and George became infatuated early in their lives. Both acquaintanceships are begun when the girls are permitted, under differing circumstances, to play with the boys. Pip's socializing is maneuvered by Miss Havisham who encourages Estella to "beggar" Pip as she—Mrs. H. herself—had been "beggared" in her courting days. Pip departs only after the stigma of his origins has been ingrained ("I was a common laboring boy; [I knew] that my hands were coarse; that my boots were thick; that I was much more ignorant than I had considered myself. . . ; and generally that I was in a low-lived bad way"). This debut of Pip with Estella is echoed in *Tono-Bungay* during the first meeting at tea beween the twelve-year-old George and the eight-year-old Beatrice Normandy who calls attention to George's dirty hands and frayed collar.

By such encounters—the teatime-among-servants scene in *Tono-Bungay* and any of Pip's interviews with Mrs. Havisham—do Wells and Dickens reinforce the distance a poor lad under Victoria had to rise for any possibility of social mobility. From the gossipy small talk of the pensioned ex-servants who visit George's mother at Bladesover House, one senses the fear of gentry. In the petty contempt of the hired help for their betters,

Wells reveals a rarely articulated detestation of the System. Dickens is less subtle. At the point in *Great Expectations* where Pip suffers the humiliation of presenting his indentures, Dickens paints decadence in broad strokes. It is felt in Miss Havisham's dusty lace and in the fire which, in approved Victorian-novel style, levels country-houses and caste alike. Only a kind of residue of noblesse oblige keeps Miss Havisham from dissolving in flames before our eyes.

Bladesover in *Tono-Bungay* is, of course, the Uppark of Wells's child-hood (*E,* 33). It had been there in the 1850s that Sarah Neal met Joseph Wells. She was engaged as a maid on the estate of Sir Henry Featherston-haugh; the man she was to marry worked as a gardener. Years later, when it became obvious to the mother of three that the failure of Joseph Wells's shop was only a matter of time, she accepted a call to return as a stroke of heavenly fortune. Her other two sons safely apprenticed to drapers, Sarah Wells took her youngest, thirteen-year-old Bertie, with her and became housekeeper at Uppark in 1880.

The change in outlook from a shopkeeper's window to below stairs in a manor house was salutary for the youth. Bertie took more from Sir Harry Featherstonhaugh's fossil of a dying age than the son of a domestic had the right to expect. Not only did the dislocation close, at least temporarily, the almost inevitable path to being a tradesman, but it enabled Bertie to encounter books in profusion for the first time. In the late Sir Harry's li-brary, the boy made the acquaintance of the lucid satire of Voltaire, the unexpurgated *Gulliver*—a reading which established Wells's lifelong debt to Swift—and the liberating air of Plato's *Republic.* Despite the attenuated social life, Wells would one day write of the Uppark days that his life there became charged with potency, for the house "retained a vitality that alto-gether overshadowed the insignificant trickle of upstairs life" (*E,* 106).

But Bertie's deliverance from the fate of his brothers was only tempo-rary. Almost as unquestioning as her belief in God and Savior was Sarah Wells's belief in drapery. From the habit of servility came her conviction that the best of positions for a young man lay in wearing a black coat and tie behind a counter. So the last-born son of Joseph and Sarah Wells was made to put his books away, give up drawing, painting, and every sort of free delight, and slip almost unprotestingly into the mold cast for boys of his class. Thrown aside, too, was the boy's first attempt at fiction, the writing and illustrating of a gaily tragic tale, "The Desert Daisy." Begun shortly before his mother returned to Uppark, it involved an ill-starred romance, a thieving bishop (the clergy never came off well in any of his early work, published or unpublished), and a bloody conflict between the

Kingdoms of Spade and Clubs. There were gore and violence—infants hurled at the enemy like projectiles, dismemberment practiced with relish. Thematically, Wells was already cutting his teeth on what would become familiar morsels: the satirization of royalty, government and church, the army, and even—without stinting—himself. The books, those to be read as well as those to be written, were apparently left behind as Bertie Wells, turning fourteen—a Pip without any great expectations—was set down from an uncle's dogcart and apprenticed to a fate proper to his place.

There is little point in tracing his half-dozen or so "starts" in life—to use the word Wells employs in the early pages of his autobiography. His education was desultory and fragmentary, alternating as it did in its adolescent phases with abysmally unhappy periods of apprenticeship, first to drapers and later to dry-goods dealers and druggists. Wells, in a moving segment of *Tono-Bungay*, tells how George Ponderevo—his history showing insubordination, unjust charges of pilferage, and unpopularity wherever he was apprenticed—got up early one Sunday morning and walked nearly twenty miles to Bladesover to proclaim to his mother that the latest drapery experiment had to end.[6]

Wells learned firsthand about the Alfred Pollys, Artie Kippses, and Teddy Ponderevos. He came perilously close to living out the life of Mr. Polly, his most lasting creation, without that little man's saving recourse to arson. He might have remained an underpaid science teacher like Mr. Lewisham, with a schema for life that would have included marriage and children, but not a lifelong chafing against convention in a hundred books. He might have had, with his Artie Kipps, only vague intimations of greatness without the pull of literary success that elevated him to a kind of world statesmanship of letters: confrontations with Theodore and Franklin D. Roosevelt, Lenin, Stalin, and most of the other figures who shaped human destiny during the first third of the twentieth century, such as are virtually closed to even the most eminent of today's literati.[7]

H. G. Wells escaped anonymity through a door few men of letters used before him and only an occasional C. P. Snow has used since. He began to pass examinations and to show unusual ability in science; when he was eighteen, he was offered a scholarship at the Normal School of Science, South Kensington, to train as a teacher.

Haven and Huxley

The Normal School was only five years old when, on a September morning in 1884, Bertie Wells, only recently arrived in London for the first

time, matriculated at South Kensington. He termed the occasion "one of
the great days of my life." He believed he had reached "the fountainhead
of knowledge." This was no overstatement, especially since the fountainhead proved to be Thomas H. Huxley.

At the time Wells arrived Huxley was in his sixtieth year and exhausted
to the point of illness by his brilliant campaign as Darwin's public spokesman and as a passionate battler for science education. Seventeen years later
Wells recalled that he only attended one course of lectures by Huxley and
had spoken to him but once, holding open the door and exchanging a
simple "good morning."[8] Although Huxley died in 1895, the year of *The
Time Machine,* and is not known to have recorded an impression of his most
famous student, what Wells drew from that year of study he would spend
a lifetime dramatizing in story after story.

One can well imagine the impact on the young biology student of
stories current among the older assistants about times only recently past
when Charles Darwin had entered the lecture auditorium to hear his
friend. Darwin had been dead less than two years, and Huxley was still a
decade away from delivering his lecture on "Ethics and Evolution" at Oxford University.

Fifty years later Wells could still write of his year in elementary biology
and zoology under Huxley that it "was beyond question the most educational year of my life. It left me under that urgency for coherence and
consistency, that repugnance from haphazard assumptions and arbitrary
statements, which is the essential distinction of the educated from the uneducated mind" (*E,* 161). But, more specifically, it was from Huxley that
Wells drew the cosmic pessimism that marked his scientific romances from
the beginning. Norman and Jeanne MacKenzie are particularly cogent on
this point. Huxley's example and his teachings, they declare, provided
Wells with "the vital link between the evangelical beliefs in which he had
been brought up and the scientific ideas which he absorbed as a student.
For the remainder of his life he held these two systems together in a dy-
namic relationship. . . . Neither Darwin nor Huxley nor Wells after them
. . . believed that progress was inevitable. . . . And both Huxley and
Wells were plagued by haunting doubts whether in fact it would oc-
cur. . . . This dualism lay at the heart of Huxley's belief, as it was subsequently to run through Wells's scientific romances, his novels and utopias,
and his sociological and prophetic writings."[9]

As early as 1915 Van Wyck Brooks saw the imprint of Huxley on the
scientific romances of Wells. Huxley espoused a theory of evolution in
which the world and the universe, society and nature, are viewed as oper-

ating at cross purposes, with man pitting mind against matter. The only chance for social and ethical progress is the "checking of the cosmic process at every step" and the replacement of it by the ethical. But, as Houston Peterson notes, Huxley has "no fantastic hopes" for the efficacy of man's assault on the cosmos. [10] He sees no necessary millennium, not even a better life on earth, in the theory of evolution. For him, the theory points to a time when the cosmic process will destroy man. If, as Huxley believed, evolution involves a "constant remodeling of the organism in adaptation to new conditions," retrogressive change is both as possible and practicable as progressive. The course of earthly life is like the trajectory of "a ball fired from a mortar," and "the sinking half of that course is as much a part of the general process of evolution as the rising."

The dread potential for destruction held by forces outside man was gleaned by H. G. Wells in the laboratory and made palpable in those cosmic phenomena so dear to his heart: colliding comets, invading Martians, monstrous creatures seen in the Time Traveller's kaleidoscope of the earth's dying. "It has always been a fixed conviction with Wells that man personal and man social is dancing on a volcano," wrote Brooks at a time when the emergent image of Wells as the jolly apostle of scientific materialism, the forger of new (and invariably better) worlds for old, was taking hold of the liberal imagination. Brooks was not to be blinded by the popular view of Wells to the more compelling truth that grave warnings, even hopelessness, lay at the storyteller's spiritual center.

If the starting-point of Wells's literary career is a series of scientific romances that invoke through myth and symbol their creator's fear that man could well be doomed by a hostile universe, the middle period shows Wells discarding the cosmos for the individual. Most of the novels that follow the golden trio of *Kipps, Mr. Polly,* and *Tono-Bungay* exhibit Wells wrestling unsuccessfully with the conflicts of his persona. Under a heavy film of doctrinaire musings are revealed such Wellsian alter egos as the politician Remington in *The New Machiavelli* and the scientist Trafford in *Marriage,* men who come to grief through irrational compulsions within themselves.

In his search for a congenial persona, the influence of Huxley on Wells became much more than cerebral. Viewed through a dual lens as hero and as awesome abstraction, Huxley became the basis for the earliest shape of the Wells self-image: Herbert George Wells, Man of Science. Huxley loomed from lecture-platform vantage as the prototype for the first of Wells's fictional heroes, the scientist who would do battle with Jekyll-Hyde and Dr. Frankenstein.

It is in the translating of the treacheries of evolution into scientific romance that one finds the authentic mood of H. G. Wells. One turns to the early tales where Huxley-Wells as knight-errant plays at war with alien forces in time and space. These visions, whose surface pyrotechnics conceal antiutopian intimations, brought H. G. Wells to the attention of the literary world and may eventually prove his most lasting contribution to it.

Chapter Two
Evolution Transformed: The Scientific Romances

The convergence of the biggest idea of the nineteenth century—the theory of evolution—with a mind that was capable of grasping and extending it in all of its biological, philosophical, social, and poetical ramifications made possible the earliest—the best-known—writings of H. G. Wells. Although Wells subtitled his autobiography "discoveries and conclusions of a very ordinary brain," it was the distinctive cast of that brain—nurtured in the laboratory yet tuned to the music of new spheres of possibility—that enabled its possessor to savor Darwin's ideas, then transform them into aspirations to untold vistas.

I have already discussed the impact of natural evolution which the eighteen-year-old Bertie Wells first felt when he attended the lectures of T. H. Huxley at South Kensington in 1884 and 1885. It is certainly true that by the 1890s the concept of evolution had lost whatever polemical value it may have possessed. Evolution had destroyed the conventional theology. However, it was a scientific notion whose implicit consequences went far afield from Godhead into the worlds of ethics and social organization. For the intelligent nonspecialist reader of Wells's day who could never understand *The Origin of Species* or attend such lectures as Huxley's "Evolution and Ethics," the theory "had to be translated into the particular language of fiction. It had to be imparted to the reader by means of characters caught in the web of a fictional structure, and deriving "life" from the language they used and the situations in which they were placed."[1]

J. P. Vernier goes on to note that many of the later "discussion novels" elucidate the same views on evolution as the scientific romances that will be reviewed in this chapter. These latter, he remarks, retain the kind of fascination that only literature can exert; the former are now forgotten. But one should also point out that the impetus for the scientific fantasies—the stories, long and short and never out of print—came from even earlier writings, his "scientific journalism." These, as cataloged by those tireless Wellsians Robert M. Philmus and David Y. Hughes, amounted to more than two hundred items published between 1887 and 1898. Anyone who has been charged with the editorial smoothing out of scientific papers to make them intelligible to the nonspecialist knows the difficulties. However, as Philmus and Hughes demonstrate in their editing of *Early Writings by H. G. Wells* (1975), nearly all of student Wells's technical papers are readable, some "have intrinsic worth as literature," and all are potentially of value for understanding the scientific romances and the later utopian writings. He made a credo of the critical spirit of scientific inquiry; the same credo illumines his fiction.

One does not have to be a student of science generally, or of biology particularly, to infer the extraordinary relocation Wells experienced when Huxley lectured on evolution. The newly posited entanglement of species in the destinies of one another reopened the question of man's relation to the entire universe because "it rendered the idea of isolation . . . anachronistic, if not obsolete."[2]

When the philosophical artilleryman in *The War of the Worlds* observes that earthlings must seem to the Martians as alien and lowly as monkeys seem to his own species, Wells is dramatizing the notion that the process of natural selection provides a gauge for comparison between any two creatures. William Golding, among others, powerfully contested this idea of human progress, but it is an article of faith that Wells extrapolates in book after book. What he applies to the animate in evolutionary theory Wells applies to the spatial and, as Philmus and Hughes note, if the conceptual bridging of distances could be inferred from Darwin's theories, "the telescoping of time was a necessity. Evolution enlarged human consciousness of time: most obviously, because for the theory to be true this planet must be older than anyone before Darwin had supposed it to be. . . . And once human consciousness opens itself to the possibility of conceiving the entire past of the evolutionary process, why not attempt to project the course of that process a . . . greater 'distance' into the future?"[3] The important words are the last two—"the future." The most abiding of Wells's passions, the shape-of-things-to-come, began with a sense of the plasticity of space and time. But if it lent buoyancy to the scientific romances, it was ballast for the late books. William Clissold, the narrator of Wells's longest and, except for *Tono-Bungay,* most ambitious novel, looks out the window and meditates about something he calls "flux universal." Instead of being tormented out of faith and, like Matthew Arnold before him, into seeking after some sharer of the human condition, the Wells speaker waxes mystical, messianic, and monotonous: "I see the nearness of an order . . . like the order of a garden, of a workroom, of a laboratory, a clean life and a direct life and a powerful life for men; the jungle and all its sufferings gone

at last for ever. . . . [Lives] will be passing beyond egotistical conflict . . .
the age of jealousy . . . the age of fear. . . . To-day already in a thousand
aspects of their lives people . . . are anticipating this new phase, this completely adult phase of human life."[4] Wells would lose such postures. But
nothing is lost from his translations of human evolution into those "atrocious miracles" (Borges) by which his imagination redeemed passage in
time and space.

The best of his scientific romances have come down to us with the freshness of adventure stories. Their most insistent qualities are those of myth.
Such romantic ideas as travel into past and future time, Martian invasion,
invisibility, and lunar voyaging may not have originated with Wells; but a
lifetime after he gave expression to them, he is still their principal spokesman. To an older generation of science-fiction readers, the photographs of
Major Edward White taking his space hike in the summer of 1969 and the
accelerating reports of UFO sightings throughout the 1970s may have
seemed, in a curious way, familiar. Looking at the pictures of the American
astronaut astride the universe in a kind of cosmic sleepwalk recalls imagery
from *The First Men in the Moon,* written by Wells in 1901.

Stories like *The Time Machine, The Island of Dr. Moreau, The Invisible
Man,* and *The War of the Worlds* may be read only as thrilling stories. Yet
all the scientific romances have Swiftian overtones and can be viewed on
several levels. In considering five of these works in some detail, it will be
best to look simultaneously at all sides of the early Wells—the imaginative
storyteller and mythmaker, the futurist skeptic invoking a fin-de-siècle
promised land.

The Time Machine (1895)

Today, with satellite balloons twinkling by with timetable exactitude
and with men being sped into orbit in two ideological hemispheres, it may
be difficult to imagine the impact of a work like *The Time Machine* in its
period. With it, H. G. Wells made "the shape of things to come" a romantic phrase. But this first of Wells's scientific romances may be read, as
youthful readers all over the world still affirm, entirely as a thrilling story
of cosmic adventure in which the Time Traveller invents a machine of
gleaming nickel and quartz that carries him along the Fourth Dimension,
first to the world of 802701 A.D. with its degenerate descendants of man,
and then on to the earth in its death agony.

The short novel opens at the home of a man identified only as "the Time
Traveller." The host expounds on a theory of Time as the Fourth Dimen-

sion. He shows his small circle of friends first a working model, then the actual Time Machine. A week later the narrator goes again to the home of the Traveller, and this time the assembled group is told of his first and only flight into time. On the saddle of the machine he had flung himself far into futurity, stopping at the year 802701. He finds the Thames Valley a magnificent garden; London has disappeared save for gigantic but crumbling palaces of granite, marble, and aluminum. Mankind has differentiated into two races, the Eloi and the Morlocks. The Eloi are fragile, childlike people and, with the exception of Weena, a girl he saves from drowning, take little interest in him or in his machine. The machine is mysteriously stolen, and it is only then that he realizes the existence of the Morlocks, a bestial people who live in caverns and passages beneath the surface of the earth and who allow the Eloi to possess the earth on sufferance. They feed and clothe the Eloi from long habit, and prey upon them for their meat. After several adventures with the Morlocks, during one of which Weena is killed, the Traveller recovers the machine and travels once more into the future, until more than thirty million years have passed and the earth has at last come to rest with one face to the dull red sun, now so near as to obscure one tenth of the sky. Then he comes back, stopping his machine at eight o'clock on the evening of the day of his departure. Most of his guests incline to the belief that his tale is "a gaudy lie," and a few days later he sets out again with camera and knapsack to secure proof of the reality of his time-traveling. From the instant of his departure he is never seen again.

This plot summary, familiar even to the children of parents who no longer read Wells as avidly as their own parents did, does scant justice to what a leading science-fiction writer, Arthur C. Clarke, called one of the two works of science fiction that are also literature.[5]

For a generation yet to hear of Albert Einstein, the opening pages of *The Time Machine* provided an introduction to the possibilities of the Fourth Dimension which in 1895 was not elsewhere available outside of scientific journals. The reader is initiated convincingly into the shaded-light-and-fireplace world of the Time Traveller and his friends. The technique is one Wells's critics were to insist he borrowed from his ideological opposite number, Kipling; but, whatever the source of the device, it succeeded in providing a firm transport from ordinary contemporary life to an imaginative world beyond the ken of the late Victorian bourgeoisie. By ushering his friends gathered about the shaded light into the world where a fourth dimension is possible, Wells shows himself to be essentially not, as Oscar Wilde had once said, "an English Jules Verne," a forecaster of new inventions based on old models or, as with Poe, a searcher after "effects." Rather, using the currency of narrative fiction, he became the supreme communicator in his time of the possibilities of science.

Wells is quite explicit about what caused the collapse of man's utopian dream. Huxley, he says, was justified in his fears that mankind ultimately would be powerless to control the evolutionary process. For a time, perhaps for centuries, the millennium-promising balance between capital above ground and workers below was achieved. But it was destroyed because the Upper Worlders, the descendants of nineteenth-century capitalists, ignored Huxley's most salient warning: "If we may permit ourselves a larger hope of abatement of the essential evil of the world . . . I deem it an essential condition of the realization of that hope that we cast aside the notion that escape from pain and sorrow is the proper object of life."[6]

After the ancestors of the Eloi achieved security and freedom from danger, they lost the initiative that stems from struggle; their descendants evolved, therefore, to "mere feeble prettiness" and became the delicate Eloi. Only the knowledge of machinery prevented the Morlocks from enervating into vegetablelike creatures; but, when starvation ultimately became a world problem, Huxley's fears were realized with the reversion of the Morlocks to a state of cannibalism. The agency of destruction, Wells makes perfectly clear, was a materialist, technological society of the kind to which he, in the later phase, seemingly gave willing endorsement:

I grieved [muses the Time Traveller] at how brief the dream of human intellect had been. It had committed suicide. It had set itself steadfastly toward comfort and ease, a balanced society with security and permanency as its watchword. It had attained its hopes—to come to this at last. Once, life and property must have reached almost absolute safety. The rich had been assured of his wealth and comfort, the toiler assured of his life and work. No doubt in that perfect world there had been no unemployed problem, no social question left unsolved. And a great quiet had followed.[7]

The H. G. Wells of unforgettable stories like *The Time Machine* believed that men were as base and cruel as the Morlocks or as acquiescent as the Eloi. The world might easily become Dr. Moreau's island where, as will be shown in the next section, science produced destruction and death.

Escaping the Morlocks by reentering the time machine, the Traveller stops his conveyance for a look at the expiring world. Wells's picture of the world in lethargy is unforgettable. He has propelled his Traveller thirty million years ahead to a world in which man has disappeared. Although the huge sun obscures a tenth of the heavens, the air is bitter cold and snow is falling. Not even the gigantic crablike creatures, seen earlier in his journey, remain. The Traveller sees the last animated creature, a round thing the size of a football, trailing tentacles against the blood-red water.

In reading these passages, called by Nicholson "among the most significant (for the humanist) in the popular literature of the last sixty years,"[8] one thinks of T. S. Eliot's Prufrock and his evocation of world's end desperation: "I should have been a pair of ragged claws scuttling/across the floors of silent seas." In horror at his vision of the full circle of evolution, the Traveller climbs weakly into the saddle of the machine, the hands spin backward upon the dials, and presently he is back in the comfortable "Now" of his London home.

V. S. Pritchett confidently asserts that *The Time Machine* "will take its place among the great stories of our language." He sees in it a hearkening back to the early eighteenth century and to the highest traditions of English narrative literature.[9] Winston Churchill found the story "not unworthy to follow . . . in the train of *Gulliver's Travels.*"[10] Pritchett, however, places Swift's imaginative range and style in a loftier position; he says they stem from a humanity "denied to Wells because he arrived at the beginning, the crude beginning, of a new enlargement, whereas Swift arrived toward the end of one."[11]

The truth of Pritchett's synthesis is underscored by the knowledge that the origins of the story are rooted firmly in Wells's years as a student at the Royal College of Science. In 1887, the year he completed his courses under Huxley and others, Wells began work on a fantastic novel called "The Chronic Argonauts." Serialized in fragmentary form in the *Science Schools Journal* in April, May, and June of 1888, it was the first draft of *The Time Machine,* which did not appear for seven more years. *The Time Machine* was an instant success; over six thousand copies were sold within a few weeks. Although no overnight phenomenon, Wells clearly managed to capture the public ear at the very beginning of his literary career. No sooner had *The Time Machine* and his first collection of stories, *The Stolen Bacillus,* appeared than he was deluged by inquiries from publishers. Writing to his mother, he said: "I've had letters too from four publishing firms asking for the offer of my next book. . . ."

Although not widely reviewed, *The Time Machine* received favorable notices. One anonymous reviewer called it the most bizarre of fantasies since Stevenson's *Dr. Jekyll and Mr. Hyde* and lauded Wells for producing that rarity, a new thing under the sun. The ninety years that have passed since its publication have seen no refutation of this tribute. Wells was the first writer to employ the idea of time as the fourth dimension in a story; and, so far as can be discovered, he invented the idea of traveling through time by means of a mechanical device.

The Island of Dr. Moreau (1896)

It cannot be said, as with *The Time Machine,* that the second of Wells's major scientific romances falls outside the main stream of English narrative fiction. As numerous critics have pointed out, *The Island of Dr. Moreau* owes immediate debts to Kipling's *Jungle Book,* to Mary Shelley's *Franken-stein,* and to the already-mentioned *Dr. Jekyll and Mr. Hyde.* Wells himself thought it a better book than *The Time Machine;* and, in terms of the shock-ing imagery of the work, his appraisal was accurate. *Moreau* is hard on the nerves, for the horror is more explicit than is usually possible in a clearly allegorical work.

Simply as a narrative, the story has scenes that are more suspenseful than anything found in its predecessor. A half-mad scientist, Moreau, has con-verted a Pacific island into a zoological laboratory. His fiendish work is discovered by another scientist, Edward Prendick, who has been ship-wrecked and is picked up by a drunken assistant of Moreau. Prendick soon learns that there is nothing idyllic about Moreau's atoll retreat. The island-ers are all grotesques. Despite semihuman appearance, they are unmistak-ably jungle creatures. They chant a Law which has been taught them by Moreau:

> Not to go on all-Fours; *that* is the Law.
> Are we not Men?
> Not to suck up Drink; *that* is the Law.
> Are we not Men?
> Not to eat Flesh nor Fish; *that* is the Law.
> Are we not Men?
> Not to claw Bark of Trees; *that* is the Law.
> Are we not Men?
> Not to chase other Men; *that* is the Law.
> Are we not Men?[12]

At first, Prendick, given a glimpse of Moreau at work on one of the creatures, assumes his aim is the transformation of men into animals and that he (Prendick) will be next. Only after he hears the latter part of the littany does he glean the whole truth:

> *His* is the House of Pain.
> *His* is the Hand that makes.
> *His* is the Hand that wounds.
> *His* is the Hand that heals.
>
> (*S, 105*)

"A horrible fancy came into my head [reasons Prendick] that Moreau, after animalizing these men, had infected their dwarfed brains with a kind of deification of himself" (*S, 105*).

From this point, the story is the continuation in the life of that first Wellsian persona, the Time Traveller of the earlier story—what Bergonzi calls the enlightened post-Darwinian scientist. The book, for the first time, projects a major confrontation which appears repeatedly in the scientific romances. Prendick seeks to overthrow Moreau's island laboratory and to release the beast-men from their bondage to pain and terror. He, like Wells, had studied under Huxley; and he held high the Huxleyan banner which proclaimed that the future could be shaped only by man's ethical control of the blind impulses of nature. Thus Prendick is made to stand for Huxley; Moreau, for Frankenstein.

The novel, illumining in fictional form Huxley's fears for the fate of Homo sapiens, tells its story and delivers its myth-message in terms exemplified by a long line of island-allegory works, whose landmark is Shakespeare's *Tempest* and whose most recent addition is William Golding's *Lord of the Flies*. The genre's finest prose practitioners from Defoe to Golding have used the coral island as an elemental setting for parable and myth. Although neglecting to mention *Dr. Moreau*, Carl Niemeyer had brilliantly traced the sources of *Lord of the Flies* (1954) to *Robinson Crusoe* (1719) and to R. M. Ballantyne's *The Coral Island* (1857).[13] Whereas the two earlier works extol the innate virtue of man, *Lord of the Flies*, like *The Island of Dr. Moreau*, traces the defects of society back to the defects of human nature.

Golding's book echoes the Ballantyne fable in its use of a group of castaway children who assume adult responsibility without adult supervision. Ballantyne endows his shipwrecked boys with pluck and resourcefulness so that they are able to subdue tropical islands as triumphantly as England imposes empire and religion on the lawless natives of the island. Golding, in an elaborate allegory of the end of civilization, leaves his boys to fend for themselves and shows that the beast, latent in all of them, may be subdued—and then only temporarily—by the organized institutions of civilization.

There are no children in *Dr. Moreau*, but the Wells book, written sixty years before *Lord of the Flies,* is an equally savage reaction against rampant optimism. Both authors develop, in the mythopoeic way that is their trademark, the idea that man is a savage, not intrinsically different from the Paleolithic brute. Humanity, as dramatized in the two novels, is but animal—rough-hewn to a reasonable shape and in perpetual conflict between instinct and injunction. "Morality in this view," writes Leo J. Henkin, "is simply the padding of social and emotional habits by which society keeps the round Paleolithic savage in the square hole of the civilized state."[14] *The Island of Dr. Moreau* is a dramatization of this idea and is also a fictional elaboration on an article Wells wrote the same year, "Human Evolution, an Artificial Process." Wells assumes in *Moreau* that the gulf between animality and humanity is capable of being bridged by a surgeon's knife; Moreau's hybrids, walking on two feet and chanting their formula-like litany of the Law, slowly slip back into savagery. The beast folk, in Anthony West's words, "under Dr. Moreau's scar tissue . . . remain animals interested only in the satisfaction of their appetites."[15]

In Golding's novel, only one of the marooned boys, Simon, understands that there may indeed be a beast within each of the lads ("However Simon thought of the beast, there arose before his inward sight the picture of a human at once heroic and sick"). His intuition is verified in the mystic confrontation between Simon and the lord of the flies, a sow's head mounted on a stake. The sow has been killed savagely by the children. In worshipping the head, the youngsters satanically enthrone their own power of blackness. While the others hide from the truth behind masks, Simon hears the words of the "Lord": "Fancy thinking the Beast was something you could hunt and kill! You knew, didn't you? I'm part of you? Close, close, close! I'm the reason why it's no go? Why things are what they are?" Tragically, Simon is murdered by the boys because of their insane belief that he is the beast, the beast which he alone has exorcised through understanding.

In both books, the surviving representatives of civilization are rescued. In the later novel, Ralph leads a minority camp among the boys that is devoted to keeping the coral island at peace and to following the "rules." The British Navy arrives at the eleventh hour to save Ralph from the other camp, led by Jack Merridew, which is devoted to savagery and hunting. But until the rescue Ralph and all he represents—that is, "parliament" or "human order"—was defeated, and Golding appears to be saying that adult society is lost in an even more hopeless way. In *The Island of Dr. Moreau,* Prendick's escape is even narrower. He is forced to become one of the beast people—the slayers of Moreau—until he can find a boat and set himself adrift. Returning to civilization, he, like Captain Gulliver after he has come back from the land of the Houyhnhnms, is horrified by contact with humans because their animal nature will never escape his memory. The island assumes its allegorical identity in his mind; it is the world where the brute in man is covered by the flimsiest of facades: "Then I look about me at my fellow men, and I go in fear. I see faces keen and bright, others dull or dangerous, others unsteady, insincere; none that have the calm authority of a reasonable soul. I feel as though the animal was surging up through them; that presently the degradation of the Islanders will be played over again on a larger scale" (*S*, 155).

For the two mythmakers, Wells and Golding, the beast in man will not inevitably backtrack into the jungle with the coming of rescue boats. Dr. Moreau's failure to make beast into man and the reversion of the boys into beasts are symbols of Thomas Huxley's fear that man may be the victim rather than the master of the cosmic process, both in nature and within himself. Wells endorsed Huxley's pessimistic declaration that "even the best of modern civilization appears to me to exhibit a condition of mankind which neither embodies any worthy ideal nor even possesses the merit of stability."[16]

The Island of Dr. Moreau was soundly thrashed by the critics for its sensationalism. The *Athenaeum* devoted a long unfavorable review to the book without bothering to spell out its theme. A *Saturday Review* critic declared, "The horrors described by Mr. Wells in his latest book very pertinently raise the question how far it is legitimate to create feelings of disgust in a work of art."[17] Wells later described the book as "an excuse in youthful blasphemy. Now and then, though I rarely admit it [he said], the universe projects itself towards me in a hideous grimace . . . and I did my best to express my vision of the aimless torture in creation" (*S*, ix).

The Invisible Man (1897)

None of the others can match the high spirit of Wells's third scientific romance, *The Invisible Man,* but the influence of Huxley is equally strong. The name of the scientist here has changed from Prendick to Kemp, and the setting from the coral isle to Iping Village in Surrey. Prendick battled a stranger, Dr. Moreau, but Kemp confronts a former science college classmate, Griffin, who has learned the secret of invisibility. The story's distinctive merits stem from Wells's complete grasp of the Scottish meaning of "weird": something that actually takes place. The story is an adept balance between the unbelievable—the predicament of the Invisible Man—

and the ordinary—the routine life of Iping Inn. The peculiar problem is Dashiell Hammett's "old chestnut"[18]—making the reader feel that what cannot happen does happen though it should not—and the writer's problem is compounded by Wells's need to make the reader believe in invisibility without seeing it. To accomplish this feat, Wells presents the invisible Griffin through the eyes of the villagers. His introduction is a montage of increasingly bizarre effects: the hurrying figure swathed in bandages and wig, its mouth a gaping hole; its trouser legless, its sleeve empty. It is a mesmerizing business; and, as Norman Nicholson puts it epigrammatically, "we believe in all things visible and invisible." *The Invisible Man,* in its early pages, is as picaresque as the rural adventures of the bicycling Hoopdriver in *The Wheels of Chance,* the first of the comic novels. The Coach and Horses Inn of *The Invisible Man* derives from the same landscape as the Fishbourne Hotel in the richly humorous *History of Mr. Polly.* The ingenious explanation of how Griffin effected invisibility demonstrates once again Wells's ability to project the possibilities of science. Griffin, while working on the subject of optical density, has hit upon a course of treatment whereby the refractive index of human tissues may be equalized by that of the atmosphere, thus making the body invisible.

Griffin's undoing, like Moreau's, stems from a megalomania that has convinced him that his discovery will endow him with unlimited power. Bernard Bergonzi is correct in stressing that, since Griffin's invisibility stands for Wells's apprehension of the possibilities of science, Griffin's fate must be seen as a rebuke to the pretensions of science and, perhaps, the end of the young Wells's own identification with a romanticized species of scientist-magician, one that is notably apparent in the characterization of the Time Traveller.

H. G. Wells, spinner of fables and maker of myths, is never so much in evidence as in the final scene, in which the Invisible Man, naked and in flight, is battered to death by the whirling spades of a desperate posse. Wells, the detached Huxleyan spokesman observing mankind rather than men, sees the dead Griffin physiologically—molecularly—and, at last, for just an instant, as human: "It [the transformation to visibility] was like the slow spreading of a poison. First came the little white nerves, a hazy grey sketch of a limb, then the glassy bones and intricate arteries, then the flesh and skin. . . . Presently . . . his crushed chest . . . the dim outline of his drawn and battered features [and finally] there lay, naked and pitiful on the ground, the bruised and broken body of a young man about thirty. . . ."[19]

This passage, one of the most memorable in all of Wells's books, is comparable to the glimpse of the dying world in *The Time Machine*. No writer of his day put so much power into an essentially detached viewpoint. In his first three scientific romances Wells sees humans as stripped of their distinctly human qualities, just as Griffin is stripped of clothing to maintain transparency. Once again, as in *The Island of Dr. Moreau*, Wells is saying that not even the development of the secret of invisibility is in itself a guarantee of progress. Griffin has studied natural science and has become as pitiless as the elements. The cosmic process, declares Wells, in an echo of Huxley, is at odds with the ethical process. *The Invisible Man*, then, is a warning of what could happen if science, in the persons of the Griffins and Moreaus, is not controlled. The instruments of saving the world are the enlightened, humanity-based Kemps and the Prendicks.

The War of the Worlds (1898)

The *War of the Worlds* is the archetype of all B-grade films that present giant creatures from another world who invade the earth armed with death-ray guns. The imagery of the novel is so vivid that it is no wonder film scenarists have always thought of outer-space invasions in Wellsian terms. Moreover, one grasps from this novel the essential technique of all of Wells's scientific romances, *Dr. Moreau* excepted: the pinning of strange events to an everyday locale. The attraction of *The Invisible Man* lay in placing the astounding dilemma of Griffin within the slow village life of Iping. In *The War of the Worlds*, the narrator sees the effects of the Martian invasion on a village in Woking, a place familiar to Wells because he once retreated there to convalesce from illness. Wells wrote in his autobiography of bicycling about the district and "marking down suitable places and people for destruction by my Martians."

Combined with a faultless adherence to down-to-earth physical details is a sense of time; the chronology of invasion is attributable about equally to a boy's imaginative grasp of war games and to a man's foreboding vision of terrestrial resistance turned to panic:

About three o'clock there began the thud of a gun at measured intervals from Chertsey to Addlestone. I learnt that the smouldering pine-wood into which the second cylinder had fallen was being shelled in the hope of destroying that object before it opened. It was only about five, however, that a field gun reached Chobham for use against the first body of Martians.

About six in the evening, as I sat at tea with my wife in the summer-house talking vigorously about the battle that was lowering upon us, I heard a muffled detonation from the common, and immediately after a gust of firing. Close on the heels of that came a violent rattling crash, quite close to us, that shook the ground; and, starting out upon the lawn, I saw the tops of the trees about the Oriental College burst into smoky red flame, and the tower of the little church beside it slide down the ruin. The pinnacle of the mosque had vanished, and the roof-line of the college itself looked as if a hundred-ton gun had been at work upon it. One of our chimneys cracked as if a shot had hit it, flew, and a piece of it came clattering down the tiles and made a heap of broken red fragments upon the flowerbed by my study window.

I and my wife stood amazed. Then I realized that the crest of Mayberry Hill must be within range of the Martians' Heat-Ray now that the college was cleared out of the way.[20]

This extraordinary grasp of moment-to-moment detail made the novel easy prey for Orson Welles when in 1938 he converted it into the script that panicked a national radio audience. Welles changed the setting from a British district to Grover Mill, New Jersey.

Wells, apostle of the possible, registers himself in *The War of the Worlds* as the archenemy of the smug heralders of a new-century utopia in which the Union Jack would always prevail. "With infinite complacency," he writes in the opening paragraph of this novel about the routing of civilization, "men went to and fro over the globe about their little affairs, serene in their assurance of their empire over matter." Even as they luxuriate in a mental inertia of "all's well," keener intelligences from Mars covet the earth and lay plans to conquer it.

The same cautionary message, told in fable, is sounded in the previous romances: man has no right to take control of the cosmic process for granted. Wells warns the reader to look at what happened to Mars—"not only more distant from life's beginning but nearer its end." The conditions on Mars became increasingly uncongenial to higher life, Wells speculated, citing dropping temperature, thinning atmosphere, water drying up. Eventually, the planet was forced to search space for some buffer to cosmic annihilation. Once again Wells reinforces his convictions by presenting a picture of the expiring planet of war as a preview of earth's fate: an earth moving in Huxleyan inexorability along the declining parabola of evolution.

Wells, in effect, gives the reader a step-by-step report on how a breakup of metropolitan society would come about. Whereas *The Time Machine* and the yet-to-come *First Men in the Moon* are conceived poetically—that is, the myths of time travel and of moon visitation are rendered in such a way as to suspend the demands of verisimilitude—in *The War of the Worlds* the mythopoeic mood is exchanged for the methods of documentary realism. The Martian invasion is treated as an event of contemporary history.

It is not necessary to review the invasion in detail. Suffice it to say that the Martians are octopuslike creatures who are as far above mankind in intellect and command of machinery as humans are above animals. The Martians stride over the earth in machines of impregnable armor and devastate town and country with searchlights projecting rays more destructive than those of radium. They feed on human blood, and they force humanity, if it is not to perish or become as docile as the Eloi, to seek subterranean refuge. In the robotlike calculations of the Martians, Wells again underscores Huxley: evolution may produce creatures with superior brains, but it will not inevitably lead to a millennium.

In one of Wells's best passages of dramatic sociological speculation, a courageous artilleryman speaks of what life will be like for the survivors: "The tame ones [of us] will go like all tame beasts. . . . The risk is that we who keep well will go savage—degenerate into a sort of big, savage rat. . . . You see, how I mean to live is underground. I've been thinking about the drains. . . . Then there's cellars, vaults, stores, from which bolting passages may be made to the drains. And the railway tunnels and subways. Eh? You begin to see? And we form a band—able-bodied, clean-minded men. We're not going to pick any rubbish that drifts in. Weaklings go out again" (*S*, 371–72). The artilleryman's formula is suggestive of the fallout fears of a more modern day that Wells did not quite live to see. In *The War of the Worlds*, the worldlings are relieved of the necessity of putting survival conditions to the test by the intervention of an unexpected ally, the most minute of rescuers: the microbe. The invaders from Mars, lacking immunity to terrestrial diseases, are annihilated by one of them.

The possibility of life on Mars was part of the folklore in Britain at the end of the nineteenth century. The first volume of Camille Flammarion's *La Planète Mars* had appeared in 1892, thus making, as Bernard Bergonzi suggests, "a convenient and plausible superhuman adversary for mankind." Passages in chapter 1 of Wells's novel are probably imitations of Flammarion; they describe the physical conditions of Mars and are strikingly similar to descriptions in Flammarion's books. Wells's theories of the superhuman qualities of the Martians were also in line with those of the American astronomer Percival Lowell, who in 1896 advanced the idea that the canals on Mars were the work of intelligent beings.

But H. G. Wells's "scientific" knowledge of Mars, impressive as it was, has in the years since the book's publication become secondary to the message that underlies the romance—a message few of Wells's early readers understood. The novel continued his practice of bludgeoning the complacent bourgeois. He who had forced his mean little undernourished and illness-ridden body out of dingy shops was at century's end, by dint of the scientific romances, forcing himself on literary society.

Who can say how many of Wells's dread forebodings in these four novels had their origin in Huxley's laboratory and how many in severe social maladjustment? The H. G. Wells of 1897, barely thirty but soon to be famous, was encountering difficulties in gaining acceptance in the cultivated world with its necessary insincerities and demand for credentials. It may be that the early Wells might have welcomed some such social upheaval concomitant upon invasion or similar catastrophe. As he wrote to his close friend George Gissing that very year, he might see in such an event, "a return to the essential, to honorable struggle as the epic factor in life. . . ."[21]

At any rate, the assertions of the coarse artilleryman, though somewhat discredited later in the novel, mark perhaps a beginning toward a new, sociological Wells—one who, within less than a decade, would project in a landmark utopian book, *A Modern Utopia,* a thoroughgoing blueprint for world revolution in the hands of an intellectual and physical elite, the Samurai. If sociology ruined H. G. Wells, the beginnings of that forty-year penchant may be gleaned even in a masterful scientific romance like *The War of the Worlds.*

The First Men in the Moon (1901)

The First Men in the Moon has the same deceptive simplicity as *The Time Machine.* As the story of an imaginary journey into space, it represents, according to Mark Hillegas, "the highest point in the development of the cosmic voyage in the nineteenth century."[22] On perhaps its most profound level, the novel, and especially a long Gulliverian colloquy between the moon voyager and the Grand Lunar, is rich in satire. Although nearly always paired with Jules Verne's *From the Earth to the Moon,* the story draws more fundamentally from Swift; it shares with *Gulliver's Travels* a portrayal by parable of life on earth, or, in the case of Swift's disciple, of life within the rigidly class-divided structure of English society. Finally, the story stands at the apex of that handful of works that reveal what Nicholson calls Wells's "poetic gift." Nowhere in popular literature can one find so moving a description as that of the landing on the moon at the dawn of a lunar day—T. S. Eliot termed it "quite unforgettable"[23]—or so vivid a picture as that of the gigantic anthill of the moon's interior, with its blue-lit passageways and tunnels lying above the great swirling, luminescent central sea that laps around the moon's core.

Cosmic journeys were literary staples as early as the seventeenth century. The most famous of eighteenth-century voyagers—Crusoe and Gulliver— chose water as their element. Jules Verne preceded Wells with his *From the Earth to the Moon* (1865), a book to which Wells acknowledged a greater debt than to any other nineteenth-century story of a cosmic voyage. But, as Hillegas points out, "it is difficult to pin down the numerous similarities and determine which are the result of direct borrowing by Wells and which are due to the feeling of a common tradition by the two authors."[24] Indeed, the differences are more to the point. Arnold Bennett was the first major writer to demur from the view that Wells was an English Verne. Bennett pointed to Verne's preoccupation with machinery over men; his stockpiling of unimportant scientific facts at the expense of story movement; the abortive nature of the voyage which relieved him of any necessity for those lunary descriptions which so distinguish the book; the absence of a philosophical base.[25]

Verne immersed himself in mechanics. His method was to place his three explorers in a padded projectile and to shoot them from an enormous gun, the barrel of which was a well, sunk nine hundred feet in the ground and charged with four hundred thousand pounds of gun-cotton. Verne amassed, in the interest of scientific fidelity, material better suited to the lecture room: "The Armstrong cannon employs only 75 pounds of powder for a projectile of eight hundred pounds, and the Rodman Columbiad uses only one hundred sixty pounds of powder to send its half-ton shot a distance of six miles." The Frenchman went to great lengths to work out the mathematics of setting off his projectile. He, in effect, left to a better writer the lunar landscape by having his projectile deflected off course and finally reversed back to earth.

Wells, that better writer, took up where Verne left off. Verne was interviewed in 1903 and asked about Wells's moon novel. He scoffed at Wells for "inventing" and wanted to be shown gravity-resisting Cavorite.[26] The Englishman, on the other hand, was always fair to Verne.

Verne wished only to make his fictional product scientifically merchandisable. Wells threw such caution to the winds. Never in his scientific romances did he worry about technicalities. Without a machine equipped for the purpose, there would have been no time travel; but Wells gives little description of the time-girdling conveyance. He brings to *First Men* the invention of "Cavorite," a gravity-resisting substance that enables his moon-voyagers, Bedford and Cavor, to travel to the moon; and he permits Bedford eventually to return. Cavorite is moored tenuously to the laws of physics. The writer Bedford, the narrator, says from the outset that he took no notes while Cavor explained his theories.

As was his custom, Wells domesticates his setting, keeping it firmly Kentish. And Cavor is neither Frankenstein nor Moreau, but compounded of features drawn by Boz: "He was a short, round-bodied, thin-legged little man, with a jerky quality in his motions; he had seen fit to clothe his extraordinary mind in a cricket cap, an overcoat, and cycling knickerbockers and stockings . . . He gesticulated with his hands and arms and jerked his head about and buzzed. He buzzed like something electric. You never heard such buzzing. And ever and again he cleared his throat with a most extraordinary noise."[27] Cavor foreshadows Artie Kipps and Mr. Polly. The man comes alive as Verne's cosmic voyagers never do.

No less realistic are the strokes Wells uses to disclose that there is life on the moon. His deft touches never leave the reader without solid associations:

I have said that amidst the stick-like litter were these rounded bodies, these little oval bodies that might have passed as very small pebbles. And now first one and then another had stirred, had rolled over and cracked, and down the crack of each of them showed a minute line of yellowish green, thrusting outward to meet the hot encouragement of the newly risen sun . . .

Every moment more of these seed coats ruptured, and even as they did so the swelling pioneers overflowed their rent-distended seed-cases, and passed into the second stage of growth. With a steady assurance, a swift deliberation, these amazing seeds thrust a rootlet downward to the earth and a queer little bundle-like bud into the air. In a little while the whole slope was dotted with minute plantlets standing at attention in the blaze of the sun. . . .

The movement was slower than any animal's, swifter than any plant I have ever seen before. How can I suggest it to you—the way that growth went on? The leaf tips grew so that they moved onward even while we looked at them. The brown seed-case shrivelled and was absorbed with an equal rapidity. Have you ever on a cold day taken a thermometer into your warm hand and watched the little thread of mercury creep up the tube? These moon plants grew like that. (S, 425)

Passages like this can only derive from the marriage of scientist and literary artist. Wells clearly drew on what must have been his feelings the first time he looked into a microscope at South Kensington. He used myriad images remembered from the study of botany, making a kind of collage full of suggestive effects. Wells never quite lost this gift for rendering evolution—the growth of species, human, animal, or plant—poetically. It shimmers through the early pages of *The Outline of History* in those sections devoted to prehistoric man.

The action of the story properly starts when the voyagers find that there is not only plant but human life on the moon. For Wells's purposes, supercreatures like the Martians will not do. This time the Selenites, far from towering over the earthlings, like the tentacled invaders of *The War of the Worlds,* are antlike. Like Swift's Lilliputians, whose descendants they assuredly are, they capture the Gullivers from earth. Cavor and companion are taken inside the moon; after a grim struggle that suggests the Time Traveller's battle with the Morlocks, they escape. The two separate, and Cavor is again made prisoner. Bedford finds the sphere and returns to earth. The rest of the story is told by virtue of an invention that necessarily eluded Verne: wireless. Cavor's messages are devoted to a description of the moon-creatures—the insect breed which by vocational specialization has developed into a species with hundreds of varieties, each adapted for a single job.

Here Wells delves further into an idea that fascinated him as early as *The Time Machine* and *The War of the Worlds,* an idea that finds expression in all the utopian novels which he wrote until almost the end of his life. Wells believed that the specialization brought on by scientific advances would cause structural modifications of the individual. In *First Men,* for instance, the machine-minders have enormously developed hands; and memory-men, there being no books or writing on the moon, have enormous craniums and shrunken torsos. In a much later novel of Wells's more sanguine phase—*Men Like Gods* (1923)—the utopians wear no clothes, their lives having progressed to a state of unalloyed bliss.

No such optimism tempered the mood of the man who closed out his major scientific romances with *The First Men in the Moon.* The society of the Selenites reflects Huxley's cosmic pessimism at its blackest by exposing planned civilization at its worst. The adaptation and control of the organism produces efficiency in the moon-people and resolves instability caused by the struggle for existence, but human considerations are muted. In fact, it is impossible not to read into *The First Men in the Moon* a Wellsian commentary on Marxist theory. Georges Connes in *Étude sur la Pensée de Wells* (1926) draws a reverse analogy between revolution as promised by Marx and the evolvement of Wells's lunar society to a state of greater control by the few and stricter obedience by the many. Revolution, in fact, is rendered impossible by the acquiescence of the Selenites to superefficient specialization. The satire contained in Cavor's wire, telling how young Selenites are compressed in jars with only their elongated hands free to be trained for machine-minding, hints at Wells's suspicion that a society that makes its members into automatons is the worst kind of slave system. Efficiency has replaced morality.

The kind of technological utopia with which the popular image of Wells is associated was anathema to him in the five major scientific romances. Not efficiency but "freedom of mind"—the peace of Plato's idealism—is at the center of Wells's utopia. At the end of the book, Cavor's messages end. It is clear he has been slain by his captors. Unwisely, he had allowed the Selenites to glimpse earth's imperialistic tendencies, its penchant for war. In the fear that Cavor might "contaminate" the Selenites, the Grand Lunar found no alternative to killing him. Cavor's fatally revealing interview with the Grand Lunar appears to have been modeled after Gulliver's audience with the king of Brobdingnag. Lacking Swift's end-of-era misanthropism, Wells, writing at the start of a technological age, was content to warn readers of the dangers of unchecked scientific materialism.

Chapter Three
Literary Edison:
The Short Stories

H. G. Wells was only one of a large number of English storytellers who bear witness to the richness of short fiction in the 1890s. Writing during the next decade, he gathers "like a mixed handful of jewels drawn from a bag" some two dozen names for special mention and doubts, except for Conrad, if any—Kipling and James included—will come up to the quality of their 1890s stories. "It seems to me this outburst of short stories came not only as a phase in literary development, but also as a phase in the development of the individual writers concerned."[1]

In the 1890s, the golden age of the English short story had begun. Kipling's stories of Anglo-Indian life were opening a new and exotic dimension to readers worldwide. Poe and his theory of the well-made story had became a pattern for imitation, and a flourishing Maupassant community had come into existence on the English side of the channel. Wells's range is narrower than Kipling's, only rarely does Wells achieve effects anywhere near Poe's, and he is incapable of the irony underlying the deceptively simple studies of the French master. But from these three H. G. Wells discovered the technique of the short story. "I was doing my best to write as the other writers wrote," he acknowledges in his autobiography, "and it was long before I realized that my exceptional origins and training gave me an almost unavoidable freshness of approach" (E, 428).

Wells came to realize that his knowledge of science gave him a vantage point for writing a kind of story that was out of the reach of Kipling, Poe, and Maupassant. He soon occupied himself writing tales of the strange, which frequently described and usually extended some innovation of science or technology. In a progressive age, his visioning in 1903 of tank warfare ("The Land Ironclads") and of aerial flights early as 1897 ("The Argonauts of the Air") combined the topical with the novel in affairs. Only two months after the flying-machine story had been published, a flight similar to the one detailed in the story, also climaxed by an accident, took place over Berlin. Camille Flammarion was one of the first to describe modern types of aircraft in fiction, but Wells pioneered in making a mishap in a flying machine the object of treatment in a story.[2]

Early readers of Wells's tales, then, had the impression that they were being let in on something that had just happened, was happening, or was about to happen. However, the best stories transcend the merely topical. These, like the scientific romances, have the power to imbue the reader with a sense of personal freedom. Spirits soar; inhibitions fade. And the mood is sustained as it is only rarely in Wells's realistic novels.

Something Wells told an Australian radio audience in 1938 about his "prophetic" fiction is doubly applicable to his short fantasies. Often a story "starts as a joke . . . and does not attempt to be anything more," he observed. "There is a shock of laughter in nearly every discovery. . . . and if a writer keeps at the level of that first laugh, he will save himself a lot of trouble."[3]

H. E. Bates, himself a master of short fiction, was one of the first to see the twinkle of the eye. He praises Wells as "a great Kidder. . . . a man who succeeded in telling more tall stories than any writer of his generation yet, by a genius for binding the commonplace to some astounding exploration of fancy, succeeded in getting them believed."[4] The stories may well be, as Frank Swinnerton has said, the "most characteristic" of Wells's works.

The impetus to write these stories was first provided by Lewis Hind, then (1894) the editor of *Pall Mall Gazette,* who invited the twenty-eight-year-old Wells to contribute a series of "single-sitting" stories. Fifteen were published as a book in the same year (1895) that *The Time Machine* came out. Ingvald Raknem, after exhaustive research into the early criticism that heralded Wells, observes how much in fashion the twenty-nine-year-old author was: his *Stolen Bacillus and Other Incidents* was one of fifteen collections of stories reviewed in the *Athenaeum* of 21 December 1895.[5]

William Bellamy offers an interesting explanation for the prevalence of quality short fiction over longer in the 1890s. He places the phenomenon in the larger context of the fin de siècle, which he defines as less a matter of years than of mood. Crisis is the keynote, a "cultural anxiety" which for Bellamy "seems to have inhibited" the large statement.[6] The major self-contained works are novellas—Wilde's *Picture of Dorian Gray* (1891), Conrad's *Nigger of the "Narcissus"* (1897), Wells's *The Time Machine* (1895), and James's *Turn of the Screw* (1898). If a representative mind of the previous generation like Matthew Arnold's could respond to the post-Darwinian vanishing of God by turning to his fellow humans for consolation in poems like *Dover Beach* and *To Marguerite,* the fin-de-siècle man, of which Wells is representative, turns to "unconscious interests,' to which short stories were more responsive than novels. Wells's preoccupation with the bridging of cosmic consciousness and visionary unconsciousnes dates from these early stories.

> Mr. Hind's indicating finger had shown me an amusing possibility of the mind. I found that, taking almost anything as a starting point and letting my thoughts play about it, there would presently come out of the darkness, in a manner quite inexplicable, some absurd or vivid little nucleus. Little men in canoes upon sunlit oceans would come floating out of nothingness, incubating the eggs of prehistoric monsters unawares; violent conflicts would break out amidst the flower-beds of suburban gardens; I would discover I was peering into remote and mysterious worlds ruled by an order logical indeed but other than our common sanity.[7]

Bellamy does not regard it as coincidental that the coming century's most penetrating "peerer"—Freud—should have begun his investigations into the psyche in the 1890s: "It might be argued that the associative activism of Wells the short-story writer and Freud the psychoanalyst relates to a post-Darwinian breakdown in man's sense of a sequential universe. For *fin-de-siècle* man, disinherited and in crisis, sequential logic fails."[8] A sense of exhilaration, of anything is possible, even of awe takes over for logical progression. In "Under the Knife" (1896), Wells describes escape from the body in exuberant terms. A lovely flower displays predatory inclinations in "The Flowering of the Strange Orchid" (1894). Strange creatures threaten rationally based men in the comic "Aepyornis Island" (1894). These stories, whatever theories their emergence drew forth as the century came to its end or now, one hundred years later, showed an enormous capacity for sheer fun.

The Fantasies

"The Stolen Bacillus," the title story of Wells's maiden collection, not only is representative but is also the first of his "single-sitting" stories. It contains seedlings of *The Invisible Man, The War of the Worlds,* and *The History of Mr. Polly.* A bacteriologist tells a romantically inclined anarchist that he has imprisoned cholera bacillus in a test tube—enough, if introduced into the drinking supply, to bring pestilence to London. The anarchist, intent on destruction, steals the bottled cholera. The scientist pursues him by horse-cab and a maid-servant, anxious that the scientist not catch his death, brings up the rear carrying his coat. The scene flares into comic disarray, not unlike Mr. Polly's burning of the Fishbourne Hotel, with the three-way race described by a group of Cockneys. In his haste, the anarchist cracks the tube and, bent on martyrdom, drinks the potion. The bacteriologist confesses to his maid that he had only tried to astonish his visitor; that, far from being cholera bacillus, it was the bacterium bringing out blue patches in monkeys.

The story bears the early hints of Wells's penchant for superimposing exotic material from the laboratory on the prosaic lives of the lower middle class Wells knew so well. "The Stolen Bacillus" also reveals a strain of jolly humor amid the most serious of possibilities, one which Wells was to retain in his writings and in his life almost to the end. The anarchist and the scientist appear ludicrous to the spectators, the dire aspects of the chase notwithstanding. Griffin in *The Invisible Man,* with all his transparency, rampaged more picaresquely than formidably until he went berserk and had to be destroyed.

A famous story, "The Man Who Could Work Miracles" (1898), is archetypal of a vast literature about unprepossessing souls unexpectedly endowed with the power to upset their worlds. The clerk Fotheringay was an early model for Thorne Smith's Topper. Topper cavorted invisibly, but Fotheringay had real room for enterprise: his supreme windfall lay in conjuring up miracles. But as with so many who lack the proper combination of élan and restraint for the proper use of divine powers, Fotheringay let his reach exceed his grasp. Requesting that the earth stop rotating, he precipitated a scene of comic confusion as every object about him fell off into space.

The Parables

If Wells in those early stories gave dramatic and sometimes bizarre expression to his feelings about the infinite plasticity of things, he was also capable, within the confines of the short story form, of spinning parables to illustrate his distrust of perfected civilization. In a story like "The Lord of the Dynamos," the symbolic implications became more emphatic than in the "trick" fantasies. The first paragraph dramatizes one of Wells's polemical positions—hatred of Empire. The reader is introduced to the uncivilized-civilized white man, the characteristically wooden product of technological society, and to his "burden" who will rise against oppression and destroy:

The chief attendant of the three dynamos that buzzed and rattled at Camberwell and kept the electric railway going, came out of Yorkshire, and his name was

James Holroyd. He was a practical electrician but fond of whisky, a heavy red-haired brute with irregular teeth. He doubted the existence of the Deity but accepted Carnot's cycle, and he had read Shakespeare and found him weak in chemistry. His helper came out of the mysterious East, and his name was Azuma-zi. But Holroyd called him Pooh-bah. Holroyd liked a nigger because he would stand kicking—a habit with Holroyd—and did not pry into the machinery and try to learn the ways of it. Certain odd possibilities of the negro mind brought into abrupt contact with the crown of our civilization Holroyd never fully realized, though just at the end he got some inkling of them.[9]

Holroyd is pictured as a brute of the sort who, seventy-five years before the story saw print, had imposed an uncongenial order on the aboriginal population of Tasmania and had concluded by forcing its extinction. Wells acknowledged that conversations with his brother Frank about Tasmania had led to *The War of the Worlds*. At about the same time, his mentor Huxley was citing the extinction of the natives of that country as a tragedy of evolution.[10]

Holroyd and Azuma-zi, white man and "white man's burden," are opposed on all points: the positivism of the one contrasts with the superstitious nature of the other. Like Yank in O'Neill's *Hairy Ape*, Azuma-zi learns to worship the dynamo but for all the wrong reasons:[11] "Holroyd delivered a theological lecture on the test of his big machine soon after Azuma-zi came. He had to shout to be heard in the din. 'Look at that,' said Holroyd; 'where's your 'eathen idol to match 'im?' And Azuma-zi looked. For a moment Holroyd was inaudible, and then Azuma-zi heard: 'Kill a hundred men. Twelve per cent on the ordinary shares,' said Holroyd, 'and that's something like a Gord!'" (*F*, 279). Wells fastens the electrician's religious intimations to the dynamo: it is a god to him because of its "kill-a-hundred-men" power and of its importance to the capitalist enterprise Wells would soon deride at length, if symbolically, in *The Time Machine*.

The climax of "The Lord of Dynamos" is approached with a kind of dread inevitability rarely seen in Wells's longer fiction, except for *The Island of Dr. Moreau* and *The Invisible Man*. No polemic holds up the narrative; one feels the tightening of suspense. The native, under Holroyd's sneering tutorship, becomes a worshipper of the dynamo; and, by tribal custom, he must ritualize it. Azuma-zi one night grasps the lever and sends the armature in reverse. There is a struggle, and Holroyd is electrocuted. His death is taken to have been accidental, and a substitute arrives. For Azuma-zi, the newcomer is to be a second sacrifice. This time the Asiatic is foiled; to avoid capture, he kills himself by grasping the naked terminals of the dynamo. The conclusion is fittingly phrased in myth of undeniable power: "So ended prematurely the worship of the Dynamo Deity, perhaps the most short-lived of all religions. Yet withal it could at least boast a Martyrdom and a Human Sacrifice" (*F*, 286).

"The Lord of the Dynamos" is almost pure Kipling, and one feels a wave of sympathy for the misled Azuma-zi. Certainly, the story broadly conceives the meeting of the twain, East and West—the aboriginal Tasmanians and the British colonials. The work, writes Bernard Bergonzi in his brilliant book on Wells the mythmaker, recalls the early Joseph Conrad and *Heart of Darkness*, a novel not yet published when Wells wrote "Lord of the Dynamos" in 1894. Whether more Conradian or Kiplingesque is less important than that the story, like others among the handful by Wells that are consistently anthologized, can be read simply as a good yarn as well as for profounder implications beneath the parable.

In another of his earliest stories, "The Remarkable Case of Davidson's Eyes" (1895), Wells turns for the first time to the theme of what Bergonzi calls "the rootlessness and mental and emotional fragmentation of the modern intellectual." More simply, Wells was preoccupied from the beginning of his career with the conflicting compulsions of art, which he saw as alienating the practitioner from the mainstream of life, and with the teaching of ideas, which increasingly he came to see as his proper business. The publication in 1886 of *Dr. Jekyll and Mr. Hyde*, Stevenson's vivid reiteration of Poe's "William Wilson," dramatized an emergent end-of-century myth: the discovery of the unconscious mind. In his later idea novels, Wells directly acknowledged a debt to Carl Jung and his conception of the struggle in men's minds between Consciousness and the Shadow, Jung's feeling of living simultaneously in two different ages and of being two different persons.[12]

In "The Remarkable Case," an undistinguished young scientist named Sidney Davidson suffers a dislocation of his vision while conducting an experiment. While he continues to be bodily present in London, he lives *visually* on an uninhabited isle somewhere on the other side of the earth. Wells's fancy in a story of this kind is inventive beyond compare. When Davidson is taken downhill in London, his vision similarly descends on the island, so that at certain points he sees and describes a strange maritime world of luminous fishes; but he can still hear people passing in the London street and a newsboy selling papers. Normal vision returns, and the extrasensory world disappears. Years later a photograph proves to Davidson that the island did indeed exist, and the testimony of a ship's officer anchored offshore verifies the duality of Davidson's former life.

"The Story of the Late Mr. Elvesham," in which a young medical student named Eden enters into a kind of Faustian pact with an elderly stranger named Elvesham and enters the old man's body without losing his own mental identity, can also be taken as a play on the theme of spiritual schizophrenia.

By the time Wells stopped writing stories, the theme of self-alienation had flowered into a giant contempt for *ars pro arte*. Wells's last story, "The Pearl of Love" (1925), rejected that year by the editors of the *Saturday Evening Post* but subsequently published in England, dramatized the folly of projecting aesthetic means for spiritual ends.[13] Twenty years before "The Pearl," however, Wells had practically stopped writing short stories. Two of his latter ones, among his best known, provide a poetic rendering of Wells's own personal obsessions as man and artist.

"The Beautiful Suit," first published in *Collier's* (April 1909) under the title "A Moonlight Fable,' superficially follows the manner of a fairy tale by Oscar Wilde. A boy is presented by his mother with a shining suit but is constrained from wearing it, except on special occasions, by the poor woman's innate caution—a reference perhaps to Wells's own mother and to her sense of Victorian propriety. But the boy dreams of the fuller life he believes wearing the suit will bring him. One moonlit night he unwraps the precious gift, dons it, and in an ecstasy of fulfillment, plunges into what was, by day, a duck-pond but which to his enchanted night-sense "was a great bowl of silver moonshine . . . amidst which the stars were netted in tangled reflections of the brooding trees upon the bank" (*F*, 138).

The scene is suggestive of a familiar imagery in Wells: a "darkling" forest ("darkling," almost Wells's favorite word, occurs countless times in his books and finally in the title of his penultimate novel) is bent on consuming the wanderer but is capable of being cleared by dint of superior guidance. To the boy's starry eyes, his suit equips him for his journey; but next morning his body is found in the bottom of a stone pit, "with his beautiful clothes a little bloody, and foul and stained with the duckweed from the pond [but] his face . . . of such happiness . . . that you would have understood indeed . . . he had died happy . . ." (*F*, 139).

In "The Door in the Wall," written in 1906, three years before "The Beautiful Suit," Wells's little boy has grown up. He is Lionel Wallace, a cabinet minister and an early foreshadowing of the ill-fated politician Remington in *The New Machiavelli*. Wallace's misgivings are less realistic than Remington's. He is haunted by a childhood memory of a door that leads into a garden containing all the things success has denied him— peace, delight, beauty. Three times Wallace rejects the door before yielding to its promise and, at the end, falls to his death, like the boy in "The Beautiful Suit," but in an excavation pit.

The story was written at a time when a widening of the author's social experience and meteoric rise in earnings must have produced uncertainty about the direction of his literary career or, to use the word Wells borrows from Jung, about his multiple personas. His first marriage had failed, and his second one, while made tenable by an understanding that he would always be free to pursue extramarital relationships, was never entirely satisfactory. Only a few years earlier Wells could write to Arnold Bennett that the *Strand Magazine* paid one hundred twenty-five pounds for a short story and *Pearson's* fifteen pounds per thousand words to serialize *The Sea Lady* (1901).[14] Even earlier Wells was earning rates equal to those accorded the well-established Thomas Hardy.[15] By 1905, when *Kipps* appeared, he was being compared to Dickens. Men on both sides of the Atlantic—literary figures as various as Oscar Wilde, Henry James, Ambrose Bierce, and William Dean Howells—were welcoming Wells to the front rank of young English literati.

Bernard Bergonzi, a modern student of the early Wells, while finding it possible to draw Freudian implications from "The Door in the Wall," is much more illuminating when he detects in the story an allegory tied to warring natures within the writer:

The beautiful garden behind the closed door . . . can be readily taken as a symbol of the imagination, and Wallace as a projection of Wells's literary personality. At the start of his career as a writer he possessed a unique imagination, which flowed in a number of brilliantly original romances; yet after a few years he turned to realistic fiction, and then to works in which he tried to dragoon his imaginative powers for specifically didactic or pamphleteering purposes; at which the quality of his original imagination deserted him. Here, perhaps, we see the implication of the closed door, glimpsed from time to time, but never opened again. . . .[16]

The Mythmaker as Artist:
Two Versions of "Country of the Blind"

"The Country of the Blind," the last of the stories that will be discussed, is more than Wells's finest achievement as a writer of short fiction. Of all his vast array of works, this story best states H. G. Wells's philosophical position in terms of the techniques of the literary artist. Wells's conception of the world was mystical and his hopes for it, as viewed in all his authentic novels and stories, dark. In 1904, when he wrote "The Country of the Blind," Wells had already approached the divided trail.

What probably tipped the scales toward books like *Utopia* over books like *Kipps* was a destructive Fabian interlude—to be discussed fully in chapter 5—that led Wells to see humanity less and less in terms of the individual and more and more in collective terms. His first essay for the Fabian Socialists was written about the same time as "The Country of the Blind." The latter is the outcry of the artist to the demands of the propagandist.

More effectively than anywhere except in certain of the scientific romances and in the last pages of *Tono-Bungay*, "The Country of the Blind" blends the riches of the humanist storyteller and the mystic visionary. To the mythmaker at the heart of Wells, no imagery proved so obsessive as that of this story. From his student days under T. H. Huxley down to his deathbed conviction that mankind had played itself out, Wells viewed mankind darkly: as struggling in an evolutionary whirl to achieve a millennium of beauty, but always forced back into some sealed-off country of the blind.

Essentially, the story is a pessimistic restatement of Plato's Allegory of the Cave. The mountaineer Núñez comes unawares on a fastness deep in the Andes, where for centuries the inhabitants have been sightless and where the idea of seeing has disappeared. At first, Núñez brazenly assumes the truth of the proverb, "In the country of the blind, the one-eyed man is king" and he confidently expects to become master. However, he finds that the blind inhabitants have developed other faculties; that in a land where no one sees, the sighted are actually handicapped. Eventually Núñez is forced to submit and his submission includes giving up his eyes, regarded by the blind as grievous and useless appendages. As Núñez rebels and endeavors to escape over the mountains, he is obliged to leave behind the woman, Medina-saroté, he has come to love.

Like the prisoners of the cave, the blind have made the remote valley a symbol of estrangement. They can no more conceive of a world outside their valley than the chained cave dwellers of Plato could imagine anything beyond the flickering shadows on the wall. Their mental inertia—and Wells wrote in a score of novels that bondage to empty tradition is the earmark of the uneducated mind—becomes apparent in the first dialogue between the newcomer and the blind:

"And you have come into the world?" asked Pedro.
"*Out* of the world. Over the mountains and glaciers; right over above there, half-way to the sun. Out of the great big world that goes down, twelve days' journey to the sea."

They scarcely seemed to heed him. "Our fathers have told us men may be made by the forces of nature," said Correa. "It is the warmth of things and moisture and rottenness—rottenness."(*F,* 171)

The opposition between light and darkness—truth and superstition—is nowhere more forcefully depicted than in the contrast between the sighted Núñez and the unseeing: "They told him there were indeed no mountains at all, but that the end of the rocks where the llamas grazed was indeed the end of the world; thence sprang a cavernous roof of the universe, from which the dew and the avalanches fell; and when he maintained stoutly the world had neither roof nor end as they supposed, they said his thoughts were wicked" (*F,* 177). And later: "Núñez had an eye for all beautiful things, and it seemed to him that the glow upon the snowfields and glaciers that rose about the valley on every side was the most beautiful thing he had ever seen" (*F,* 187).

The glow of the greater world that wreathed the narrow valley was, metaphorically, H. G. Wells's challenge to the unnameable hordes of humanity content to live in their determinist furrows. Even in *Kipps,* a triple-decker novel seemingly written by another part of the mind that produced "The Country of the Blind," Wells is preoccupied by the imagery of sight and shadow: "As I think of [Kipps and Ann] lying unhappily there in the darkness, my vision pierces the night. See what I can see. Above them, brooding over them . . . there is a monster . . . like all that is darkening and heavy and obstructive. . . . It is matter and darkness, it is the anti-soul, it is the ruling power of this land, Stupidity. My Kippses live in its shadow" (*W,* 8:415).

However, it is not Núñez's fate, as it was Wells's lifelong dream, to save the country of the blind from its torpor of ignorance. Rather he is subjugated by the sightless hordes; humiliated by them; and though he escapes the valley, defeated.

Bergonzi finds in "The Country of the Blind" a mythical anticipation of the brainwashing techniques of modern totalitarianism.[17] Núñez, driven by hunger and sleeplessness and despair, agrees to conform to the blind rationale. His final surrender comes, when he reluctantly agrees to the condition of his blind overlords that he allow "those irritant bodies"—his eyes—to be removed by surgery. Núñez, however, rebels at the prospect of blindness, begs his lover Medina-saroté to flee the valley with him, is refused, and dies, a worthless outcast. Meanwhile the blind world goes on, self-satisfied.

A revealing postscript to "The Country of the Blind"—indeed to Wells's brief phase as full-time literary artist—was provided a third of a century after his original writing of the story. In 1939, the Golden Cockerell Press of London, for a limited and numbered edition (280 copies), asked Wells to update his famous story.[18] But, to grasp the significance of what Wells did to his finest effort in short fiction, it is necessary to jump ahead briefly. By 1939 Wells's voice had grown shrill with warnings that the world, it appeared, had failed to heed. The same year that he revised "The Country of the Blind," he had made his last voyage to the United States. His pleas for a world state were heard by thousands with the respect due an elder statesman of letters. W. Somerset Maugham recalled the twilight phase in a memoir that concludes: "[Wells] was mortified that people looked upon him as a has-been. . . . When they listened it was . . . with the indulgence you accord to an old man who has outlived his interest." The world in 1939, even as the Andean valley reincarnated by Wells, *was* cracking.

The revision of "The Country of the Blind" runs parallel to the original until the final page when Núñez, having made his escape, sees along the vast rock a fresh scar. As certain of coming doom as his creator in his own agonizing last years, Núñez contemplates risking his life by returning to the valley. He considers falling at the feet of the blind people; pleading "Believe in my vision. Sometimes such an idiot as I can *see.*" Only the sight of a moving crack of disaster spurs him to action. Wells describes the sound of destruction as "like the shot of a gun that starts a race." The metaphor is vintage of the man who described humanity's race between education and catastrophe.

In a tacked-on epilogue, Wells reveals that Núñez and his beloved Medina-saroté won the race. They lived to tell their tale—among Núñez's people. Wells concludes on an ironic though not surprising note for a writer who soon afterward, under sentence of death in a mortal illness, would view the seeing world as "going clean out of existence, leaving not a wrack behind . . ."[19] Wells switches focus to Medina-saroté, now the mother of four. Her life saved by her husband's vision, she expresses no desire to see. Her last words are also the revised version's last: "The loveliness of *your* world is a complicated and fearful loveliness and mine is simple and near. . . . It may be beautiful . . . but it must be terrible to *see.*" Wells appears to be saying that blindness is the only bearable antidote to the coming catastrophe. He has reversed Plato's allegory by letting one of the prisoners of the cave (or valley of the blind) return from the light—unchanged. While Medina-saroté may not have *seen,* she knows sight saved her life; yet she still prefers the illusions of the cave—blindness.

The contrast between the two versions of his most well-known short story tells more about the fatal ambivalence in Wells than can be learned from the millions of words of hack journalism that occupied him during the fallow half of an intensely productive literary life. That Wells should at the end of his life go back to one of the acknowledged minor classics of his golden period and rewrite it to conform to a growing misanthropy is one more index to the truth that he failed to resolve the conflicting claims of the artist and the public educator. Although he flawed his imperishable story, he also provided undeniable evidence at the eleventh hour that his dark conception of the world—the conception that pervaded *The Time Machine* and *The Island of Dr. Moreau*—could no longer sustain the optimism of his journalism and would, in the end, overwhelm him.

Chapter Four

"Spiritual Guttersnipe":
The Comic Novels

Critics are right who see the early H. G. Wells as firmly in the tradition of the "angry young men."[1] It could not be otherwise. His childhood had been shattered by the cruelty of Victorian society, which seemed bent on relegating him to the trash heap of drapery. A rebel's attitude, or a criminal's, was the concomitant. However, in the case of Wells an early sense of the absurd in his relationship to society was wedded to a sustaining stoicism in the face of one illness after another. This special alchemy transmuted his anger into warmly sympathetic characterizations like those of Polly and Kipps.

Wells had already filtered his warnings to a somnambulant bourgeoisie through his scientific imagination; they took the forms of time-traveling and invisibility, possibilities of human development amid the common lot. Now it remained for him to turn from the nightmares inherent in contemporary science to those inherent in the human condition. From the start, Wells had refused to give in to the twin traumata of his youth: his father's insolvency and the draper's trade. If the greater world outside the tradesman's shop would not admit him willingly, he would force his way:

But when a man has once broken through the paper walls of everyday circumstance . . . he has made a discovery. If the world does not please you *you can change it* altogether. You may change it to something appalling, but it may be you will change it to something brighter, something more agreeable, and at worst something much more interesting. There is only one sort of man who is absolutely to blame for his own misery, and that is the man who finds life dull and dreary. . . .

This quotation sounds like the later Wells and like one of those exhortative tracts that always promised a pot of gold if only society would legislate a rainbow. Instead, it comes from Wells's most enduring novel. Appearing as it did near the end of *The History of Mr. Polly* (1910) (see *W*, 17:212), it spurred that dyspeptic little man to "clear out": to leave the

41

shop he despised, his bed and his snoring wife, Miriam; to strike out against the petty middle-class world he had accepted without question.

With the appearance of *Kipps and Mr.Polly,* Wells was hailed as a new Dickens. Some of the similarities may be noted. Dickens kept up a relentless attack on Marshalsea Prison where his debtor father languished; Wells during his best period held the terrain of the small tradesman as his true north and harangued at the cage that enslaved his spirit. Wells celebrated his father in Mr. Polly, just as Dickens did his in Mr. Micawber. Both writers gloried in what E. M. Forster calls, without disparagement, "flat" characterizations in which habits of speech and dress are stockpiled.[2]

However, in their feelings about the relationship of the individual to society, the differences between Dickens and Wells are more revealing than any likenesses. Dickens insisted that all it took for the world to become better would be for the Uriah Heeps and Merdles to be better people. Wells discounted individual evil—there are almost no villains in his novels—and insisted that what people *did* in society was vital. After all, had not science and his talent for it delivered him? For Dickens, workers and society would flourish if everyone behaved like Tiny Tim. For Wells, it was the organization of society that, if it did not corrupt, certainly paralyzed men from making the proper use of themselves. Dickens loved—or hated—the objects of his inspired caricatures; but Wells acknowledged late in his life what all but a select few of his books bespoke: "For all my desire to be interested I have to confess that for most things and people I don't care a damn" (*E, 20*). When Dickens exalted goodness and gave Heep his "comeuppance," the sparks flew; he cared. As Wells intruded more and more directly on the actions of his novels, his voice drowned out the individuality of his characters. If he cared at all about the Britlings and Clissolds—those repositories for Wells's later thrashings with his persona—his feelings were concentrated on the fidelity with which *they* represented *him.*

But for a brief time—the period placed by Orwell between the publication of *The Time Machine* (1895) and that of *Mr. Polly* (1910)—Wells did care for the figures in his tableau. If fortune denied him that wide sympathy for humankind that placed a Dickens or a Balzac in the first rank of novelists, Wells unquestionably caught in a handful of early comic novels enough of the poetry of the human spirit to move Norman Nicholson, despite his disappointment with the later books, to proclaim that Kipps and Mr. Polly "have in them more of the stuff which endures than the characters of any of Wells's contemporaries or successors."[3]

Kipps (1905)

It is true that Kipps and Polly—as well as Hoopdriver, Wells's bicycling draper's assistant who in *The Wheels of Chance* (1896) rode ahead—are no less projections of Wells than the writers, scientists, politicians, and teachers of the later idea-novels. These three are the products of Wells's temperament—egotistic and romantic—before it battled for its life with an intellect that tried to persuade him that the egotistic and romantic had to go. Hoopdriver, Kipps, and Polly all struggle against the imperfections of the human condition that pose also as defects of Victorian society. Implicit in their dreams of a tradesman's Elysium are the pangs of the angry young sociologist in Wells. But the novelist's insights that have enshrined Kipps and Polly in the permanent gallery of memorable characters worked as minutely and as unseen in the early Wells as the zeal to preach loomed large in the later.

Artie Kipps and Mr. Polly are specimens of the muddled inferior material with which the subsequent Wells, or any other sociological messiah, would have to deal in reworking society. Although never intrusive, the autobiographical tendency in Wells is unmistakable. *Kipps,* especially in its early scenes, borrows incidents Wells had experienced as a draper, as well as childhood impressions Wells later recorded in his autobiography. The first chapter, a brilliant précis of the massive first third of the "big" novel, *Tono-Bungay,* due to be started the next year, is an account of the circumstances that thwarted a lower-middle class youth at the end of Victoria's reign:

> When Kipps left New Romney, with a small yellow tin box, a still smaller portmanteau, a new umbrella, and a keepsake half-sixpence, to become a draper, he was a youngster of fourteen, thin, with whimsical drake's tails at the poll of his head, smallish features, and eyes that were sometimes very light and sometimes very dark, gifts those of his birth; and by the nature of his training he was indistinct in his speech, confused in his mind, and retreating in his manners. Inexorable fate had appointed him to serve his country in commerce, and the same national bias towards private enterprise and leaving bad alone, which had left his general education to Mr. Woodrow, now indentured him firmly into the hands of Mr. Shalford of the Folkestone Drapery Bazaar. (*W,* 8:34)

At this point Wells has changed little but the names of people and places. Kipps's story after he left the drapery has nothing in common with that of Wells, yet the author's presence is felt in several later chapters. He breaks in on the narrative, airs a grievance, prods with a criticism. The personal note is discernible in many places, especially in the discourses on socialism and the housing problem.

Bertie Wells saved himself from the Emporium by scholastic brilliance leading to a series of science scholarships; but Kipps is ordinary and after seven years' apprenticeship only the swift stroke of fictional incident can save him. He comes into a fortune—twenty-six thousands pounds left him by his paternal grandfather. The gift comes on the heels of a riotous drinking scene which has resulted in Kipps being dismissed by Mr. Shalford.

Under the guidance of Chester Coote, the nouveau-riche Kipps joins Folkestone high society and marries Helen Walsingham, who belongs to a county family and is related to an earl. Kipps, a sadly displaced person among the upper crust, perseveres; he pretends to accept standards he knows to be false. But finally, in desperation, he runs off with his childhood sweetheart, Ann, now a Folkestone housemaid. Eventually he marries Ann, and they set up house. The path of the second marriage is rough, strewn with ludicrous quarrels over the propriety of receiving and returning "calls." In *Kipps* Wells deals superficially with problems of marriage and remarriage that he later treated in detail in a long series of novels beginning with *Love and Mr. Lewisham* (1900) and ending with *Apropos of Dolores* (1938).

In *Kipps,* Wells's verve is unimpaired, but his imagination is not nearly so rich and varied as in the scientific romances. When Artie Kipps loses his fortune—speculated away by his first wife's lawyer brother—Wells turns to the dangers of free enterprise in the hands of incompetents like Kipps, a theme he was to pursue much more memorably in *Tono-Bungay.*

Another stroke, a second fortune stemming from an investment, saves Artie and Ann. By now Kipps has recognized his place, and the money makes no change in him. In a sense the System has triumphed over Kipps. American critics, Ingvald Raknem reports, characterized the novel as disagreeable: "The appalling vulgarity of English lower-class society, its absolute aloofness from everything that gives a spiritual meaning to life, this utter imperviousness to ideas of any kind, are the impressions that chiefly remain after reading *Kipps.*"[4]

What has vindicated the novel for later critics, especially when viewed in the perspective of Wells's gradual alienation from his characters, is the involvement of the author in Kipps's uneasy subservience, his clumsy, though essentially true-to-life, gropings toward self-realization:

"Artie," said Ann.
He woke up and pulled a stroke. "What?" he said.

"Penny for your thoughts, Artie."

He considered. "I really don't think I was thinking of anything," he said at last with a smile. "No."

He still rested on his oars. "I expect," he said, "I was just thinking what a Rum Go everything is. I expect it was something like that."

"Queer old Artie!"

"Aren't I? I don't suppose there ever was a chap quite like me before." (*W*, 8:450)

As long as Wells, the man and the novelist, maintained Kipps at the center of his being, there is no danger of the sage overrunning that which in Wells was supremely ordinary. But, along with his identification with Kipps, there is a restless current of proprietary condescension. It is as if the coming giant Wells were giving the tiny Wells—Kipps—a pitying pat on the head and turning from the Kippses and Anns, with whom his romantic temperament was in perfect correspondence, to the collective forces of society, to which his restless intellect was urgently being summoned: "I think of [Kipps and Ann] lying unhappily there in the darkness. . . . Above them . . . a monster . . . it is the antisoul, it is the ruling power of this land, Stupidity. My Kippses live in its shadow" (*W*, 8:415).

This statement, from near the end of *Kipps*, charts the course of H. G. Wells. He will engage the monster of Victorian stupidity in mortal combat. He will bring, as no other writer of his time, a sense of liberation to his generation. He will, as C. E. M. Joad put it, "take the wrappings off the lay figures of Victorian respectability, pass through their ribs the rapier of [his] wit."[5]

Kipps was developed from the later part of a typescript entitled *The Wealth of Mr. Waddy,* which Wells sent to his agent James B. Pinker in January 1899. This incomplete material, which Wells later assumed to have been lost, was found among his papers and published in 1969. The MacKenzies report that "Wells changed his mind about the book . . . shifting the emphasis from [Mr. Waddy] the irascible man of property in a wheel chair to the fortunes and misfortunes of [Kipps] the draper's apprentice who inherits his wealth."[6] Mr. Waddy is merely an offstage presence in *Kipps*. From the point at which Kipps learns of his inheritance, the later book follows the broad outlines of the earlier. What altered Wells's plan to write a 200,000-word *Mr. Waddy* was the disappearance of the old Victorian three-decker. This shift in publishing convention was, in this case, salutary. Wells wrote to Pinker that the new work had become "the complete study of a life in relation to England's social condition." Like *Tono-Bungay,* its almost immediate and more ambitious successor as a condition-of-England novel, *Kipps* successfully fused the lot of the genteel poor and their agonizing efforts to find a place for themselves in Edwardian England.

The History of Mr. Polly (1910)

The History of Mr. Polly represents an advance in Wells's Cockney hero. Polly is more vigorous, both in his dreams and in his rebellion, than Kipps. If Kipps was the Wells that might have been without the latter's burning desire to cut a figure in the world, Polly is more like Bertie's father, Joseph Wells, who stargazed and dreamed of a better life. The elder Wells never rose out of the mire of his class and trade. Polly does.

Mr. Polly is Thurber's Walter Mitty carried to the tenth power—or millionth. He dreams like Mitty, but he also speaks in a frantically rebellious series of fractured "suffixiations" of incomprehensible enchantment: "Sesquippledan verboojuice" is his rendering of something he invoked in the hope that his lingual ignorance would be taken for whim. "In Mr. Polly," writes Vincent Brome, "Wells was . . . in the full-blooded Dickens tradition, rebelling against the frustrations of the human personality . . . kicking hard at the dumb elephant of education, but possessed more than anything with the essence of Polly, the man as a man."[7]

Wells begins his novel squarely in the middle. Mr. Polly is thirty-seven—a miserable, hopeless man—suffering from a severe attack of indigestion. In his later, more urgent concept novels, Wells rarely delayed the rush of ideas to describe a character in the throes of dyspepsia. In his description of Mr. Polly, Wells showed a real knowledge of the details of life, the needs and troubles of the poor. After Mr. Polly endures his lot for fifteen years, he revolts. He intends to commit suicide and to burn his house down, thus providing his wife Miriam with a double insurance. The suicide does not come off but the fire is a great success, spreading from Mr. Polly's own shop to half a dozen other establishments. Excited by his own handiwork, he gallantly rescues an old woman and becomes the town's hero.

Then Polly quietly sneaks away. For his wife, even on his wedding day, Polly has felt "alarm, desire, affection, respect—and a queer element of reluctant dislike" (W, 17:133). She becomes after marriage limply unhelpful, utterly irritating, perpetually ready to scold. Mr. Polly, after his "bit of arson," knows Miriam has her insurance money. He means to have life. He is a born romantic, a poet forced by miseducation to disregard every known turn of language. Polly's rebellion was particularly well thought out and particularly wholehearted. He meant to gain his freedom and was unaffected by the fact that arson is a crime. Few readers, then or now, would condemn Mr. Polly's desertion of his wife, his deceit in allowing her to think he was drowned, or the preliminary arson. Wells was always an advocate of marshaling action to alter intolerable circumstances. The salvaging of Mr. Polly justified the means: a disconnected dyspeptic became a contented, healthy man.

But what of Miriam? What of the wife whom he abandoned? When Polly skips off, she is able to use the insurance to set up a teashop (in the variant from life, Wells established his first wife in the laundry business). Polly's rationale includes this "ode" to the folly of trying to bridge irreconcilable connubial interests: "It isn't what we try to get that we get, it isn't the good we think we do that is good. What makes us happy isn't our trying, what makes others happy isn't our trying. There's a sort of character people like and stand for and a sort they won't. You got to work it out and take the consequences" (*W,* 17:279–80).

All the characters in *Mr. Polly* are comic, and they are real. Among Polly's relatives is the wise Uncle Penstemon who classes his dreamer nephew as "the marrying sort":

> "You *got* to get married," said Uncle Penstemon resuming his discourse. "That's the way of it. Some has. Some hain't. I done it long before I was your age. It hain't for me to blame you. You can't 'elp being the marrying sort any more than me. It's nat-ral—like poaching or drinking or wind on the stummick. You can't 'elp it and there you are. As for the good of it, there ain't no particular good in it as I can see. It's a toss-up. The hotter come the sooner cold; but they all gets tired of it sooner or later. (*W,* 17:148)

The exuberance of the book is Dickensian, yet it is without a trace of the plodding booby-traps of syntax that slow that master's novels for the modern reader. Much of Wells has dated, but not a paragraph of *Polly.* The novel is, as Sinclair Lewis wrote in 1941, as contagious as ever, "the eternal story of the kindly, friendly Little Man, whose heart and courage would anywhere . . . lift him from behind the counter of the Gents' Furnishings Shoppe, and lead him out to find a wayside world that is perpetually new and surprising."[8]

With Mr. Polly, Sidney Dark reminds the reader, Wells proved himself seer enough to realize that "tragedy and comedy are all to be found on everyone's doorstep [and they] jostle each other wherever two or three men are gathered together."[9] However, this truism H. G. Wells all too quickly forgot.

Chapter Five
Wells at the Crossroads: *Tono-Bungay*

The great crisis in Wells's life as a literary artist and as a man came neither in his thirties nor in his sixties. For H. G. Wells, the divided trail came in his early forties when, with thirty volumes already published and status as a public figure well in hand, he chose the Shavian preference, classically expressed in the preface to *Man and Superman,* to be a force recognizable only in one's own time. The body of work produced by Wells before his forty-fifth year was, as Orwell has pointed out, the fruit of a first-rate literary talent. It was not accompanied, however, by even a jot of reverence for the life of the conscious literary personage visioning immortality.

Mrs. Humphry Ward wrote to Henry James that she found Wells "coarse," and James wrote back that he liked H. G.'s "cheek," a word admirably describing Wells's attitude toward the canons of art James held sacrosanct.[1] Wells's writings are replete with satirical comment on the pretensions of the literati. The vein began with one of his earliest pieces, an essay (contributed in 1893 to the *Pall Mall Gazette*) suggesting that literary capacity is engendered by indigestion and proposing that chemical food be exploited for its unwholesomeness and salutary effect on literary aspirants. Wells's penchant for ridiculing the pompous solemnity of the artist was climaxed in 1911 with the publication of *Boon* and its famous burlesque of the manner of Henry James. A James novel, he wrote, "is like a church lit but without a congregation to distract you, with every light and line focused on the high altar. And on the altar, very reverently placed, intensely there, is a dead kitten, an egg shell, a bit of string."[2] Wells's badinage against the literati was largely defensive; it was prompted by their patronization of him "to the limit of endurance." The extent to which criticism wounded him can best be gauged by his tendency for the next thirty years to strike back at what he took to be an irresponsible campaign to bury him as a novelist of stature.

The foregoing should not create the impression that all of the growing pains of the young writer were exclusively literary. Wells was also learning

48

the pitfalls of the author who is also a celebrity. He did not see until they almost wrecked him that his private acts were inseparable from his published acts and ideas in the molding of a reputation. His autobiography, which deals candidly and at length with his life up to 1904, barely mentions in passing a five-year Fabian phase (1903–8) which brought him to the brink of social ruin. He devotes only two pages to "the crowded meetings. . . , the gathered 'intelligentsia'—then so new in English life—the old radical veterans and the bubbling new young people. . . ." It was Wells's relations with the "new young"—the new young suffragettes, the Fabian daughters and bluestockings in particular—that helped plunge the obstreperous socialist crusader into disrepute and discreditation.

Beatrice Webb, after her first meeting with him, recorded in her diary that "Wells is an interesting though somewhat unattractive personality except for his agreeable disposition and intellectual vivacity. . . . Altogether it is refreshing to talk to a man who has shaken himself loose from so many of the current assumptions and is looking at life as an explorer of a new world."[3] The social geography of the "new world" that Wells was exploring proved quite other than Beatrice Webb envisioned and more by far than she and the other Fabians bargained for. It was a new world of woman's emancipation, and in Wells's case it would be more audacious than brave. One of the "current assumptions" from which he was shaking loose was monogamy. The Fabians, "more like an extended family than a political organisation," were not ready for a nonmonogamous member in their midst.

Norman and Jeanne MacKenzie have provided the fullest and most reliable account we have of the effects of Wells's determination to practice what he preached as a force for suffragism. It is beyond the scope of this study of the writing Wells to chronicle the philandering Wells. Where the two coalesce is part of the business of the next chapter. It is sufficient here to note his tendency to allow his obsession with polygamous relationships to pour openly into his fiction. Another way of saying this would be the observation that Wells actively espoused feminism as a novelist and as a man. Kingsley Martin, long-time editor of the *New Statesman,* goes so far as to declare that the emancipation of women was the crusade on which Wells had the most influence and that *Ann Veronica* is his most important book. The latter "hastened the notion of the 'equal mate,' the splendid girl striding fearlessly side by side with her man. . . . It sounded fine, especially as the adventures included free sex relations and we had not then discovered the difficulties that arise when both partners are free to experiment and both try to do a job and have a family at the same time."[4]

In every facet of his life Wells wanted things both ways. He had an "arrangement," never codified, with his Jane that he would be free to pursue any amorous inclination while she would continue to be his wife, the mother of their two sons, his amanuensis and tireless hostess in charge of the bustling social life that befitted a famous man. He began to insist that the public persona bore no necessary relation to the private one, and that any attempt to demonstrate links between what he wrote and his own private life was as wrongheaded as it was intrusive.

The Fabian adventure illustrated the disaster that awaited Wells when sides of his public and private selves came into conflict. He joined in February 1903, sponsored by Shaw and Graham Wallas. He appeared a welcome newcomer, a good instrument, especially to the Webbs, for popularizing ideas. To them he had an affinity for just their kind of efficient, middle-class socialism. The Fabians, in turn, presented for Wells the only base available to him for portfolio as an intellectual and a prophet.

But the Fabians were ruled by an Old Gang who were the most genteel of revolutionists seeking to achieve a socialist society without provision for birth pangs or militant intent to wipe the slate clean. Such a one as Wells, who throughout the Fabian years was working on a novel about the decay in the condition of England and irresponsible takeover by a capitalist misadventurer and the fraud of his vehicle called tono-bungay, was inevitably attracted away from the Fabian moderates and toward certain eccentrics who scurried around the edges of the progressive movement. These were people who believed in sexual permissiveness, people like Hubert Bland, one of the Fabian founders, his wife, Edith Nesbit, and their beautiful daughter Rosamund, about whom more in the next chapter.

Although there are many tributes to Wells's influence on the Fabians— a long-time secretary[5] of the group called *New Worlds for Old,* written by Wells while a member of the Fabian Executive, the best recent book on English socialism—the five-year interlude was destructive to both the creative artist and the man. Although Wells railed at their parochialism and left them finally over a dispute with the Old Guard about methods of expanding their influence, he involved himself in a long series of intramural skirmishes that continually deflected his aim from more primary matters in the life of a novelist of widening scope.

When the showdown came, Wells was soundly thrashed in parliamentary debate. Shaw, who led the onslaught, later declared that he smote down his inexperienced adversary to save Wells embarrassment, as well as to protect the reputations of some of the older Fabians whom Wells had maligned. Shaw, who was intensely competitive and could not have helped but recognize the arrival of an equal, summarized the interlude by saying that the Old Gang did not extinguish Wells; he annihilated himself.[6] In after years, while never quite forgiving Shaw for what he regarded as a needlessly prominent role in his discreditation, Wells confessed that his frustrations in the Fabian Society reinforced his bias against all human planners. He later embraced enthusiastically and then violently rejected, in their turn, the Labor party, the League of Nations, and the Soviet Union. No artist ever gave more of himself to the issues of his day. However, his panaceas were invariably visionary by-products of his creativity. Leonard Woolf tells an amusing story about how badly Wells took the words of a critic that he did his thinking with his imagination.[7] Of Wells, no truer words were ever spoken. Those of his ideas that are remembered at all were given fire by his imagination. He would in a few years embark on his mammoth *Outline of History* as an indefatigable lobbyist for a World State. Yet nothing of that gigantic scheme to sell an idea survives with the vividness of those end-of-world scenes in *The Time Machine,* whose first version was penned by an unknown science student. Membership in the Fabians forced Wells to formulate endless "what-I-believe" slogans uncongenial to the intuitive artist.

First and Last Things (1908)

Out of the welter of essays stemming from the Fabian phase (the title of his first excursion, "The Questions of Scientific Administrative Areas in Relation to Municipal Undertakings," gives an idea of what the Fabians put him up to) came *First and Last Things,* Wells's most fruitful effort at a systematic statement of his philosophy. As early as 1891, Wells had written an article for Frank Harris and the *Fortnightly Review* called "The Rediscovery of the Unique." Now, fifteen years later, Wells reiterated his denial of scientific precision as possible in questions of human relations:

Now I make my beliefs as I want them. I do not attempt to distil them out of fact as physicists distil their laws. I make them thus and not thus exactly as an artist makes a picture so and not so. I believe that is how we all make our beliefs, but that many people do not see this clearly and confuse their beliefs with perceived and proven fact. . . .

The artist cannot defend his expression as a scientific man defends his, and demonstrate that they are true upon any assumptions whatsoever. . . .

. . . I adopt certain beliefs because I feel the need for them, because I feel an often quite unanalyzable rightness in them. . . . My belief in them rests upon the fact that they work for me and satisfy my desire for harmony and beauty. They are arbitrary assumptions, if you will, that I see fit to impose upon my universe. (*W,* 11:216–17)

This credo, of course, is that of the artist, whatever his medium. From this position there should follow, as a freshet flows from a mainstream, a disposition to regard each human, the raw material for literary art, as unique. However, following a statement of belief that so befits the creator of a Kipps and a Mr. Polly, Wells swerved from the acceptance of individuality as uniqueness to a belief in a superhuman synthesis transcending and absorbing individuality:

The essential fact in man's history to my sense is the slow unfolding of a sense of community with his kind, of the possibilities of co-operations leading to scarce dreamt-of collective powers, of a synthesis of the species, of the development of a common general idea, a common general purpose out of a present confusion. In that awakening of the species, one's own personal being lives and moves—a part of it and contributing to it. *One's individual existence is not so entirely cut off as it seems at first; one's entirely separate individuality is another, a profounder, among the subtle inherent delusions of the human mind.* . . .

You see that from this point of view . . . our individualities, our nations and states and races are but bubbles and clusters of foam upon the great stream of the blood of the species, incidental experiments in the growing knowledge and consciousness of the race. (*W,* 11:248–50; my italics)

Although Wells anticipated and denied the charge that his statement was mystical, it is difficult to reconcile the Mind-of-Race with the minds of those raw, lower-middle-class types whose chronicles were building Wells a solid reputation as a novelist of power. It was clear that in *First and Last Things* H. G. Wells was formulating a rationale for the kind of art to which he planned to devote himself. In 1911 he would astonish the literary establishment with his emancipation proclamation for the Novel. "We [novelists] are going to write," he declared, "about the whole of human life . . . about business and finance and politics and precedence and pretentiousness and decorum and indecorum, until a thousand pretenses and ten thousand impostures shrivel in the cold, clear air of our elucidations."[8] Wells's credo, as both philosopher and novelist, should have presented fair warning of the spate of "dialogue" and "idea" novels that were to come from his pen.

However, at about the same time—1906—that he was writing Fabian drafts of the essays later revised into *First and Last Things,* Wells set to work on an ambitious novel upon the accepted lines. It occupied him for nearly three years, a one-book effort unmatched in his career. *Tono-Bungay* found Wells thinking the only way he found congenial—with his imagination. Certainly, with the highest expression his art could summon, he wrestled with the dilemma implicit in *First and Last Things:* the intellect of the man trained in science versus the intuition of the man fitted by nature to be an artist. When, in 1922, Wells prepared special prefaces for the twenty-eight-volume Atlantic Edition of his works, he acknowledged that, with one exception, "it is far truer to call [my books] Journalism than Art." That exception was the novel he called *Tono-Bungay.*

Tono-Bungay (1909)

Tono-Bungay combines to advantage the three strains for which Wells is noted: the spokesman for a generation escaping from Victorianism; the scientific romancer who, having already made "the shape of things to come" a magic phrase, would now fashion metaphors for the Life Force from material as likely as soaring gliders and as unlikely as battleships; and the portrayer of warm human characters in the manner of, though with distinct differences from, Dickens.

Although in significant ways that are only lately being studied *Tono-Bungay* belongs in a modernist context, it is as a transitional work that the novel can best be approached initially. William C. Frierson anglicizes the German romantic word *Bildungsroman* into "life-novel" and fits Wells's best book into that tradition,[9] a distinguished line that reaches back to Goethe's *Wilhelm Meister* (1796), Dickens's *David Copperfield* (1850) and Thackeray's *Pendennis* (1850) while looking forward to Lawrence's *Sons and Lovers* (1913), Maugham's *Of Human Bondage* (1915), and Joyce's *Portrait of the Artist as a Young Man* (1916). Its hero, George Ponderevo—like Paul Morel, Philip Carey, and Stephen Dedalus—is the personification of a consciousness that seeks a certainty against the severity of all its tests. Again and again this kind of hero makes a crucible of every level and phase of society, and always life crowds in.

In the sense that both seek to assess the condition of England, *Tono-Bungay* joins loosely the tradition of George Eliot's *Middlemarch* (1872). Dorothea Brooke recapitulates the intellectual development of her age and places the reader on the threshold of the twentieth century. *Middlemarch* looks ahead to a society that is to become increasingly secular, scientific, and commercially specialized. As a boy living belowstairs in an estate called Bladesover, Wells's George Ponderevo becomes secularized early, inclined to follow the liberating force of scientific discovery late, and a survivor of the commercial charlatanry of tono-bungay in between. Eliot's study of provincial life is horizontal, nostalgic; it presents a rich microcosm that, in the wedding of Dorothea Brooke and Will Ladislaw, rescues the Victorian age from puritanism, or what Matthew Arnold called Hebraism, by a new Hellenism. Dorothea's two marriages symbolize a journey of the unleavened mind from impressionability to practical wisdom and humane sympathy. Wells' condition-of-England novel is vertical, futuristic; it presents a rocketlike macrocosm that enables Ponderevo to survive the wreckages of an unsuccessful marriage and love affair, the "woosh" and sputter of tono-bungay, and, finally, to be the human emblem for something Wells leaves unspecified except as "the one enduring thing."

Perhaps it is instructive to note here that Henry James, while appearing to admire both books, judged *Middlemarch* as "set[ting] a limit . . . to the development of the old-fashioned novel" and faulted *Tono-Bungay* on its quality of "saturation." Both novels, certainly, are sprawling with characters and incidents. But, with *Middlemarch,* David Daiches observes, the labyrinthine coheres by its very tortuousness. "[T]he careful reader has only to take up one end of a thread and he will find it leads him in and out, through character after character, situation after situation, and not simply in terms of the fitting together of the plot but in terms of the way the ironies and the wisdom work, of anticipations and parallels and illuminating reflections from one element to another."[10] And, with *Tono-Bungay,* as a recent but already famous essay by David Lodge shows, diction, not always considered Wells's strong suit, shapes and integrates. "I suggest that if we read *Tono-Bungay* with an open mind, with attention to its language, to the passages where that language becomes most charged with imaginative energy, we shall find that it is an impressive, and certainly coherent, work of art."[11]

The first third of *Tono-Bungay,* a fictionalized transcript of the opening (and best) chapters of *Experiment in Autobiography,* sends George through a Victorian grotesquerie compounded of adolescent love and servants' gossip. The love scenes between George and Beatrice, a niece of the lady of the house, bear a striking resemblance to those in *Kipps,* which preceded *Tono-Bungay,* and in *Mr. Polly,* which followed. Invariably the object of George's heart's desire (or Artie Kipps's or Alfred Polly's) is viewed as on a pedestal. It is revelatory how much these scenes—the only convincing love scenes Wells ever wrote—are alike in this vertical sense. In the following quotation George, from the vantage of success and scandal, is recalling the time he, at fourteen, first kissed and embraced Beatrice:

I recall something of one talk under the overhanging bushes of the shrubbery—I on the park side of the stone wall, and the lady of my worship a little inelegantly astride thereon. Inelegantly, do I say? You should have seen the sweet imp as I remember her. Just her poise on the wall comes suddenly clear before me, and behind her the light various branches of the bushes of the shrubbery that my feet might not *profane,* and far away and high behind her, dim and stately, the cornice of the great facade of Bladesover rose against the dappled sky. (*W,* 12:41)

Profane is italicized because it is crucial to Wells's idealizing of the love relationship between his heroes and heroines. George Ponderevo, coarse son of a servant, and Kipps and Polly, bumpkins both, but redeemed by an inner poetry, fear they *profane* the women they covet. It was also the word Henry James, undoubtedly without intent to wound the socially maladjusted Wells, used to describe the manner in which Wells handled a love scene in his later novel, *Marriage.* "Profane" appears in the midst of what, to Wells, were barbs of betrayal in James's essay on Bennett, himself, and the other younger novelists. It moved Wells to lash back with *Boon,* the lampoonery of James that ended their friendship a few months before the latter's death. This, however, is not the place to take up in detail the James-Wells quarrel, a matter to be dealt with in chapter 7.

The reunion of George and Beatrice in *Tono-Bungay* comes years later. Ponderevo has seen his marriage wrecked, and his career threatened by the scandal of tono-bungay, a preposterous bottled health elixir; he is now a successful builder of battleships. But Wells's positioning of George and Beatrice in the reunion scene is unchanged from the adolescent dream. Beatrice still sits on a citadel above and beyond her partner: "At the further corner from the cedar she perched herself up upon the parapet and achieved an air of comfort among the lichenous stones. 'Now tell me,' she said, 'all about yourself. . . . I know such duffers of men. . . . You've climbed'" (*W,* 12:389). But the Wellsian hero has not climbed out of an adolescent, almost puppy-lovelike relationship with his inamorata. The scene ends quickly; Beatrice is summoned away. The love object in all of Wells's early novels is unattainable. In *Kipps* the pattern recurs. Artie asks Ann if she will be his girl:

Towards dusk that evening they chanced on one another at the gate by the church; but though there was much in his mind, it stopped there with a resolute shyness until he and Ann were out of breath catching cockshafers. . . . Ann sat up upon the gate, dark against vast masses of flaming crimson and darkling purple, and her eyes looked at Kipps from a shadowed face. There came a stillness between them and quite abruptly he was moved to tell his love.

"Ann," he said. "I *do* like you. I wish you was my girl. . . . I say, Ann: will you *be* my girl?" (*W*, 8:26)

She consents but, as in *Tono-Bungay*, the hero must try and fail in a first marriage (the fate, too, of his creator) and learn that the nouveau riche needs more than money to break through the bastille of the Victorian class structure. In *The History of Mr. Polly*, Polly is prevented by a wall from fulfillment. Here in a first meeting betwen Polly and Christabel, the latter stares down at the undersized stranger as

she sought to estimate his social status on her limited basis of experience. He stood leaning with one hand against the wall, looking up at her and tingling with daring thoughts. He was a littleish man, you must remember, but neither mean-looking nor unhandsome in those days. . . . He had an inspiration to simple speech that no practised trifler with love could have bettered, "There *is* love at first sight," he said, and said it sincerely.

She stared at him with eyes round and big with excitement.

"I think," she said slowly, and without any signs of fear or retreat, "I ought to get back over the wall."

"It needn't matter to you," he said; "I'm just a nobody. But I know you are the best and most beautiful thing I've ever spoken to." His breath caught against something. "No harm in telling you that," he said.

"I should have to go back if I thought you were serious," she said. . . . (*W*, 17:105)

Their idyll is—characteristically—interrupted; resumed in twenty minutes; and interrupted again. In all, their acquaintance lasts ten days. The abortive—the unfulfilled—adolescent male fantasy is at the heart of the love interest in Wells's major trilogy. As mere partners in these dreams, the women have no life of their own. It is a measure of Wells's limitation as a novelist that, in the long series of novels about marriage, Wells projects a *knowledge* of women but no *feeling* for them. Remington's first wife in *The New Machiavelli* is remembered only because of her last letter which cuts so close to the truth of the essentially destructive nature of free love.

The latter portions of the novel chronicle comic-serious adventures with a fraudulent patent-medicine whose name Wells may have drawn in part from Bacon & Bungay, the huckstering publishers in Thackeray's *Pendennis* who often pegged the prices in the literary marketplace, and with an ill-fated search for a do-all elixir known as "quap." If Wells has been rightly called the star reporter of his day, it has not been sufficiently stressed that he also understood, with a sophistication astonishing for its time, the coming age of advertising and the hard-sell, the spirit of public relations and publicity. Wells appears always to have understood the power of the graphic arts to sway men's minds. As early as in *The First Men in the Moon,* it is a column of "mean little advertisements" in *Lloyd's News* that are suspended before the earth-departing Mr. Bedford as he and Cavor ascend toward the moon (*S,* 416).

The purveyor of Tono-Bungay quackery is a bubbling sprite of an uncle, Teddy Ponderevo, who in at least two respects is a chip off his creator's block. He, like the early Wells, has escaped from pill dispensing and is an outsider storming the bastions of society. An early scene between George and his uncle is a capsule of Victorian mores under bombardment from the New Spirit, which threatens the innocence of the Edwardian era:

"Well, George!" he said, quite happily unconscious of my silent criticism, "what do you think of it?"

"Well," I said, "in the first place—it's a damned swindle!"

"Tut! tut!" said my uncle. "It's as straight as—It's fair trading!"

"So much the worse for trading," I said.

"It's the sort of thing everybody does. After all, there's no harm in the stuff—and it may do good. It might do a lot of good—giving people confidence. For instance, against an epidemic. See? Why not? I don't see where your swindle comes in."

"H'm," I said. "It's a thing you either see or don't see." (*W,* 12:177–78)

The novel, written in first person and presented almost entirely in flashbacks, gets properly started with the introduction of Uncle Teddy. He makes his entrance as a small druggist in a dead country town. He quickly exhibits to his nephew "the temperament of a Napoleon of finance spoiling for conquest"—a meteor in the making. Teddy Ponderevo is the sort of outsider-adventurer Wells liked, although such living counterparts as Bottomley and Birkenhead, Ramsay MacDonald and Zaharoff, would wither and die among the elite bores of Wells's utopias.[12] Writing several decades before advertising magnates would begin to appear in English and American novels, Wells does not make the mistake of caricature. Ponderevo, a fraud to be sure, is never the doer of direct villainy like Merdle, the other pioneer financier of fiction, in *Little Dorrit.* Even his charlatanry is tempered by a taste for the business. He glosses over his shady dealings with such phrases as "Romance of Commerce" or "Room for Enterprise." Wells cannot avoid a kindly tolerance for Teddy, his brother in arms. But since, to the burgeoning socialist in Wells, Teddy and tono-bungay represent the dangers of irresponsible capitalism, the author employs an altogether balanced nephew to be the uncle's conscience: "You don't mean to say you think doing this stuff up in bottles and swearing it's the quintessence of strength . . . is straight?" (*W,* 12:178).

Harry T. Moore, in a foreword to a paperback edition of the novel, properly notes that the book transports the reader to today's world of slogans that bark out at him from the television screen. For, after Uncle Teddy scores a first success with tono-bungay, he hucksters a soap. What, continues Moore's analogy, "gurgles more invitingly or foams more bewitchingly on our television screens than, respectively, patent medicines and soap?"[13] But Teddy, given the gift of high finance, as Griffin in *The Invisible Man* was given the gift of transparency, comes to a pathetic demise. Teddy threatens to disorganize the industrial fabric of England, just as Griffin bid well to destroy Iping Village. Both go beyond their depth and become menaces to be eliminated.

Tono-Bungay effectively links the comic-novel triumphs of Wells's past with the tract-novels of his next vein. For all his ambition and unscrupulousness, Teddy never loses the innocence of a Hoopdriver or of a Kipps. The fall of the Ponderevo empire, his patent-medicine sham world in bits around him, is described by Wells with a moving concern for the single human soul. Teddy's meeting with nephew George at the moment of bankruptcy brings out the finest in Wells:

I discovered that his face was wet with tears, that his wet glasses blinded him. He put up his fat hand and clawed them off clumsily, felt inefficiently for his pocket handkerchief, and then to my horror, as he clung to me, he began to weep aloud, this little, old world-worn swindler. It wasn't just sobbing or shedding tears, it was crying as a child cries—It was—oh!—terrible.

"It's cruel," he blubbered at last. "They asked me questions. They kep' asking me questions, George." (*W,* 12:473–74)

Ponderevo's death comes ignominiously enough in a forgotten French village. More than one critic has suggested that Wells drew on memories of the deathbed vigil spent with his friend, the novelist George Gissing, to describe the poignant fade-out of a late Victorian tycoon (*E,* 493). "So ended all that flimsy inordinate stir . . . that was George Gissing," wrote Wells in a memorable but widely misunderstood epitaph for the man closest to him among fellow writers at the turn of the century. With the fictional event—the death of Uncle Teddy Ponderevo—the "inordinate stir" became the meaningless "push and promotions . . . the excitements, the dinners and disputations" of the human rocket's upward thrust. Wells had deep affection for Gissing but regretted what he considered the waste of a potentially important writer who unduly depreciated life. So, too, the fictional Uncle Teddy is shown to be defeated by the failure of his lower-class, village-druggist background to equip him for the tycoon's role thrust upon him by tono-bungay.

Tono-Bungay comes closest of any of the novels to being a spiritual biography; it is closer, certainly, than *William Clissold,* a catalog of issues that occupied the world and Wells between the great wars. The last chapter of *Tono-Bungay* evokes symbolically and poetically the entire spirit of the novel. Using an ocean destroyer as his contemporary time machine—George Ponderevo has survived a trap of the new century, irresponsible capitalism, and has become a builder of great ships—Wells portrays the inexorable and explosive quality of the coming age in the wake of the vessel:

They [the ships] stand out bound on strange missions of life and death, to the killing of men in unfamiliar lands. And, now behind us is blue mystery and the phantom flash of unseen lights, and presently even these are gone, and I and my destroyer tear out to the unknown across a great grey space. We tear into the great spaces of the future and the turbines fall to talking in unfamiliar tongues. Out to the open we go, to windy freedom and trackless ways. Light after light goes down. England and the Kingdom, Britain and the Empire, the old prides and the old devotions, glide abeam, astern, sink down upon the horizon, pass—pass. The river passes—London passes, England passes. . . . (*W,* 12:528)

Such closing passages reveal how close Wells's first biographer was to the mark when he described the novel as "thought adventure."[14] And what an adventure in thought maturation George has experienced! By the end of the novel he is a poet whose literariness belies the insisted-upon untidiness of his expression at the beginning ("I warn you this book is going to be something of an aggomeration . . . contain[ing] all sorts of irrational and debatable elements that I shall be the clearer-headed for getting on paper"). But it is not clear how much of his settled articulateness George attributes to the purgative effect of his confessional or whether he credits it wholly to his actual experiences. At any rate, by the end of the novel, George has thrust free of temporal circumstances:

I have come to see myself from the outside, my country from the outside—without illusions.

We are all things that make and pass, striving upon a hidden mission, out to the open sea. (*W,* 12:529)

The experience of *telling* his story and the reader's experience of *reading* it have merged in an impulse to sheer possibility. At the end of the disastrous quap episode, George had linked the cancerous effects of radioactivity to the decay of a diseased culture. The reader visions with George the passing of Bladesoverian—that is, hierarchical—assumptions where reactions were semiautomatic and assured.

Finally, *Tono-Bungay* is a book that speaks to the modern sensibility. The poetic conceit of the final pages—Wells's notion of the Thames as the river of life—or, perhaps, of life as a river that is subject to unknowable laws and choices—is echoed in at least one contemporary time-jump novel. It is curious that John Fowles has never mentioned Wells. In *The French Lieutenant's Woman*, Charles Smithson, marooned in the midst of the Victorian era a generation before George Ponderevo, is also viewed as the man between. Both are men who have lifted one leg out of one time frame and are about to put it down in another of whose substance they are uncertain. Like *Tono-Bungay*, Fowles's novel ends in a dramatizing of "post-cultural man" through imagery of the sea. In Fowles's case, it is borrowed from Matthew Arnold's poem "To Marguerite": "[L]ife . . . is not a symbol . . . not one riddle and one failure to guess it, is not to inhabit one face alone or to be given up after one losing throw of the dice; but is to be, however inadequately, emptily, hopelessly into the city's iron heart, endured. And out again, upon the unplumb'd, salt, estranging sea."[15]

Charles Smithson dabbled in paleontology and once believed himself a student and even a creature of Evolution. He lost everything at the end—his fortune, his name, his inner assurance—but he gained a sense of the possibilities of his own autonomy. George Ponderevo—created by a one-time student of Huxley—appears at the end to have placed his faith in his X2—his battleship/destroyer, Wells's emblem for the power of science. Arnold Bennett found an epic quality in the last words of *Tono-Bungay*. Certainly they are the most poetic—and powerful—of any Wells wrote. But in making science his Destroyer, he seems to have put aside the grave doubts about science that he learned from his mentor. The actual ambivalence of his position will provide the subject matter for every book he wrote after this, the best of them.

Chapter Six

New Women for Old: Wells and Feminism

Socialism and Sex: Suffragettes and Samurai

All his life Wells enjoyed boy's games—especially war games. However, he had little preparation for the two-front holding action he would fight with the Fabians. The MacKenzies devote the exact middle of their biography to "Passions and Passades" but sum up his problems in a single striking sentence: "At the same time that he was engaged in political intrigues against the Fabian Old Gang, he was involved in an emotional intrigue in the Fabian Nursery."[1] The asexual Webbs and Shaw, not to mention the Fabian fathers, watched as Wells's liaisons with the Fabian daughters intensified. Increasingly he tried to salve his wounds at the hands of their elders in the flattery of "pretty young things." And if, as in the affairs with Rosamund Bland, Amber Reeves, and Cicily Fairfield (Rebecca West), he encountered ardent desires to break loose from upper-middle-class conformity, H. G. Wells and his writings promised deliverance. Beatrice Webb, as usual, recorded the problem in her diary: "an aptitude [in Wells] for 'fine thinking' and even 'good feeling' but a total incapacity for decent conduct."[2]

In the indecent-conduct department, there was that which Wells inappropriately labeled, in a letter to Shaw, as the "Bland affair." It was, if not his first major infidelity, certainly his first major Fabian indiscretion. Hubert Bland, Fabian Old Gang founder and eleven years Wells's senior, was a Jekyll-Hyde figure who outwardly supported conventional domestic behavior but secretly practiced shameless philandering. Edith Nesbit was seven months pregnant when they married. It was only three years later that she discovered Bland had never broken an engagement to a lady who was the mother of his illegitimate child, Rosamund. Edith had even been persuaded to adopt the girl before she learned that Bland was the father.

The Wellses and Blands had long been on visiting terms, and Rosamund often played Daisy to Wells's Gatsby in lawn parties at Spade House. "A beautiful girl . . . with a natural complexion that needed no make-up," Rosamund was singled out for special attention by a tireless host.

The MacKenzies report that the liaison was broken off before it came to threaten his marriage. Hubert Bland, who was as given to effective public oratory as Wells was unsure and bumbling, used the occasion of an interruption of the lovers' planned flight to read Bertie a formal lecture at Paddington Station. He made it clear he would expose H. G. publicly if he pursued his daughter any further.

But public exposure appeared to bother him less and less. His next affair—with a brilliant Cambridge graduate named Amber Reeves—was carried out in brazen openness. Least prudent of all, the novelist who had implied his enthusiasm for polygamy as early as 1906 in a *menage à quatre* in *In the Days of the Comet* (1906), now came out for it openly in *The New Machiavelli* (1911), whose heroine was Remington's mistress Isabel, an undisguised portrait of Amber Reeves, and whose pilloried Altiora Bailey was, in every detail, Beatrice Webb.

This is not the place or the book to detail the checkered publishing history of *The New Machiavelli* or the narrow survival of Wells's marriage in the wake of the Amber Reeves scandal. The MacKenzies cover both in fascinating detail. Suffice it to say that Frederick Macmillan refused to publish the novel—he "farmed it out" to a lesser firm—and Amber refused to let Wells divorce Jane and marry her although she was carrying his child. She chose to engage herself to an old friend who had previously proposed and now repeated his offer in full cognizance of her affair.

The most famous—the most lasting—of Wells's affairs was with Rebecca West, his intellectual—and perhaps literary—equal. Something of the lacerating effect of the relationship on both partners is revealed in Gordon Ray's *H. G. Wells and Rebecca West* and in Anthony West's recently published *H. G. Wells: Aspects of a Life*. Dame Rebecca provided Gordon Ray with access to more than eight hundred letters that Wells wrote to her. Only five of her letters to him survive. They were lovers for about a decade—1913–23—and the ups and downs of the relationship prescribed something of the same course as any addiction for which, eventually, cure must be sought. Her less-than-laudatory review of *Marriage* brought them together for the first time late in 1912. ("He found a slim, sturdy girl of nineteen. . . . a *brune adorable*. . . . The keen intelligence, passionate sympathy, and pungent wit that had attracted him in her writing were equally present in her person, and he was soon deeply interested in her.")[3]

Despite a tacit arrangement with Jane that he might wander when his needs dictated, Wells by now had grown wary of mistresses generally and of suffragettes in particular. Anthony West's report on his parents as lovers can be summed up in a sentence. Rebecca allowed him to chase her until she almost caught him.

For most of their decade as lovers, Rebecca and H. G. are "panther" and "jaguar," respectively. These, Ray points out, "were far more than mere affectionate nicknames. . . . They emphasized the ruthless withdrawal from society that the relationship entailed, the fact that [they] were not part of the pack and did not acknowledge its law. Instead they were 'carnivores' living apart in their hidden 'lair,' going forth to 'catch food,' and meeting 'at the trodden place in the jungle.' Wells's other life became a mere 'showcase.' . . ."[4]

Animosity among big cats is well known, and panther and jaguar could not escape it. The birth in 1914 of Anthony Panther West made for complications between them whose full truth is difficult to ascertain. The Gordon Ray-Rebecca West volume suggests that Wells in his fifties had become increasingly self-centered, often restive, unreliable, and irascible. That she remained his mistress for a decade after Anthony's birth was traceable, Rebecca insisted, to H. G.'s inability to cope without her. Naturally, through it all, the young writer-mother brooded over her fate. Ray writes: "Instead of the full and exciting life in the center of English literary society that might have been hers, she was spending her youth virtually in hiding, always in a false position, always having to act a part."[5]

Wells, who would have married Amber Reeves in his early middle-age, now knew better in his late. He resisted Rebecca's demands that he divorce Jane and marry her. Throughout the decade, according to Anthony West, it was his mother who was the aggressor, hoping always for Jane Wells's death. By the time Jane did die (in 1927, when he was sixty and Rebecca thirty-four), H. G. had found consolation elsewhere—in Odette Keun, a crusading, frequently deported Dutch woman whose un-Englishness proved more *en rapport* with Wells than Rebecca West. They argued over Henry James, and in *The Strange Necessity* she devoted two pages to Wells and two hundred to Joyce and Proust. Although they had long since ceased to be lovers, the mid-1920s found them in bitter, often public, rancor. Finally, in 1929, she waged a bruising though successful legal battle to adopt the fifteen-year-old Anthony. As World War II approached, their relationship turned cordial again. The final letter in Ray's book, written in 1946 to Wells's daughter-in-law a week after his death, acknowledged that "I loved him all my life and always will. . . ."[6]

The New Machiavelli (1911)

Wells called *The New Machiavelli* "a queer confused novel . . . one of my worst and one of my most revealing" (*E, 661*). Written directly after *Tono-Bungay* and *The History of Mr. Polly,* it was less carefully wrought than the former and showed how easily the satire of the latter could be transformed into lampoonery. More than any previous work, the new novel illumined the path Wells's fiction would take for the next forty years.

George Ponderevo is reincarnated in *Machiavelli* as Remington. But, in place of the intellectual voyager, Wells ushers in the first of a long line of Wellsians—men full of good intentions and eager to rebuild the world. Remington, most of all, reveals Wells's almost Byronic self-adulation. He is a New Republican, Wells's new breed of politician-thinker, who strides forth to battle in the arena of Westminster; savors the heady potions of socialism; imbibes its dream, but distrusts its practitioners to the point of hatred; leaves his wife; and ends in disgrace.

The novel was viewed in 1911 as a roman à clef. One critic remarked that *The New Machiavelli* was the book in which Wells betrayed some of his best friends.[7] Wells duly registered his objections to criticism that was "incapable of the fine but real distinction between giving a similar figure and . . . 'putting people into a book.'"[8] Nevertheless, the smoke from Wells's fiery departure from the Fabians had not yet cleared, and it was inevitable that minor characters in his political novel should be taken as models of living antagonists.

But what made *Machiavelli* one of Wells's most self-revealing books was its deeply pessimistic commentary on the chances of idealism when in conflict, not only against centuries of muddleheaded, political thinking, but against irrational impulses within the idealist. Remington is defeated by his own instinct to break the law. The maker who would reform the system into a socialist Elysium is also the breaker who destroys himself by choosing a mistress instead of a career. Remington's choice gives the book a thematic unity and points out, more clearly than any other novel that Wells wrote, how little faith he actually had in the triumph of schemes that rule out existential aspects in men.

Wells depicts the world of Westminster as essentially formless. Against this sympathy for the resistance of men to order he pits the zeal for planning of Oscar and Altiora Bailey, flimsily disguised counterparts of his old Fabian friends, Sidney and Beatrice Webb:

> At the Baileys' one always seemed to be getting one's hands on the very strings that guided the world. You heard legislation projected to affect this "type" and

that; statistics marched by you with sin and shame and injustice and misery re-
duced to quite manageable percentages . . . [and] you felt you were in a sort of
signal box with levers all about you, and the world outside there, albeit a little
dark and mysterious beyond the window, running on its lines in ready obedience
to these unhesitating lights, true and steady to trim termini.

And then with all this administrative fizzle, this pseudo-scientific administrative chatter, dying away in your head, out you went into the limitless grimy chaos
of London streets and squares . . . a vague incessant murmur of cries and voices,
wanton crimes and accidents bawled at you from the placards . . . and you found
yourself swaying back to the opposite conviction that the huge formless spirit of
the world it was that held the strings and danced the puppets on the Bailey stage.
(*W*, 14:232–33)

Wells sacrifices Remington to the triumph of the "huge formless spirit"
of life. The passage reveals Wells's distrust of some of man's instrumental-
ities as antidotes to the chaos of his condition. *The New Machiavelli,* a representative work of his middle period, echoes *The Island of Dr. Moreau* in
its view of the world as "nothing but a mere heap of dust, fortuitously
agitated"—the mechanistic view. In the tract-novels—the planned societies—of his sterile final period, Wells assumed the stance of one who believed in inevitable progress, in an evolution in which the mind would be
orderly and vital. Remington (Wells) certainly did not believe this way in
1911. Although Remington is pictured as blaming his failures in politics
on a lag between his political progress (too fast) and his education (too
retarded), what he is really saying is that the economic and social disorder,
the incoherence and planlessness, the unequal struggle of reason with the
natural energies and instincts of human life, are in large part characteristic
of the way of the modern world.

The New Machiavelli by Wells's own admission among his most "revealing" novels, is a deeply existential work. Remington's external passion for
order is at war with the irrationality at his core. The novel bares the conflicting passions that nagged H. G. Wells at forty-five. "You are always
talking of order and system," writes Margaret to Remington a week before
he leaves her for another woman, "but by a sort of instinct you seem to
want to break the law. . . . You are at once makers and rebels, you and
Isabel too. You're bad people—criminal people . . . and yet full of something the world must have. . . . It may be there is no making without
destruction, but . . . it is nothing but an instinct for lawlessness that
drives you . . ." (*W*, 14:557–58). Raknem suggests that Wells probably
inserted this letter at the end of the novel because he had a bad conscience.
Margaret's complaints are such as Jane Wells could justifiably have made.
Certainly Remington's taking of a mistress could be compared to Wells's

own practice before, during, and after the writing of *The New Machiavelli*.
Wells reveals in his autobiography that, a few years after his second marriage, he asked to be released from his marriage vows. Arnold Bennett once
noted that Wells placed photographs of three of his mistresses on his man-
telpiece beside that of his wife.[9]

But Remington is more than Wellsian self-projection. He is a monument to the proposition that the world is inhabited by error-prone, passionate, jealous creatures who are given to excesses beyond their control.
Remington, like Wells, would be uneasy in a world state geared to perfect-
ibility; and Remington would as surely be banished from it as he was from
Westminster. Moreover, *The New Machiavelli*, along with the below-sur-
face insights into its author provides revealing documentation for the political historian. Wells was among the first to show in a novel the force of
education in liberalizing the minds of the political intelligentsia in Edwardian England. Men, according to Remington, "are becoming increasingly
constructive and selective. The past will rule them less, the future more.
It is not simply party but school and college and county and country that
lose their glamour. One does not hear nearly as much as our forefathers did
of the 'Old Harrovian,' 'Old Arvonian,' 'Old Etonian' claim to this or that
unfair advantage or unearned sympathy. . . . A widening sense of fair play
destroys such things" (*W*, 14:323).

Remington assaults the world of British politics as Ponderevo did the
world of commerce. He projects the enthusiasm and idealism so characteristic of his creator. He has been, unlike Wells, to Cambridge; is taken
under wing by the Baileys, as Wells was sponsored by the Webbs; and
joins the young Socialists, as Wells joined the Fabians and the Coefficients.
Wells's grasp in this novel of the three-tiered structure of British politics is
enlightening. He gives a picture of flux and chaos. The old conservatism
appeared undermined because it was joined to old Westminster traditions,
and seemed not at all alive "to the greatness of the Present and to the vaster
Future." The Liberals showed clearly what they were against; the trouble
was to find out what on earth they were for. The third party, the Socialists,
had become "a sort of big intellectual No-Man's Land." Finally, the Labor
party had a constructive program, but most of its members were hostile to
education and, except for an obvious antagonism to employers and property owners, almost destitute of ideas.

The book emerges, at one level, as a rationale for Wells's lifelong inability to mesh his ideas with those of any individual or of any group. At the
height of despair over the Fabians, Remington speaks for Wells and his
disenchantment with British Socialists: "When you think of the height

and depth and importance and wisdom of the Socialist ideas, and see the men who are running them. . . . A big system of ideas like Socialism grows up out of the obvious common sense of our present conditions. It's as impersonal as science. All these men—they've given nothing to it. . . . We mustn't confuse Socialism with the Socialists . . ." (*W*, 14:342).

The novel also displays Wells as at once contemptuous of politicians and fascinated by them. He is equally divided in his feelings about the new type of suffragette heroine epitomized by Altiora Bailey. Wells called them the "Marcella crop" after the title character of Mrs. Humphry Ward's influential novel: women who have dropped from their shoulders the Victorian draperies of timidity, false modesty, and propriety—who have rolled up their sleeves to battle for industrial and economic amelioration. Wells's picture of Altiora—a kind of intellectual Valkyrie—is cruel but not without grudging admiration:

She had much of the vigour and handsomeness of a slender impudent young man, and an unscrupulousness altogether feminine. She was one of those women who are wanting in—what is the word?—muliebrity. . . . She was entirely unfitted for her sex's sphere. She was neither uncertain, coy nor hard to please, and altogether too stimulating and aggressive for any gentleman's hours of ease. . . . Yet you mustn't imagine she was an inelegant or unbeautiful woman, and she is inconceivable to me in high collars or any sort of masculine garment. But her soul was bony, and at the base of her was a vanity gaunt and greedy! (*W*, 14:220–21)

Interesting as Remington's observations on politics and the Baileys are to political clinicians, there is another facet to *The New Machiavelli*. It provides an early view of the rising tide of feminism and the battle of the sexes. Margaret is the first of what André Maurois calls those "half-Fabian, half-aristocratic Amazons"[10] who in one Wells novel after another join their mates in battling the class structure. Margaret's meeting with Remington, a promising young Liberal-Socialist, is arranged by Altiora Bailey. Margaret is intelligent, beautiful, idealistic; and she has enough money of her own to help him in his political career. They marry, but something clouds their married life. Despite Wells's reluctance to come to artistic grips with Lawrentian themes, he clearly intends to blame their troubles on sex. Remington describes the conflict: "My quality is sensuous and ruled by warm impulses; hers was discriminating and essentially inhibitory. I like naked bodies and the jolly smell of things. She abounded in reservations, in circumlocutions and evasions, in keenly appreciated secondary points" (*W*, 14:276).

It is impossible not to see in this novel, as in *Tono-Bungay,* a catharsis for the failure of Wells's first marriage. In October 1891 the twenty-five-year-old Wells married Isabel Mary Wells, a cousin. She insisted on a long engagement as Marion does in *Tono-Bungay.* Once they were married, the cloud noted in *Machiavelli*—Remington's sensuality versus Margaret's reserve—darkened their relationship. Wells confessed to "an unalterable difference . . . in our nervous reactions. I felt and acted swiftly and variously and at times loosely and superficially, in the acutest contrast to her gentler and steadier flow. There was no contact nor comparison between our imaginative worlds . . ." (*E,* 297) Moreover, Remington falls in love with Isabel Rivers, just as Wells fell in love with Amy Catherine Robbins. Since it would be several years before Remington's first wife could give him a divorce, Remington runs away with Isabel. In Edwardian England, divorce for a politician was career suicide; Remington knows, therefore, that his action will ruin him.

Wells has described his desire for other women fully in this novel. So central is this sexual uneasiness to the fabric of a whole succession of Wells's novels from *Tono-Bungay* and *Machiavelli,* down to the last tired reiterations of *Babes in the Darkling Wood* thirty years later, that a recent critic, Montgomery Belgion, sees in Wells's hostility to monogamy the key to his zealousness for social reform: "As his stories show, he credited other people with no independent existence. So he could but think of himself. The one entity of which, apart from himself, he was conscious was the environment, and . . . he felt that this environment required to be 'tamed.' Having tried monogamy and found it irksome, when he saw that monogamy went on being respected in the environment, he was impelled, as part of the 'taming,' to try to get monogamy generally condemned and discarded."[11]

This view is a perceptive one, as far as it goes; but it is shortsighted. One side of Wells unquestionably saw an opportunity to convert ideas into action by living openly out of wedlock with a series of suffragettes and lady writers in London during his struggling Fabian days, and in his villa in the south of France during the 1920s and 1930s when his was one of the most famous names in the world. But the line of novels that started with *The New Machiavelli* and *Ann Veronica,* both literary causes célèbres, has a deeper intention than advocacy of free love. They are, writes Kenneth Rexroth, "about matrimony, about the mysteries and difficulties and agonies and tragedies and—rarely—the joys of the search for a true 'life of dialogue.'"[12]

Wells had stressed as early as 1905 the need for this life of dialogue. In *A Modern Utopia,* he writes:

"A man under the Rule who loves a woman who does not follow it, must either leave the Samurai to marry her, or induce her to accept what is called the Woman's Rule, which, while it exempts her from the severer qualifications and disciplines, brings her regimen into a working harmony with his."
"Suppose she breaks the Rule afterwards?"
"He must leave either her or the order."
"There is matter for a novel or so in that."
"There has been matter for hundreds."[13]

The general problem of marriage—more exactly, the relation of one individual to another—is the concern of all of Wells's longer novels. From *Love and Mr. Lewisham* in 1900 to *Babes in the Darkling Wood* in 1940, Wells wrestled with one variation after another on the theme.

Brome has said, with entire truth, that the freedom of the sexes "was first made articulate by Wells, laughingly reaffirmed by Shaw, developed in lyrical unrestraint by Lawrence, and given a cynical sanction—if not smear—by Aldous Huxley."[14] In *The New Machiavelli,* despite the tempered lampoonery of Beatrice Webb, Wells showed himself to be firmly feminist—and more. His early works developed out of a curious linking of the evolutionary zeal of T. H. Huxley, the imaginative riches of Poe and Verne, and the "flat" caricaturing of Dickens. But Wells's private code in relation to marriage and plural associations was straight out of Shelley by way of Rousseau.[15] "I was entirely out of accord with the sentimental patterns and focussed devotions adopted by most people about me," Wells writes in his autobiography. "Regardless of every visible reality about me of law, custom, social usage, economic necessities and the unexplored psychology of womanhood, I developed my adolescent fantasy of free, ambitious, self-reliant women who would mate with me and go their way, as I desired to go my way . . ." (*E,* 147). Most of Wells's heroines are charter members of this delectably unreal class of intellectual Valkyries. In his most infamous heroine he solidified his adolescent fantasy. In creating Ann Veronica, he whipped up a storm in the country that had created Mrs. Grundy.

Ann Veronica (1909)

Ann Veronica "came like an angel of freedom, a very determined audacious angel, into the lives of endless young women" during the second decade of the twentieth century.[16] There was an electric reaction to this novel, which called for sexual license sixty years after Hawthorne's Hester

Prynne had quietly accepted the emblem of the scarlet letter. It was no overstatement to say that the underlying conflict of centuries was thrust into the open at the point in the novel where Ann Veronica announces her intention of attending an unchaperoned dance in London and of spending the night in a hotel, and her aunt utters that apprehensive phrase, "But, my dear!" (*W*, 13:11). In Edwardian England, girls had to be chaperoned; none questioned the dicta of their fathers. It was also a time when no decent girl worked for a living, expressed political opinions publicly, or dared be seen with a suffragette.

Odette Keun, a once close friend who has expressed her disenchantment with Wells in an overwrought but perceptive memoir, described the impact, especially on young women of her generation, of a book like *Ann Veronica:* "Into this foul and insupportable nightmare leapt [Wells] . . . to thrust and cut and hack . . . at the tentacles, the octopus, the whole evil, heavy, stupid, brutal frame in which we were imprisoned. . . . We were being delivered."[17] For Ann Veronica, a daughter of the English middle-class—a class that considered the Wells of 1910 to be a distinct outsider— defies her father, flees her home to live apart, becomes a violently partisan suffragette, and eventually throws herself into the arms of the man she loves.

There is no way to know exactly how many daughters left home to follow the path to fulfillment forged by Ann Veronica. Wells said only that advanced young people in Sweden, Bulgaria, Russia, and Austria "learned to their amazement that there were young people like themselves in England." The novel, he wrote, was not so much criticized as attacked "with hysterical animosity by people who did not like the heroine or who disapproved of her thoughts and ways" (*W*, 13:ix). As a result, the book was banned by libraries and preached against by earnest clergymen. There was not only a bad press and public denunciation but attempts to ostracize Wells socially. St. Loe Strachey's diatribe is characteristic of the criticism leveled at Wells. The novel was reprehensible, Strachey wrote, not so much because it discussed sexuality frankly but because in describing Ann Veronica sympathetically Wells was demolishing the Old Victorian standards:

The Book is based on the negation of woman's purity and of man's good faith in the relations of the sexes. It teaches, in effect, that there is no such thing as a woman's honour, or if there is, it is only to be a bulwark against a weak temptation. When the temptation is strong enough, not only is the tempted person justified in yielding, but such yielding becomes not merely inevitable but something to be welcomed and glorified. . . .

It is not for nothing that the world has learned to think of a woman's honour as involving a peculiar sacrifice. The general Vice of Mankind is right when, if it speaks of a woman's dishonour, it means thereby a sacrifice to her purity in mind and body.[18]

In other words, what rankles Strachey is Wells's refusal to accept the double standard. However, Wells's attack was not against that standard but against social mores that refused to allow women to act as human beings. There is nothing promiscuous about the virginal Ann who falls in love and shows it. In fact, in Wells's handling, the evil lies less with the woman than with the man.

Ann Veronica was smeared but not subjected to the direct suppression of Shaw's banned play of a decade earlier, *Mrs. Warren's Profession*. Read today, the novel presents a heroine too innocent and trusting to be believed; she has nothing of the brittle brilliance of Vivie Warren or of the lyrical flights into passion of Lady Chatterly, for whom she paved the way. If Ann is the best realized of any of Wells's noncomic women characters, this is not to say she comes alive with the vibrancy of a Kipps or a Polly. Her motives are too carefully analyzed, thought processes too exhaustively explained, for her to be an artistically rendered character. There is never a moment in Ann Veronica's soliloquies nearly so poignant as the closing scene of *Kipps* when Artie and Ann Pornick decide what a "rum go" everything is, or the one in which Mr. Polly decides against suicide when the flames are licking up about him.

Ann Veronica, for all its thematic stiffness, is never quite drowned in doctrine. Wells tries to bring the girl to life. Defiant, Ann goes to a science school in London where she falls in love with a teacher, a man named Capes, who is separated from his wife. That Wells should have dedicated the novel to his wife, Jane, is not surprising in the light of its autobiographical overtones; Wells had met her in tutorial sessions at a time when his first marriage was failing. When Ann and Capes decide, after much wrestling with conscience, to elope, one has a variation on the situation betwen Isabel and Remington in *Machiavelli.* Wells was fond of exploiting similar domestic situations from book to book by switching the angle of interest from character to character.

Although unquestionably a tour-de-force novel in an age that still considered Ibsen's plays daring, *Ann Veronica* is a markedly unsatisfactory performance. Wells does not lead Ann to any startling answer to Victorian propriety. She has demanded the right to be free, but she settles for a conventional marriage. Her conventional relatives recognize that her rebellion is condoned by her ultimate submission. Ann's "woman's role" is still what the Victorians decreed: a biological one.

Reading the novel today is such a task that the reader is hard-pressed to take St. Loe Strachey at his word when he describes the novel as "capable of poisoning the minds of those who read it." Brome writes that the book took "an audacious step in the development of the modern English novel, bringing alive the contemporary circumstance of physical love, but it seems laughingly innocent when read today and needs no defence."[19] Although Wells demonstrates conclusively that "talk" in a novel can explain the idea of love between two people, he falls desperately short in portraying passion in its higher, intenser moods. Capes, who has eloped with Ann Veronica to Switzerland, speaks with unlyrical self-consciousness to his lover: "'To think,' he cried, 'you are ten years younger than I! . . . there are times when you make me feel a little thing at your feet—a young, silly, protected thing. Do you know, Ann Veronica, it is all a lie about your birth certificate; a forgery—and fooling at that. You are one of the immortals. Immortal! You were in the beginning, and all the men in the world who have known what love is have worshipped at your feet . . . you are the High Priestess of Life'" (W, 13:375–76).

Marriage (1912) and The Passionate Friends (1913)

That Ann Veronica and Capes were not to go on to a married life of unalloyed bliss is indicated in Marriage, the novel that tells the story of Ann Veronica's fortunes in matrimony. Marjorie Pope is substituted for Ann, and Trafford for Capes. Even the minor characters are projections of people in the earlier novel. Mr. Pope becomes Mr. Stanley—both fathers of the bride—and Magnet substitutes for Manning, each an unsuccessful suitor. Marjorie's and Trafford's life together is happy until Marjorie's inclination to social climbing forces Trafford to abandon research for industry and finance. Trafford, a maturation of Wells's earliest persona—the creative man of science, a line beginning with Prendick in Dr. Moreau—is obliged to lay aside his researches in molecular physics to work out a successful process for synthetic rubber.

Trafford makes a fortune, but his affluence becomes stultifying; his life loses meaning; his marriage crumbles from within. Wells apparently, according to Edwin E. Slosson, had adopted a theory about the normal division of labor between husband and wife: the man should be an expert in the art of getting money and the woman in the art of handling it.[20] A kind of Thorstein Veblen dilemma intervenes: both Marjorie and Trafford regard their duties as ends in themselves; she, to buy things they neither want nor need; he, to be overabsorbed in business. The solution, however, is straight out of Thoreau. Their life is swamped, Wells contends, by restless activity, commercial strivings, and the loss of their identities. Their Walden is the wilds of Labrador. They live in a tent, and discuss marriage and life until Marjorie gains a new conception of the vocation of a wife. As Nicholson puts it: "She is to be a help-meet to the Wellsian cave-man, dreaming of his world state before the camp fire,"[21] for one of the rules Wells proposed for the elite of his Modern Utopia was that a man who aspired to be a leader should for a week every year go off into the desert and live in solitude.

Trafford and Marjorie extend their utopian respite to a year. The story ends happily though inconclusively, for Wells does not solve woman's problem. Trafford aspires to an equivalent of George Ponderevo's unknowable "something," the collective force that rules life:

It's something arising out of life—not the common stuff of life. An exhalation. . . . It's like the little tongues of fire that came at Pentecost. . . . Perhaps I shall die a Christian yet. . . . The other Christians won't like me if I do. . . . It's what I reach up to, what I desire shall pervade me, not what I am. . . . Salvation! . . .

This flame that arises out of life, that redeems life from purposeless triviality, *isn't* life. Let me get hold of that. . . .[22]

The novel appears to be pointing to Wells's short-lived World War I phase when he exasperated T. S. Eliot and a whole host of former disciples by contriving a series of substitute religions and even, with the publication of *Mr. Britling,* "finding God."[23]

The Passionate Friends reflects Wells's continuing preoccupation with the problem of marriage. It is also a further examination of the destructive nature of sexual jealousy, a prominent theme of *Ann Veronica* and *The New Machiavelli.* Justin, a financier, is prepared to accept marriage to Lady Mary Christian on her own terms—nonconsummation—until he learns of her love for Stephen Stratton. When Justin institutes divorce proceedings she kills herself.

Wells constructs the novel as Stratton's autobiography which he addresses to his son. Stratton's is the first-person narration, but the poignancy of a doomed involvement is all Lady Mary's. They are the "passionate friends" of the title; but she refuses to marry him because of his lack of means. On her marriage to Justin, Stratton is inconsolable and goes off to the Boer War—presumably to die. He sees distinguished service and returns to England. In the intervening four years his father has inherited land and retired. Stratton begins to move more in Establishment circles. He talks with the same prime minister—Evesham—who had a larger role in *The New Machiavelli,* and inevitably crosses paths with Lady Mary.

The scenes of their reunion are more fully realized—and believable— than those between George and Beatrice in *Tono-Bungay;* their subsequent affair and its discovery by Justin force Stratton to go abroad. After his marriage to Rachel More, he receives an unexpected letter from Lady Mary. Two years later the former lovers are reunited by chance in the Swiss Alps, a meeting that is maliciously reported to her husband by Lady Mary's companion. They meet a final time in London, when she, distressed by the upset their liaison has caused both families, announces she will live out her life in seclusion. Her suicide follows, leaving Justin and Stratton painfully aware that their conflicting claims—marriage and love—have driven her to self-destruction.

The book bears a tragic melancholia that is rare in the Wells canon. It survives Stratton's—and Wells's—obsession about the idea of a Great State. Interestingly enough, it is Mary who warns him that his world citizenry, if it is to work, must end women's servile roles and honor them for passion and sexuality that are superior to men's.

The Passionate Friends is a better novel than *Ann Veronica.* Praise for it came shortly before his death from Vladimir Nabokov.[24] In their time, *Marriage* and *The Passionate Friends* were not only savaged by status-quo adherents but by at least one of the most perceptive of feminists, Rebecca West. As to the first, Wells, in the tranquillity of autobiographical retrospect, acknowledges as "my mature persuasion" that "the distance a novel can carry a reader out of . . . moral and social preconceptions is a very short one." West, then a beginning reviewer for *Freewoman,* questioned the validity of both female principals. For her, Marjorie is *not* an archetype of the newly independent woman. Mary would not have committed suicide if she had had available to her something beyond marriage and romance: Work. "Suppose the community kept *all* its women," she quotes from one of Trafford's (Wells's) speculations. "Heavens," she protests, "I shall be inside too! I object to living under the same roof as Marjorie."

Two decades earlier another young reviewer had flayed Grant Allen's *The Woman Who Did* (1895). Allen's was a novel whose heroine actually broke convention and bore an out-of-wedlock child as "her very own." That young reviewer was H. G. Wells.

Suffragism and Biological Traps:
The Feminist and the Womanizer

It is always dangerous to infer a writer's passionate involvement in a developing movement of one period—women's emancipation at the turn of the century—as projecting a sympathy for it in a later form—women's liberation in the 1970s. We have, as has already been noted, Kingsley Martin's conviction that of all Wellsian espousals his most influential was of the New Woman. Five years after *Ann Veronica* and three after *The New Machiavelli,* Wells mounted another heroine in flight from "role tyranny" and another instance of the intrusion of sex into politics. However, much had happened to him in the years from 1909 to the outbreak of the Great War. By the time of his writing *The Wife of Sir Isaac Harman* (1914), the suffragette campaign had become "The Great Insane Movement." The scars of suffragist entanglements still festered. Certainly, as he records in his autobiography, these ladies had constituted something of a keen personal disappointment. When the movement began, Wells assumed its members would be like Valkyries, statuesque free spirits cast in the model of his early ideal females. He prepared to welcome them into his liberating spirit and into his arms. But no: "As the hosts of liberation came nearer and could be inspected more acurately," he "found reason to qualify these bright expectations." Far from comprising a "great-hearted free companionship of noble women," the suffragettes turned out to be a strident mob.[25]

A recent commentator notes a deemphasis on suffragism as the passport to Lady Harman's independence: "In fact, in the form of the derisively named Agatha Alimony, [the suffragettes] let Lady Harman down when she seeks sanctuary with them after leaving her husband: 'We mustn't mix up Women's Freedom with Matrimonial Causes. Impossible! We *dare* not!'"[26]

We remember the Agatha Alimony type from her discreditation in *Marriage.* She had surfaced in that novel at a suffragist gathering in Trafford's house, "wearing an enormous hat with three nodding ostrich feathers, a purple bow, a gold buckle and numerous minor ornaments of various origin and substance." From under this heap of millinery—designed to suggest she has more *on* her head than *in* it—she emits "deep trumpet calls," with the intention, Wells exasperatedly believes, of rallying her followers behind the banner of irrationality. Agatha wants, she declares vehemently, "to annoy scientific men." Certainly, she annoys Wells and his physicist hero, Trafford, who warns Marjorie that exposure to such feminist hot air will make her mind "liquefy . . . and slop about." For Wells, soggy idealism and slushy doctrines typify the suffragists.

For Rebecca West, even after their love had cooled, Wells was one of her cherished literary "uncles." In 1928, on the other side of the Atlantic, Freda Kirchway of the *Nation* referred to him as "the most energetic and intimate of our fathers." Both designations were acknowledgments of perishability; nieces and daughters grow away from their uncles and fathers: "The truth is, I've been disagreeing with you ever since I adopted you. First about feminism; then about marriage; then about religion. And now [with the writing of *Mr. Blettsworthy of Rampole Island*] about everything. All in all, I should say that this state of universal disagreement between us proves that you are the ideal father."[27]

Although he was their champion, Wells's view of women was complicated. While it is possible, as Kingsley Martin avers, to have more respect "for the amorous H. G., who was always genuinely falling in love, getting into scrapes and had children by more than one woman, than for the austerity of G. B. S.,"[28] it is also possible to suspect a jumble between Wells the feminist apologist and Wells the chronic womanizer.

As early as in *Anticipations* (1901), he observed that "a virile man, though he too is subject to accidents, may upon most points still hope to plan and determine his life; the life of a woman is all accident."[29] He never forgot his biology and argued that this was not a healthy situation for the race since women, much as they may liberate themselves from the duties of wives and mothers, are nonetheless the bearers of children, and it is only through them that the race continues. In *Mankind in the Making* (1903), he recommended that the state endow mothers, making motherhood worthwhile and an honorable occupation and providing women with personal independence and responsibility.

Wells hints a forecast of yet another variation—the nondifferentiation between sex roles. It is a prophecy, occurring in *Christina Alberta's Father*, for which he has received no credit. Bobby Roothing, who loves Christina Alberta, speculates that in the future there may be many women who achieve freedom, breaking away to "a real individual life—a third sex. Perhaps in the new world there would cease to be two sexes only; there would be recognised varieties and sub-divisions."[30]

Gender hybrids of our day were not prime concerns of H. G. Wells in his midlife novels. He knew there were important differences between men and women, and he sought to codify them. Marjorie Trafford in *Marriage*, who admits that women are more concerned with feeling than broad intellectual issues, represents no change from Nellie Stuart who as early as 1906 in *The Days of the Comet*, grappling with possible new relations between the sexes, admits that "a woman believes nothing by nature. She goes into a mold hiding her secret thoughts almost from herself."[31] John R. Reed, whose *Natural History of H. G. Wells* (1982) is the most rigorous synthesis of Wells's ideas since W. Warren Wagar's book more than twenty years earlier, sees the dilemma of the feminist who was also a student of biology:

> Wells wanted women to be like men in their ability to face life and their own impulses honestly, to struggle for some aim transcending egotism, and to achieve a vision of a finer, cleaner existence. But he also realized that, like men, women were confined by physical instincts, psychological fears, and social customs. Women can do what men do in the world, but they are constitutionally more inclined to sex issues and psychologically more reined in by personal reference.[32]

Thus Wells has looked beyond the usual economic and social forces and seen, for all his advocacy of feminism, biological differences as the primary activating force. Men and women must come to regard one another as equal, but different.

Another Wellsian synthesizer—though less a sympathizer—is Peter Kemp. Like Reed, he is aware of biological imperatives at work in the novels. In *H. G. Wells and the Culminating Ape* (1982), Kemp finds "uncommon excitements" generated in all the later fiction by the intersection of biological themes with "powerful obsessions" in which "Wells writes as a highly idiosyncratic personality whose very menagerie of hobby-horses and *bêtes noires* is unleashed at every opportunity. . . . His imagination piles them high with a bizarre miscellany of such things as tentacles, blood-drinkers, battling puddings, statue-women, suffragettes with squeaky voices, basements turned inside out, sex-starved dons, murderous pacifists, bicycles and bishops."[33]

There can be few writers who have portrayed more broken marriages, more misunderstandings and petty antagonisms that in life and in fiction assumed the proportions of the insurmountable. In life, he confessed to Somerset Maugham, his neighbor on the French Riviera, he could not find a mistress he could live with *or* without. Although there is no record of it, he may have compared his tolerance to that of Maugham's Gauguinesque painter Charles Strickland who, in *The Moon and Sixpence,* sought women only to satisfy his sexual appetite, not wanting them to interfere with his proper business.

In the fiction, Kemp concludes that Wells's women are either statues or slaves, goddesses or saboteurs. Men frequently lust after what *The Anatomy of Frustration* (1936) calls "a strong, quietly animated goddess-slave. Or a strong, quietly animated slave-goddess."[34] A pattern of something Kemp calls Wells's "dream of mythological promiscuity" is repeated early, when Chatteris in *The Sea Lady* (1902) witnesses a battle of goddesses between his bluestocking fiancée and a possessive mermaid, and late, in *Brynhild* (1937), when Mr. Palace is lured away from his wife into the arms of Lady Cytherea, who has played Venus to his Paris in a charade. Professor Higgins's question of Liza Doolittle in *My Fair Lady*—"Why Can't a Girl Be a Guy?"—is frequently answered to male satisfaction in Wells's novels. In *Marriage,* when Trafford gets himself into difficulties in Labrador, Marjorie works "like two men" to rescue him, muttering to herself, "Why don't they teach a girl to handle an axe?"[35] When Isabel and Remington face a crisis in *The New Machiavelli,* she declares formidably, "You and I, Master, we've got to be men."[36] The slavish note, Kemp stresses, frequently accompanies amorous exchanges. So, too, do the females sabotage the lives of the men. Lewisham in Wells's first major character novel destroys his schema in the light of his wife Ethel's final thrust as philistine and vandal. George Ponderevo can only rehabilitate himself into scientific pursuits when he has thrown off the soul-destroying Marion.

By 1914 world events were superseding for Wells even the birth of a son in his *other* household—that occupied by himself and Rebecca. World War I and Wells's preoccupations with the elaborate pamphleteering for a world state, which culminated in *The Outline of History* (1920), caused him to abandon the writing of novels about feminism and marriage.

Wells, of course, did not invent the woman of spirit. She has existed in English fiction since Pamela Andrews. That adopted Englishman Henry James had Isabel Archer confront her own sexuality in *Portrait of a Lady* (1881), but she, even with an ideal replacement waiting in the wings, vowed to continue a hopeless marriage after a self-searching vigil. James's heroine echoed fashion and George Eliot who, in *Middlemarch* (1872), spares Dorothea Brooke a devastatingly sterile married life by allowing Casaubon to die. Thomas Hardy's Sue Bridehead knew all there was to know about the fatuousness of marriage as a contract. However, in *Jude the Obscure* (1896), she was dually prevented from acting on her intimations by her own perversity and her creator's irremediable sense of an indifferent universe. Meredith also offered variations on the independent woman but their gestures were indecisive or abortive. H. G. Wells did more than any novelist until Lawrence to bring women's rights (and female rites) out of the closet. He showed female sexuality as a healthy expression of self, and he preached full freedom for women to confront their passionate natures even as he partook of them.

Chapter Seven

Masters and Modes: "Of Art, of Literature, of Mr. Henry James"

The War of the Giants

If one were of a mind to defend Wells's modus operandi as a novelist, he could do no worse than to call on the author's own words. Few authors, as George Orwell has said, had less vanity. Wells always downgraded his stature as an artist and a thinker by some temporary jockeying for position. By seeming to undervalue his own works, by comparing them to the dirty scratchings made by a beetle once imprisoned by the young Bertie Wells, he helped to blind critics to the literary brilliance of his earlier work.

Perhaps the most devastating single utterance against the Wellsian novel, one so brilliant that it never, in its day, produced a reply, was Virginia Woolf's trenchant view through a Bloomsbury keyhole of the death of characterization in the Edwardians—Wells, Bennett, and Galsworthy.[1] However, to demolish Wells, as Mrs. Woolf sought to do, on the basis, undeniably valid, that individual characterization stood for less and less in his novels as he went on, would be to overlook how vividly the intimation of his novels, even some of the lesser ones, dramatized the aspirations of the generation that was still young during World War I: "There was, conceivably, not much wisdom to be gained from [Wells]. But there was a great deal of exhilaration—the wine, of all wines, keenest on the palate of youth. And upon youth—not literary youth merely, but youth substantially and at large—no writer was to have a comparable influence until George Orwell. . . ."[2] Stanley Kauffmann, whose moving eulogy to Wells's dying voice among young readers of the 1930s is quoted above, declares that his influence declined sharply after 1925. This estimate is probably a few years on the generous side, since *Mr. Britling* (1916) was probably the last of his novels to sell in substantial numbers in the United States. Speaking as this book did for both the doomed soldier in the trenches and the grief-stricken parents, actual and potential, at home, it had a vogue few novels written during the heat of war could equal. *William Clissold* (1926) was Wells's last serious bid to right himself, but its tired frettings of an aging seer reached only the members of the generation that had grown old with him. Curiously enough, it was as a historian that Wells's meteor soared for the last time. *The Outline of History* (1919–20), whatever its reception from specialists, was an immensely popular success with sales in English of more than a half a million copies within three years of publication. Its continued use as a standard book for homes assured the presence of the famous name within the average reader's horizon. But the concentrated effort required by the *Outline* caused a three-year rupture in novel writing which, by his own acknowledgment, Wells was never able to repair. *The Undying Fire* (1919) was Wells's first and only successful experiment with a novel done wholly in dialogue; but it was also among his last well-received novels. *The Secret Places of the Heart,* published three years later, began a twenty-year languor which voluminous production, one or more a year until 1942, could not hide.

It is difficult to reconcile Wells's long sterility as a novelist with the critical acclaim he won early in his career. For fifteen years everything he touched turned to gold. First, there was the acknowledged originality and excellence of the five scientific romances described in chapter 2. Alone, however, these could not win him stature as a novelist. They were a variation of the term Graham Greene uses to describe his own early works— "entertainments"—and recognition as a novelist was not accorded Wells until the publication of *Love and Mr. Lewisham* in 1900.

"Written with greater care than any of [my] . . . earlier books," *Mr. Lewisham* never received the acclaim Wells had hoped for it. That would come five years later with the publication of *Kipps.* Nonetheless, Henry James wrote Wells of finding in *Lewisham* "a great charm and a great deal of the real thing—that is of the note of life, if not *all* of it (as distinguished from the said great deal). . . . I am not quite sure that I see your *idea*—I mean your Subject, so to speak, as determined or constituted. . . ."[3] The "determined or constituted" fabric of the novel—its adherence to the canons of the form—would forge within a few years an irreparable breach between James and his younger contemporary.

Leon Edel and Gordon N. Ray trace the meeting of James and Wells back to 1898 although, as a young drama critic on *Pall Mall,* Wells had been present three years before when James was humiliated by an audience that booed when he appeared on the stage at the opening of his play *Guy Domville.* Their ages aside—James, fifty-five; Wells, thirty-two—no more curious literary pairing could be imagined:

The paradox of [James's] life was that, although unread, he remained a literary lion. His opinions on the art of fiction were valued; he was *cher maître* to Joseph Conrad. . . . He was established as a great American man of letters who had chosen England as his home. . . .
Wells, on the other hand, was still a struggling writer. . . . By origin he belonged . . . "below stairs," but his sharp intelligence and formidable energy, conveyed to the public by a nimble pen, were allowing him to wander about increasingly in the drawing room.[4]

Edwardian England was a time when "deans" like James made it a point to welcome young writers like Wells into the fold. Dorothy Richardson and Frank Swinnerton have portrayed best the atmosphere at Spade House, Sandgate, where in 1900 H. G. and Jane Wells made their new home a central point for artists of all descriptions. Miss Richardson, especially, in her series of novels collectively titled *Pilgrimage,* conveys the rampant unsureness with which Wells, who acknowledged himself to be Hypo Wilson in her novel, strove for recognition in a literary society that Henry James ruled by a kind of age-before-glamor noblesse.

From almost the start, James welcomed Wells as, for him, by far the most interesting novelist of his generation—"in fact, the only interesting one."[5] Sandgate lay across Romney Marsh from James's bachelor quarters in Rye, and the two began to meet often. James and Wells were frequently joined by Conrad, or Arnold Bennett, or by Stephen Crane who had "borrowed" Brede House near Rye during the last year of his short life.

A James biographer, Michael Swan, may be extravagant when he suggests that the James-Wells relationship was that of father and son; but the statement makes much sense when Swan, in his perplexity over why James should have become so excited over a writer so unlike himself, asks: "Was he [James] simply recognizing genius in whatever form it should appear— or was this recognition inspired by some obscure demand of his private psychology? Did he admire Wells as the aesthete secretly admires the athlete? Wells's commonsense pragmatism attracts him in the same way that he was unwillingly drawn towards the mind of his brother William. . . ."[6] Whether James's solicitude for Wells stemmed from a total dedication to craft or from a psychic need does not concern us here. It is enough to note that the master bestowed his favors lavishly on the pupil, and the pupil received them with the deference of the aspiring pretender. Yet, as their relationship lengthened and as Wells's burgeoning fame buttressed his cockney impudence, an implication of disapproval crept into James's letters.

After James's unalloyed praise of *Kipps* ("It left me prostrate with admiration . . . a mere born gem . . . of such a brilliancy of *true* truth. . . . You have for the very first time treated the English 'lower middle' class, etc., without the picturesque, the grotesque, the fantastic and romantic interference [of] Dickens . . . [and] George Eliot"),[7] James became more reserved about *Ann Veronica;* he found the main characterization wanting in "clearness and *nuances.*"[8] Although praising the first half of *The New Machiavelli,* James excoriated Wells for the first time on "that accursed autobiographic form which puts a premium on the loose, the improvised, the cheap and easy."[9] His view of *Marriage* was almost explicitly dark: "I find myself absolutely unable, and still more unwilling, to approach you, or to take leave of you, in any projected light of criticism, in any judging or concluding, any comparing, in fact in any aesthetic or 'literary,' relation at all; and this in spite of the fact that the light of criticism is almost that in which I most fondly bask. . . ."[10]

The outlines of H. G. Wells's thorough abdication from the art of the novel became clear to anyone reading his correspondence with Henry James. James deplored long narratives in the first person because they precipitated the novel into "looseness. . . . The terrible *fluidity* of self-revelation." Two of Wells's best novels, *Tono-Bungay* and *The New Machiavelli,* are written in first person and have long monologues. James objected to having characters "talk at" the reader rather than revealing themselves through unconscious behavior or telling incident. *Ann Veronica* and *Marriage,* though written in third person, are often painfully essayistic. James excused Wells, at least on the surface, for his transgressions on the basis of the younger man's matchless vitality—James always called it, without disparagement, "cheek"—and could write to Mrs. Humphrey Ward: "I really think him [Wells] more interesting by his faults than he will probably ever manage to be in any other way; and he is a most vivid and violent object lesson!"[11]

Wells answered the criticism of mandarin critics like Henry James in the only way that he knew. All his writing life Wells had flayed Victorian obsolescence by calling for a revolution against debilitating social and political strictures. He now resorted to equivalent action in the pursuance of his craft. If his novels were deficient in the qualities Henry James said were sine qua non—and Wells, rather than denying it, said such canons omitted the fact that novels could be something else, too—then Wells would simply call for anarchy. His pleas were first made in the essay "The Scope of the Novel," published in *Fortnightly Review* (November 1911) and *Atlantic Monthly* (January 1912). They were repeated twenty years later in his autobiography in the chapter "Digression about Novels," and stated again near the end of his career in the foreword to *Babes in the Darkling Wood* (1940). Wells, in effect, sought to stretch the novel to cover almost anything that could be made interesting in the form of fiction. Behind the culminating argument put forth in the quotation below, one can hardly miss the urgency in the voice of a newly established fiction writer, who, in 1911, was aware as a professional writer that in Edwardian England it was extremely difficult to publish and get people to read anything unless it could be classified as a novel and go on the six-shilling shelf, subject to a discount of one and six-pence:[12]

And this being my view you will be prepared for the demand I am now about to make for an absolutely free hand for the novelist in his choice of topic and incident and in his method of treatment. . . . We are going to write, subject only to our limitations, about the whole of human life. We are going to deal with political questions and religious questions and social questions. We cannot present people unless we have this free hand, this unrestricted field. . . . We mean to deal with these things, and it will need very much more than the disapproval of provincial librarians, the hostility of a few influential people in London . . . to stop the incoming tide of aggressive novel-writing. We are going to write about it all. . . . Before we have done, we will have all life within the scope of the novel. (*W*, 9:379–80)

In 1914 Henry James wrote what was, in a sense, an answer to Wells's proclamation for the *Times Literary Supplement* in a two-installment article, "The Younger Generation," which he expanded for inclusion in *Notes on Novelists*, published the same year. Edel and Ray find this attempt to assess both the middle generation of writers—Conrad, Bennett, Galsworthy, and Wells—and the younger—Hugh Walpole, Gilbert Cannan, Compton Mackenzie, and a thirtyish newcomer from the Midlands named D. H. Lawrence—"in some ways his least responsible piece of criticism."[13] The essay, patronizing throughout, fails in its courtesy and syntactical deviousness to hide James's contempt for the kind of novels Wells and Bennett were writing:

We confound the author of *Tono-Bungay* and the author of *Clayhanger* in this imputation for the simple reason that with the sharpest differences of character and range they yet come together under our so convenient measure of value by *saturation*. This is the greatest value, to our sense, in either of them, their other values, even when at the highest, not being quite in proportion to it; and as to be saturated is to be documented, to be able even on occasion to prove quite enviably and potently so, they are alike in the authority that creates emulation. [14]

James damns with faint praise Wells's penchant for "absorbing knowledge at the pores" and Bennett's "density of illustration." In other words, in Wells and Bennett, Henry James saw the defects of the virtue of saturation. It left out the need for what James called a "centre of interest or . . . sense of the whole."

James then attacks in earnest when he refers to novels like *Kipps, Tono-Bungay,* and *Ann Veronica*—works he had lavishly praised in correspondence—as blunting critical judgment by their "blinding, bluffing vivacity." For *Marriage,* he reserves, however, his major onslaught: "we wince at a certain quite peculiarly gratuitous sacrifice to the casual in *Marriage* very much as at seeing some fine and indispensable little part of a mechanism slip through *profane fingers* and lose itself." [15]

The novel's "gratuitous sacrifice to the casual" was the open declaration of love between two strangers—Marjorie and Trafford—after a three-hour interlude, noted but not described in the book. The "profane fingers," though descriptive of an analogy James had drawn, could not help but have angered Wells who was sensitive to the fact that Mrs. Ward was not the only one of the mandarins who regarded him as coarse and that his reputation as something of a rake who openly cohabited with maidens without benefit of clergy might have influenced James's estimate of him as an artist.

Later, in the autobiography, Wells elaborately defended his disinclination to provide psychological preparation for a love affair that flowered on such short notice. But, in 1914, the score with James could not be settled by one of their long talks in James's garden at Rye. For his retaliatory thrust, Wells dusted off an old manuscript he had conceived as early as 1901 and had returned to periodically during his years of infamy in the wake of *Ann Veronica.* In 1914 he somewhat recast the book *Boon,* appended a chapter entitled "Of Art, Of Literature, Of Mr. Henry James"—a chaotic though frequently perceptive satire of the Jamesian novel and a cruel caricature of the man behind it.

Boon was a book Wells came to regret. There is only one reference to it in his autobiography. It was a wrongheaded effort, but an understandable one in the total picture of Wells. Under a certain surface comedy, it is the cup-runneth-over indignation of an outsider lashing out at the literary establishment. It gave violent answer to the Brahmins of London society who always considered him hopelessly "below stairs"; to the Fabians and their

"Episode of Mr. Wells"; to the "Reform Club Myth" that impugned him morally, socially, and intellectually. It followed by three years his attack on the Webbs in *The New Machiavelli*. Such angry-young-man works would have their equivalents in angry-middle-aged-man and angry-old-man effusions for the next thirty years.

The Boon aftermath is too well known to be sketched in detail here. Wells left a copy for James at his club, a gesture Edel and Ray deplore but one that Wells had followed since the publication of *Kipps* a decade earlier. James's letter of acknowledgment and the one following Wells's apology terminated their friendship and established—supremely—the Jamesian aesthetic:

> I *have* no view of life and literature, I maintain, other than that our form of the latter in especial is admirable, exactly by its range and variety, its plasticity and liberality, its fairly living on the sincere and shifting experience of the individual practitioner. That is why I have always so admired your so free and strong application of it, the particular rich receptacle of intelligences and impressions emptied out with an energy of its own, that your genius constitutes; and *that* is in particular why, in my letter of two or three days since, I pronounced it curious and interesting that you should find the case I constitute myself only ridiculous and vacuous to the extent of your having to proclaim your sense of it. . . .[16]

And, finally, James wrote: "It is art that *makes* life, makes interest, makes importance, for our consideration and application of these things, and I know of no substitute whatever for the force and beauty of its process. . . ."[17]

To nearly anyone who regards the reading of fiction as a serious pursuit in which action and characters stand as artistic artifacts to be rigorously studied, Henry James, perplexed and troubled by the neglect of his books, had triumphed over the more popular, the better-rewarded Wells. To be faced with having to rebut James's all but unanswerable rebuttal quickly squelched any justified revenge Wells might have felt in *Boon*. The following fragments from a letter he wrote three days after James's art-makes-life epistle show how easily Wells's outsider's unsureness—his seemingly short view of life and art—had cast him irrevocably into the Philistine position: "I don't clearly understand your concluding phrases—which shews no doubt how completely they define our difference. When you say 'it is art that *makes* life, makes interest, makes importance,' I can only read sense into it by assuming that you are using 'art' for every conscious human activity. I use the word for a research and attainment that is technical and special."[18]

This was a matter of sensibility. However, in the seventy years since James put down Wells the polarities of their debate are far less defined. Although his close friend and older contemporary Gissing could parody ivory-tower exclusivity in *Henry Ryecroft* and Joyce, his admired junior, could admit that Stephen Dedalus was something of a prig, words like *"art"* and *"artist"* were sacrosanct in Edwardian England. Wells's view of them was not far removed from that of a fictional former student who, like Wells, had had a scientific education. Bazarov in Turgenev's *Fathers and Children* declared that one chemist is worth a hundred poets. But, like Bazarov's, Wells's preachments were inadequate for what life decreed. Bazarov died whispering a romantic conceit into the ear of the woman who had spurned him. Wells had to accept James's counsels for perfecting the artistic form of his novels.

Long after their quarrel Wells remained impressed, though still bewildered, by James, whom he praised as "a shrewd and penetrating critic of the technique by which he lived" (*E,* 410). It has never been sufficiently stressed that professionals like James and Wells, for all the psychological prospecting of the one and the didactic thrust of the other, never stopped being novelists-in-charge. Each evoked the world as he knew it. Each felt that his version of that world was threatened by the other's contrasting version. Each managed his fiction—"stood next to God," in the words of one commentator—in ways that the practitioners of the *nouveau roman* would call obsolete.

"Every important writer's work offers us a different system of notation, which has its focal limits in abstracting from the total system of existence." If Robert Scholes's liberal dictum is right, if each significant writer employs "narrative codes" that illuminate—even elucidate—his "version of reality," then all achieved models of special representations of life merit consideration on their own terms. [19] Their fiction, as Aristotle has taught us in his elevation of a poet like Sophocles over a historian like Herodotus, offers not transcriptions of actuality but models of mimeticized actuality that is *related to,* but is fundamentally *other than,* the world that is.

James's techniques served him as means of delineating the life he saw; Wells's served equally as crystallizers. Wells saw life as involving dramatic interaction between sensibility and the flow of the times. James *ordered* impressions—regulated viewpoint—out of the necessity to encounter experience without the ability to take dramatic part in it. With James, especially in his last phase, ordered experience dominated any other aesthetic. With Wells, increasingly, any "distancing" maneuvers became impossible. Chastised but unchanged by his quarrel with James, Wells moved toward a fictional hybridization in which the imaginative and the reportorial join hands.

In the same year that Henry James died—1916—Wells published what in its time was his most famous and popular novel, *Mr. Britling Sees It Through.* The first of two sections will take up the book's topical vitality and interest. The second will bring the issues between James and Wells full circle. I shall endeavor to show that in a representative example—that is, in *Mr. Britling*—of the kind of ideological fiction in which Wells has been thought most to eschew technical refinements he was cognizant of the necessity for a controlling centrality that was a good deal more complex than a mere device for the monitoring of his own viewpoints. Specifically, I shall demonstrate that Wells installs a central intelligence of comparable galvanism to that which operates in James's last works. I shall pair Wells's commercially successful *Mr. Britling* with James's artistically esteemed *Ambassadors* (1903) as a means of illustrating the narrative viability of contrasting strategies of point of view.

Mr. Britling Sees It Through (1916): War as a Novel

"If posterity wants to know what England felt during the first two years of the Great War," wrote Sidney Dark, "there is no contemporary record . . . that will tell it so much [as *Mr. Britling*]."[20] Wells, ever a writer in a hurry, declined to wait for the war to end to reflect on it in tranquillity. He made a novel out of the war—not out of one campaign, not out of one soldier's adventures, but out of the war as a whole. Wells took for his central figure one Britling, an essayist and philosopher of advanced tendencies. In describing Britling's reactions to the war, Wells traced their development from the first angry amazement to the final extraordinary readjustment of theories and hopes.

Mr. Britling reads in places like a book of current history. References to living personalities—Lloyd George, the Kaiser, Winston Churchill, Shaw—and the transparent disguises of the well-known military and political figures all contribute to the documentary characteristic of the book. Wells frequently interrupts the flow of narrative to present a vivid communiqué on a historical event. This news-flash announces the shootings at Sarajevo, the prelude to war: "And indeed at the very moment when Mr. Britling was saying these words, in Sarajevo in Bosnia, where the hour was somewhat later, men whispered together, and one held nervously to a black parcel that had been given him and nodded as they repeated his instructions, a black parcel with certain unstable chemicals and a curious arrangement of detonators therein, a black parcel destined ultimately to shatter nearly every landmark of Mr. Britling's cosmogony . . ." (*W,* 22:59–60) The novel reads as if Wells, while keeping before the reader Britling's fictional life, also spreads out the newspaper Britling is reading. The placing of Britling's life against a backdrop of historical events leading inexorably to World War I gives the book great value as a record.

Britling, however, is clearly the work of a novelist rather than a reporter. No journal of events can legitimately pose as fiction without verisimilitude of setting and characters. Mr. Britling, as was customary for a writer who never drew his heroes from other than his own stock, is H. G. Wells; and the setting is Wells's own household during the first year of the war. Sidney Dark shows how Matching's Easy of the novel is little altered from Wells's Essex country house, Easton Glebe; and he identifies the gallery of personages in the novel by name, but the reactions, so exhaustively developed, are those of the English in general.

The spirit of the novel is the gradual forming of disillusionment as the cruel facts of war close in on civilized men who will not, until almost too late, believe in them. Wells shows his kinship to the journalist by his "arrangement" of characters. He employs an American, Mr. Direck, secretary of the Massachusetts Society for the Study of Contemporary Thought, to report an outsider's impressions of an unenterprising, sluggish, prosperous, and comfortable England on the brink of disaster. Direck is literally a reporter, and the impressions gathered through the eyes that Wells gives him tend to materialize into correspondent's dispatches.

Wells adds to his carefully planned gallery of representative figures that of Herr Heinrich, who lives with the Britlings as a tutor. The interviews with Heinrich contrast the German psyche—its definiteness and its order—with England's tendency to muddle through and America's youthful self-reliance. Sidney Dark observes the thoroughness of Wells's understanding of the American point of view, the reasons why she hesitated long before entering the war.

The novel has hardly begun when, through the eyes of Direck, one is placed in the center of a Wellsian symposium. Wells chooses for his opinion forum a representative group. Britling (Wells) is the advance-guard Republican with "ideas in the utmost profusion about races and empires and social order and political institutions and gardens and automobiles and the future of India and China and aesthetics and America and the education of mankind in general . . ." (*W,* 22:12). His antagonist in the opening dialogues is Lady Frensham, aristocratic and resistant to change, who is made to represent the body of upper-class English minds that can see no danger of the Empire's breaking down and that are violent only in their opposition to minor skirmishes waged by the suffragettes or by the advocates of Irish Home Rule. A third participant is Lady Homartyn, who represents the complacent social woman in passive resistance to post-Victorian social forces. Wells portrays her as "incapable of believing that she won't always be able to have week-ends at Claverings, and that the letters and the tea won't come to her bedside in the morning" (*W*, 22:434).

Wells craftily introduces the events leading up to war—and some of his hindsight bulletins have an interpretive brilliance only possible in a super-journalist of wide intellectual grasp who is able to look at the present from viewpoints of past and future. Britling, for all his prescience, delivers ironic commentaries on the impossibility of catastrophe. When the war does come, he records and analyzes the growing hardness of heart and the scarring over of British conscience that was destined to be reenacted, when Wells was in his late seventies, in World War II.

Wells was fifty when he wrote *Mr. Britling,* but even into middle age Wells wrote with an eye on the young. Hugh Britling, son of the title character, becomes Wells's deus ex machina for his formulation, at the end of the novel, of a faith in God. But throughout the early part of the novel Hugh is merely a part of the Wellsian symposium, a chip off the old block. Hugh's analysis of a Britain mired in tradition is full of Wellsian irony: "In England everybody talks of change and nothing ever changes. Nothing changes in England, because the people who want to change things change their minds before they change anything else. I've been to London talking for the last half-year. Studying art they call it. Before that I was a science student, and I want to be one again. Don't you think . . . there's something about science—it's steadier than anything else in the world?" (*W*, 22:66–67). And, later, to Direck, the American reporter, Hugh says: "Dad says in one of his books that over here we are being and over there [in America] you are beginning. It must be tremendously stimulating to think that your country is still being made. . . . Unless something tumbles down here, we never think of altering it and even then we just shore it up" (*W*, 22:67).

Events move rapidly to a tragic conclusion. Hugh goes to France; his letters from the trenches form much of the book. Herr Heinrich is called back to Germany for conscription, and his sentimental farewell to his English friends is one of the best things in the book. With Britling as commentator, the story moves steadily to its climax. When the fatal telegram bears the news that Hugh has been killed, Britling takes his loss in a strange spirit. He declares that he is neither angry nor depressed, only "bitterly hurt" by the end of something fine. For Wells, it is not enough to present a grieving Mr. Britling. Wells is obsessed by the human folly. However, a Wells without a solution is inconceivable. The one he offers had been strongly hinted at four years earlier in *Marriage* when Trafford referred to life as being redeemed by the flame of salvation. In *Britling,* Wells presents an embellishment. In his bitter sorrow, Mr. B.—H. G. Wells—finds God. But his God is not an omnipotent God. He is not responsible for the horrors of human life, but someday He will triumph and then horror will cease. Cruelty, injustice, and aggression are present in the world; but so also are kindness, goodness, love, and these qualities are the signs of God—the God who struggles, the God who will ultimately prevail. To a mind like Wells's—rationalistic and suspicious of spiritual values—any lengthy phase in passionate embrace of the idea that the meek will inherit the earth was hardly to be expected.

In its time, *Mr. Britling* became a household word on two continents. Mr. Britling's loss mirrored other losses of loved ones from the British Midlands to the American plains. The novel was a *succès d'estime*—Wells said it earned him twenty thousand pounds in the United States alone. Because men and women growing to maturity in the first twenty years of the new century looked to H. G. Wells for a path out of the woods, the picture of a Wells-with-a-deity was a compelling one. Years later, Wells, whose own sons were too young to serve in the war of 1914–18, wrote that enthusiastic strangers often invaded his home with the demand to see the place where he had wept when he heard of his son's death in battle.

Britling and Strether: Wellsian/Jamesian Central Intelligences

James, as is well known, made an ideal of holding his story so firmly in its frame that he could, like a prestidigitator, fully control what is *seen*. His preface to *The Ambassadors* is full of imagery from puppetry and visual illusion. More specifically, his method was the Central Intelligence, the solidly posed center which in his favorite novel resides wholly in the consciousness of the principal envoy, Lambert Strether. To read his preface is to be let in on the ways the "scenic side" can be made to serve the inner side. We see how "representational effects" so dear to the hearts of commentators from Aristotle to Conrad serve to place the reader within Strether's angle of vision. Although, syntactically, he had a curious way of showing it, James fairly bubbles over as he places before us a lifetime of trade secrets on the technique of point of view.

His major lesson, one that he had been giving Wells for years in unfailingly courteous letters and that, at the end of his life, he gave less charitably to a whole "younger generation" of fellow novelists, is to show how, through rigorous selectivity, a principal character can be accorded center stage without his creator stooping to the "terrible *fluidity* of self-revelation." Instead of giving in to the "romantic privilege" of the "I" ("never much my affair"), James explains how "the whole lumpish question" of Strether is to be evoked scenically.[21]

Certainly it is true that H. G. Wells had already by the time of his break with James become more interested in public education than in private intelligence, central or otherwise. Still, he never lost his concern for fictive plausibility. If, for James, plausibility involved a merging of the ambiguities of appearance and sense, plausibility for Wells involved a truce between strategies of *action* and—increasingly vital to him—*reaction*. Plausibility in *The Ambassadors* is whatever elaborates the fine edge of Strether's sensibility—everything directed *inward*. Plausibility for Wells, in midcareer dialogue novels like *Mr. Britling*, is whatever enabled Britling to react—an orchestration *outward*.

Mr. Britling is Wells's Condition-of-England novel for the first two years of the Great War, but its efficacy depends on a variation of the Jamesian central intelligence.

One reason for the special demand James's fictional prose makes on the reader's attention in *The Ambassadors* is that there are three levels of development—all of them subjective: Strether's awareness of events; the authorial narrator's seeing-eye arrangement of them; and the reader's perception of the relation between the two. The novel's progress is the mellowing of Strether's awareness in middle age of how much of life he has missed to the point when he recognizes and enjoys with all the taste buds of a finer sensibility the *idea* of what Europe offers him. How Strether comes, finally, to *live* his unlived life—to experience the moral perquisites of the vicarious—is the burden of the book. The epiphanic moment after his "you-must-live" advice to Little Bilham, the moment after his confession, Strether retreats. He resists in life what his creator said had always to be resisted in fiction: self-revelation. He tells the worshipful Bilham that he had wished only to promote a little "innocent gaiety" in him. Candor turns into a "proper joke."

H. G. Wells, whose effects in *Mr. Britling* are as graphic and immediate as a headline, also seeks a balanced tension between what goes on "outside"—what Britling sees and hears—and what goes on "inside"—what Britling thinks. Not even the assassination of the Austrian archduke disturbs the Sabbath calm of Britling's estate, fittingly named "Matching's

Easy." "Mr. Britling, to whom the explosion was altogether unaudible, continued his dissertation upon the common sense of the world and the practical security of our western peace" (*W,* 22:97).

Like *The Ambassadors, Mr. Britling* is the chronicle of an awakening—and a reconciliation. Where James illumines Strether's awakening by enlisting rhetorical aids he calls "ficelles,"[22] Wells is equally manipulative. While keeping before the reader Britling's fictive life of easeful contemplation, he creates a clarifying tension in it, in effect, by spreading out the newspaper Mr. Britling is reading.

The first 120 pages mount, not the title character, but an American, Mr. Direck, as the central intelligence. Wells wants the reader's first views of England to be those of an outsider whose lens, unlike Mr. Britling's, would not be fogged by the comfortable inertia of Matching's Easy. Direck is no Lambert Strether whose inner life speaks louder than words. As noted previously, he will report a visitor's impressions of a "Blimpish" England on the brink of disaster.

As James withholds the essential—the inner—Strether from his "ficelles," Wells withholds the essential Britling from Direck. Jamesian "ficelles" and Wellsian observers are only occasionally confidants. At the beginning of chapter 4, where the central intelligence of Britling takes over for the limited intelligence of Direck, Wells manages a transitional intrusion, much against the grain of the late James but, functionally, in the interests of the unity of focus James always sought:

Very different from the painful contentment of the bruised and broken Mr. Direck was the state of mind of his unwounded host. He too was sleepless, but sleepless without exaltation. The day had been too much for him altogether; his head, to borrow an admirable American expression, was "busy." . . . The impression Mr. Britling had made upon Mr. Direck was one of indefatigable happiness. But there were times when Mr. Britling was called upon to pay for his general cheerful activity in lump sums of bitter sorrow. . . .

The sorrows of the sanguine temperament are brief but furious; the world knows little of them. The world has no need to reckon with them. They cause no suicides and few crimes. They hurry past, smiting at their victim as they go. None the less they are misery. Mr. Britling in these moods did not perhaps experience the grey and hopeless desolations of the melancholic nor the red damnation of the choleric, but he saw a world that bristled with misfortune and error, with poisonous thorns and traps and swampy places and incurable blunderings. An almost insupportable remorse for being Mr. Britling would pursue him—justifying itself upon a hundred counts. (*W,* 22:121–22)

Those "counts," the authorial narrator tells us, will require a whole chapter, "Mr. Britling in Soliloquy." I have let the above excerpt, the opening of that chapter, run on because I believe Wells is maneuvering in Jamesian terrain: point of view. Ian Watt is especially cogent in revealing how idiosyncratic can be the results of James's preoccupation with rhetorical architectonics: "The dual presence of Strether's consciousness and of that of the narrator, who translates what he sees there into more general terms, makes the narrative point of view both intensely individual and yet ultimately social."[23] Wells also has shown us, through Direck's reportorial eye, the public seer. The private Britling is something else:

He was widely known, reputably known; he prospered . . . but everything was doomed by his invincible defects. Beneath that hollow, enviable show there ached waste. . . .
On these black nights, when the personal Mr. Britling would lie awake thinking how unsatisfactorily Mr. Britling was going on, and when the impersonal Mr. Britling would be thinking how unsatisfactorily his universe was going on, the whole mental process had a likeness to some complex piece of orchestral music. . . .
Was Huxley right, and was all humanity, even as Mr. Britling, a careless, fitful thing, playing a tragically hopeless game, thinking too slightly, moving too quickly, against a relentless antagonist? (*W,* 22:149–50)

Wells, characteristically, invokes the cosmic pessimism of his old teacher to problems of Britling's divided psyche. A passage like the above evokes a more explicit central intelligence than James would have accepted, but it tells a good deal about how little Wells's apostle-of-progress image truly formulated him.

Events move rapidly to the tragic conclusion that was described in the previous section. Britling's oldest son, Hugh, goes to France; his letters from the trenches form much of the latter part of the book. When the fatal telegram bears the news that Hugh has been killed, Britling takes his loss in a strange spirit. He writes to the parents of a German boy, Heinrich, a prewar visitor to Matching's Easy, and now, like his son, a war casualty: "If you think that these two boys have both perished, not in some noble common cause but against one another in a struggle of dynasties and boundaries and trade routes and tyrannous ascendancies, then it seems to me that you must feel as I feel" (*W,* 22:527). He declares himself neither vindictive nor depressed, only bitterly hurt, by the end of something fine.

In his invaluable *H. G. Wells and His Critics,* Ingvald Raknem devotes eighteen pages to the Wells-Britling relationship, concluding that "the novel is a very personal record. The whole atmosphere of the Essex country house, the principal characters, and numerous incidents in it, are presented without much alteration. . . . Mr. Britling has Wells's antipathies and sympathies . . . revealing all their characteristic traits in their writing."[24] This is well said, as far as it goes. However, the autobiographical resonances are less important than the implications of the book's original title. What Britling sees through is no less an idea than what Strether sees through. Their resolutions are appropriate for the kind of heroism with which James and Wells dealt. Strether renounces his "ambassadorship" with his wealthy sponsors in America. He stays behind in Europe, his future uncertain. What *is* certain is that, to maintain the moral ideal as befitting a Jamesian hero, he must continue to deny himself pleasure—a liaison with Maria Gostrey. It would not do for Strether to profit materially or sensually from his spiritual renunciation. The Wells hero must, as befits *his* creator, combine private and cosmic angst. Privately, he responds to despair by an awakening: "These boys, these boys, this war has killed." The words hung for a time in his mind. "No!" said Mr. Britling stoutly. "They live!"

Cosmically, Britling thus invokes "a Finite God. . . . [Someone] hitherto . . . full of the promise of a fine personality . . . a thing of the intelligence, a theory, a report, something told about but not realised. . . . There was no need to despair because he himself was one of the feeble folk" (*W,* 22:540). Britling's finding of God was a fictive imperative—a convincing peripeteia. For the English-speaking world at war, *Mr. Britling* cast private and national tragedy in a heroic mold. And the book, a generation in advance of a now established trend, made H. G. Wells a household name, a monument of something Robert Brustein has termed "news theater," the transformation of creative people into figures of the news.

Platonic Modes—the Dialogue Novel: *The Undying Fire* (1919)

In 1919, three years after *Mr. Britling* and a year after the Armistice, Wells wrote *The Undying Fire,* a modern adaptation of the Book of Job. Wells regarded it as the best of those novels that he modeled on the Platonic dialogue and which occupied him to the end of his life. Vincent Brome, writing in 1951, called it "a noble and profound religious work obscured by lesser books."[25]

Even in a novel whose text is almost wholly set between quotation

marks Wells is concerned to maintain fictive plausibility. Without Jamesian terminology, he was certainly thinking of narrative unity and coherence
in something like James's sense when he wrote to Frank Swinnerton: "But
I maintain an artificial story is a perfectly justifiable way of holding together a bunch of people if their *reactions* are real and living. Often it seems the
only way of linking them and getting them to *react*."[26] Wells's use of the
italicized words is significant. Fictional plausibility, vital to James in his
last phase as an uncompromising central intelligence, is vital to Wells as
any device that permits his characters—often his spokesmen—to react be-
lievably. In an unabashed dialogue novel like *The Undying Fire,* one would
expect dramatic plausibility to be sacrificed to talk. However, amid all the
dialogue and inner monologue, Wells recognizes that he is not a Plato
monitoring a Socrates but a novelist telling a human story.

Job Huss, borne down by pain and trouble, is staying at a dingy retreat.
Until lately he has been successful in a Wellsian way as head of a school—
Woldingstanton—where he works diligently to evolve a curriculum based
on the study of man's place in the historical and evolutionary process. Misfortune has struck, like Job's boils, from all sides. Two boys die in a school
fire; an assistant master is killed in a lab explosion: Huss's savings are lost
by his solicitor's speculations; and he and his wife receive the news of their
only son's death in France. Huss's physical pain is diagnosed as cancer; an
immediate operation is advised. On the morning of the operation Huss is
visited by two governors of the school and by Farr, the man who is to take
his place. The greater part of the novel is a record of the conversations
between Huss and his visitors, but there are also conversations, while he is
under chloroform, between Huss and God and Huss and Satan.

Years after he wrote it, Wells called *The Undying Fire* "one of the best
pieces of work I ever did. I set great store by it still." In reviving the
dialogue in a narrative form, he adds, "I was not so much expanding the
novel as getting right out of it" (*E,* 420). But it is remarkable how much,
despite the weight of Wellsian ideology the conversations and soliloquies
of Job Huss are required to carry, the book holds up as a work of the imagination. The persona of Job, that of a dedicated teacher, is an especially
congenial one for the man who was thinking, even as he finished *The Undying Fire,* that the future had become a race between education and catastrophe. Job's woes are at least as personal as they are cosmic.

Huss's long colloquy with his three visitors in chapter 4 cuts to the heart
of the same dialectic as Ivan Karamazov's recital of the Legend of the Grand
Inquisitor. Job assumes both Ivan's position—that of the skeptic—and Alyosha's—that of the believer. The reader is left with the same questions:

what happens to faith in a world where children suffer and perish and where God's "cold indifference" belies immortality? What is the good of being temperate and decent and careful during one's lifetime? Much later, Wells said of *The Undying Fire:* "It crowns and ends my theology. It is the sunset of my divinity" (*E,* 576).

And perhaps of his career as a creator of compelling characters and stories as well. One cares about Job's chances to survive the operation and even about the future of Woldingstanton and its curriculum in a way rarely matched in the later books. After the prologic exchange between God and Satan, in which God challenges his antagonist to "try Man to the uttermost [to] see if he is indeed no more than a little stir amidst the slime" (*W,* 11:51), the narrative takes firm footing on earth. Practicing what he later preached to Frank Swinnerton, Wells implements a two-front strategy. He seeks to justify his Jobian central intelligence's "cursed fluidity of self-revelation" by producing what, for him, a plausible dialogue novel needs: "reactions that are real and living." Job Huss, in deed as well as word, must be more than a spokesman for H. G. Wells. He must live in the world, too: a teacher and a man who is under sentence of discreditation and death.

Wells declared that his novel followed closely the pattern of the ancient book. What is more important is that Wells has contrived a believable situation where a schoolman with a worldview—an educator modeled along the lines of Wells's friend, the teacher of his sons, F. W. Sanderson of Oundle—would indeed fight vigorously for his school and his life. The three visitors escape caricature for anyone who has ever attended a school-board meeting. Euphemisms fill the vacuum between the trio and the stricken man whose life work they will reject by firing him. When the head hatchet-man speaks, the other two listen sycophantically. "'Go on,'" said Mr. Dad. 'Facts are facts.'" Job has resisted the trend toward narrow, technical education. Seeing "salvation through the teaching of history," Huss extends the subject by adding to it philosophy and the biological sciences.

More damaging than his teaching methods are other accusations against Huss. In public statements at the school, he has "cavilled against God's universe" (*W,* 11:73). Now his firing becomes an act done in God's name and his malignancy, a punishing God's retribution. Against these charges, Huss speaks as one whom adversity has turned inward. He recalls a time he fled the cares of his office only to be confronted, wherever he turned, by "the feeble miseries of living things." He asks, "How can there be righteousness in a scheme that afflicts them"—creatures of animal and plant life? He concludes, "Their decay and imperfection make up the common texture" (*W,* 11:64–67).

His position at this point, a third of the way through, is the same as Ivan Karamazov's: one T. H. Huxley was the first to name, the agnostic. The final two thirds chart Job's progress to faith, the Alyosha position. Word comes that the famous surgeon who is to perform the operation has been detained. The debate at bedside can continue. Wells's moving dialectic on immortality follows. Then Job finds Godhead in a metaphor that Wells first used in *Marriage* (1912) when Trafford referred to life as being redeemed by the fire of salvation. Now, seven years later, Job Huss declares: "What I am telling you now is not what I believe so much as what I feel. To me it seems that the creative desire that *burns* in me is a thing different in its nature from the blind Process of matter. . . . But this I do know, that once it is *lit* in a man it is like a consuming fire" (*W,* 11:148; my italics).

During the operation, under chloroform, Huss becomes the biblical Job who talks with God and, unlike the Old Testament version, with Satan, too. Courage burns like an undying fire within man, God tells Job; and, so long as that fire does not go out, there are no limits to man's achievements. At the close of their dialogue, God also tells Job of the fearful alternatives: "If that courage fail, if that sacred fire go out, then all things fail and all things go out—good and evil, space and time" (*W,* 11:160).

Among Wells's aesthetic manipulations, the anaesthetic has been a most useful, even artistic, device for believability. It not only justifies, fictionally, the ways of God (and Satan) to man, it makes plausible the close correspondence between Job's and God's metaphors of fire. God has become a figment of Job's dream: controlled by the dreamer. And in his vision of Heaven, H. G. Wells, reproved by Schorer for disdain of craft, tackles the same aesthetic problem as John Milton:

> for how shall I relate
> To human sense th' invisible exploits
> Of warring Spirits; how without remorse
> The ruin of so many glorious once
> And perfet while they stood; how last unfold
> The secrets of another World, perhaps
> Not lawful to reveal? Yet for thy good
> This is dispens't, and what surmounts the reach
> Of human sense, I shall delineate so,
> By lik'ning spiritual to corporal forms,
> As may express them best.[27]

Wells, past master of otherworld evocation, states his version of the challenge presented by celestial imagery:

> The thoughts that it seemed to him that God was speaking through his mind
> can be put into words only after a certain fashion and with great loss, for they were
> thoughts about things beyond and above this world, and our words are all made
> out of the names of things and feelings in this world. Things that were contradic-
> tory had become compatible, and things incomprehensible seemed straightfor-
> ward, because he was in a dream. (W, 11:154–55)

The anaesthetic-as-aesthetic enables Job, in dream, to soliloquize spec-
ulatively like Milton's angel Raphael: "What if earth / Be but the shadow
of Heaven, and things therein / Each to other like, more than on earth is
thought?"[28] For Job, "ideas [are released] from their anchorage to words
and phrases and their gravitation towards sensible realities. But [his words
were] the same line of thought he pursued through the stars and spaces
that he had pursued in [his] stuffy little room at Sundering on Sea" (W,
11:155).

The biblical Job of Uz survived his boils, saved by fate. Job Huss has
also found God; happiness crowns Wells's updated story, too. Or, perhaps,
it would not do for the heroes of successive Wellsian wartime novels to lose
sons in the conflict. At any rate, surgery reveals that the growth is non-
malignant; the diagnosis had been unsound. And Gilbert Huss, the lost
son, lives: a prisoner of war.

The writing of *The Undying Fire* set a standard for the dialogue novel
that Wells was never able to meet again although he continued in the vein
for another twenty-one years. Writing late in his life, Wells acknowledged
that his fiction in the 1920s and 1930s is "primarily discussion carried on
through living characters; it is for the discussion of behaviour they were
written and to cut out the talk would be like cutting a picture out of its
frame."[29] Had he lived to read them, Henry James might have scolded
Wells for overdoing the frame.

Any literature teacher who has tried to open up a work to receptive
students comes to know that form and content are inseparable. In this
sense, the James-Wells controversy has done literature a disservice because
it tends to divide form from content, on James's side, and content from
form, on Wells's. At his best, Wells does more in his fiction than distill
his materials down to the essence of an argument. The inherent galvanism
of James's major novels, as proved by their dramatic efficacy in recent
translations to British television, becomes more than matters of nuance of

narrative focus. Wells talked himself into a corner by his defensive self-pronouncements. James's essays on the art of the novel appear to anticipate most of the formalist problems of the genre. Yet even James was not always alert to literature's supreme moments when distinctions between form and content dissolve. For all his writings on Flaubert, James never said a word about the agricultural-fair episode of *Madame Bovary*, an early instance of something unheard-of in the middle of the nineteenth century–narrative simultaneity.

Chapter Eight
Wells and Science

The Messianic Wells:
The Scientist as Hero

It has become platitudinous to refer to Wells as the Father of Science Fiction. However, the designation becomes useful if we observe, as Roslynn D. Haynes does, that the progeny's life has followed in the train of the parent's.

> Science fantasy, as perfected by Wells, not only issued in the proliferation of science fiction in later decades, but also influenced its development. Already in the 1970s the particular type of writing usually categorized as science fiction has passed into work which is preoccupied with sociological speculation about contemporary rather than future situations and which thus appears to be approaching a coalescence with the realistic social novel. Such a progression follows the sequence of Wells's own writings. . . .[1]

This is a remarkable statement on two counts. First, so far as the popular genre now called science fiction, it acknowledges the sort of evolution that any genre must have to be taken seriously. Second, of special importance for this book, Haynes's insight, which appears at the end of her study and which best describes its modus operandi, indicates a preference to see Wells *whole*. Describing herself as "a scientist who defected to the literary camp," Haynes is the first commentator on Wells to attempt to analyze in a book his entire oeuvre under an umbrella he would have respected: namely, the influence of his formal scientific training on his writings.

Most critics before Haynes, myself included, simply echoed some such easy formulation as Vincent Brome's that "Wells had mistaken his vocation. By temperament an artist and by training a scientist, the conflict between the two remained to the end. . . ." Haynes meets Wells on his own grounds. She examines not only the conflicts *within* Wells but the "strange division of opinion" *about* him between scientists and literary critics: "[W]hile those scientists who are familiar with Wells's work have for the most part applauded his treatment of scientific interests, even, in a few cases, regarding it as germinal to their own ideas, literary critics . . . have tended to denigrate Wells's scientific ability and to dismiss his work as . . . interesting fantasy."[2]

Roslynn Haynes's in-depth distinction between scientific and poetic sensibilities goes far toward explaining, if not justifying, the kind of novels Wells had to write. Although she does not mention Joyce's *Portrait,* her sense of the implications of *Tono-Bungay*'s presentation of science and scientists as central subjects for serious literature offers a fairer basis for comparing these two novels than Mark Schorer's. Schorer places the books as north and south poles, with Joyce as the example nonpareil of the artist who placed technique in the service of "discovering" inner experience and Wells as the philistine advocate of writing tools better suited to the polemicist. Haynes stresses the ways George Ponderevo reacts to environment and the ways Wells's man-of-science persona controls the novel. "George's career thus follows a similar pattern—the diligent fervour of the young, adolescent student, striving to attain university entrance, the slackening of self-discipline when the new freedom and varied interests of a university environment are encountered, the subsequent falling away from his studies and the belated return of the mature man. . . ."[3] Stephen Dedalus, after his crises of faith, recognizes his calling to art, away from church and country, in an epiphanic vision of a plumaged girl wading offshore. He has been from the start literary, destined for exile and the poet's calling. George came to regard science as his private universe. Predictably his invocation of science-as-muse is more hortatory than Stephen's invocation of art: "Sometimes I call this reality Science. . . . something we draw by pain and effort out of the heart of life, that we disentangle and make clear. . . . I see it always as austerity, as beauty. This thing we make clear is the heart of life. . . . the one enduring thing" (*W,* 12:539). Wells's emblem for science, as we have seen, is George's destroyer, his X2, and Haynes is willing to infer irony rather than confused thinking in Wells. There should be no ambiguity here, she writes, "yet there is a cold shaft of irony at the heart of the passage, for the symbol of this penetrating drive is wholly inhuman, bereft of any moral consideration—it is George's destroyer [whose] passage down the Thames is fraught with ambivalence. While seeming wholeheartedly to approve, he simultaneously sows seeds of doubt and condemnation. . . . Nor should we ignore the stress on the very name, 'destroyer.' . . ."[4] The passage has been overexplicated. It is enough here to say that both writers will return again and again to the problems at the heart of life—art, with Joyce, and science, with Wells. The life and writings of Wells present the problems of the man of science in courtship, social intercourse, and moral conflict. Such European contemporaries as Thomas Mann and Hermann Hesse devoted long and distinguished oeuvres to the agonies of the artist in conflict with the bourgeois. George Ponderevo has much in common with Harry Haller, the title character of *Steppenwolf*. Both endure and transcend crises of identity in the very act of writing about them. Undoubtedly, for students of literature, the artist-hero is a more compelling figure than the scientist-hero. Novelists and poets write about the former as if to the manner born. To understand the scientist, one should know something about science. Wells was the first major English novelist to understand how the science-minded person coped with the world.

His scientists evolve from figures in alchemy, as with Griffin and Mo-reau, to lovers and visionaries. Although perhaps he ought not to be con-sidered a scientist at all because he never attains research credentials or even a degree, George Lewisham broke the ice *(Love and Mr. Lewisham,* 1900). Here Wells portrays his own experiences. He, too, had worn the water-proof smock, studied in the same laboratories in the Normal School of Science, and taken part in after-hour socialist debates. He, too, had expe-rienced the conflict between science studies and romantic entanglements. For Haynes, the salient feature of the novel is Wells's ambivalence about Lewisham's final situation. Having eventually relinquished his illusions about a career in research, Lewisham comes to see his mission in life in terms of his progeny, his contribution to the future of the race.

At this early stage Wells views the scientist as far beneath the pedestal on which he would later mount him. Cavor of *The First Men in the Moon,* though he has learned the gravity-resisting capability of Cavorite, is in part a comic figure—among the first absent-minded professors in literature— and in larger part dedicated to his work for its own sake, with no taint of commercialism. Cavor epitomizes the trained scientific observer, recording acccurately and without emotional involvement. The hideous conditioning process as practiced among the Selenites brings out no moral fervor but only a hope that he will learn to appreciate these methods.

Wells's first intimations that, for him, the scientist will be the hope of the world came with George Ponderevo, but for most of the novel he does not function as a scientist at all. His next qualified scientist is Capes in *Ann Veronica,* but he tosses over his research, apparently without regret, for a possible literary vocation.

Richard Trafford of *Marriage* is Wells's most fully characterized scientist in a major novel. He has studied at the Royal College of Science and at Cambridge; he will eventually become a member of the Royal Society. His difficulties arise not from any incompetence or boredom with his research, but from the conflict between his work and his social obligations. Wells describes in detail the frustrations between Trafford, dedicated to his work, and Marjorie, who fails to understand why the demands of his research should not always be subsidiary to her claims.

> When Trafford is finally forced by . . . Marjorie's extravagance to abandon his research . . . , it is a genuine sacrifice on his part, engendering a feeling of resentment against Marjorie, and leaving a void in his life. . . . Thus even Trafford, one of Wells's most mature scientists, is not permitted to find ultimate fulfillment in scientific research. Yet both before and after [*Marriage*], Wells continued to produce sociological works, often flagrantly propagandist, advocating the innovation of a world state, under the leadership and guidance, at least initially, of scientists.[5]

Haynes resolves the anomaly of Wells's scientific heroes not being allowed to be heroic by reference to his sense of mankind-in-state-of-*becoming*. Ponderevo and Trafford represent idealism that is unable to balance research and personal relationships; that cannot resolve its thrust toward the precious future while still moored in an outmoded present that is resistant to change. Only in the Wellsian utopia will such splits disappear, for then all men will have been educated to drive toward satisfaction in research along with fulfillment of responsibilities in society: "Nor, in this future utopia, will there be any division of interest between man-the-thinker and man-the-father, the biological contributor to his race—the division which torments Lewisham and Trafford. All members of Wells's future society will gladly contribute whatever talents they possess to the Mind of Race, which is both a physical and a cultural concept."[6] And, in its crusading obsessiveness, the destructor of the novelist in Wells.

The Mind-of-Race concept, as shown in chapter 5, first surfaced fully in *First and Last Things*. That 1908 treatise found Wells first confessing to a belief in a mystic community embracing mankind and the cosmos. Like Shaw's concept of the Life Force, the Mind of Race becomes, in its zeal to find a faith that gives meaning to life, messianic.

Beginning with *The World Set Free* (1913), mystical messianism begins to take over Wells's fiction. The protagonist, Marcus Karenin, is perhaps the most fully sketched character in any of the scientific romances, the first cerebral hero in a book wholly set in the future. The novel begins twenty years beyond its time—1933—with the discovery of nuclear fission by the physicist Holsten. Twenty years later the Holsten-Roberts atomic engine is perfected, disrupting existing technology and precipitating in 1956 a financial crash, which leads to war, initiated by the German invasion of France through Belgium. Wells's remarkable atomic prophecy—his forecast was less than a decade off target—will be covered in the next chapter. It is in the final section, set in the 1980s, in which Karenin, Wells's Man of the Future, is introduced. Believing himself about to die in surgery and speaking what he assumes to be his valedictory message on the Mind of Race, Karenin addresses himself to the sun:

You think I die—and indeed I am only taking off one more coat to get at you. I have threatened you for ten thousand years, and soon I warn you I shall be coming. . . . One step I shall take to the moon, and then I shall leap at you. . . . Old Sun, I gather myself together out of the pools of the individual that have held me dispersed so long. I gather my billion thoughts into science and my million wills into a common purpose. Well may you slink down behind the mountains for me, well may you cower. . . . (*W,* 21:247–48)

The operation is successful, but a week later a blood clot from the healing scar passes to his heart and Karenin dies in his sleep. His passing comes after he has shown himself to be almost the first of those late-career Wellsian ideologues who lump religion, science, and the Mind of Race in a blend that jars—never merges—with the action.

The next such is Benham in *The Research Magnificent* (1915). Martyred to his search for the "Life Aristocratic," he stands in the moonlight of the Bengal jungle, facing a tiger and lifting a lean hand to it: "I am Man," he intones; and the beast "vanished, became invisible and inaudible, with a kind of instantaneousness" (*W,* 19:48). For Edmund Wilson, the zeal of his youth set afire by the Wells of 1895–1915, the reading of that scene brought an abrupt falling-out and a determination, in the face of "such nonsense," to read Wells no more.[7]

If any idea is to be effective in a literary work, it should find expression not only in powerful final imagery like that of *Tono-Bungay.* It should not settle for unwarranted flights of unlikelihood as in *The Research Magnificent.* It ought not to be embraced only by hero-figures who are as inaccessible to the reader as they are to their fellow characters.

The Traffords, Remingtons, Benhams, and Karenins may indeed possess that wider grasp and vision with which Wells had endowed them. But their estrangement from the Kippses, Pollys, Lewishams, and Bealbys—their standing apart from "yesterday's men"—makes them poor fictive company in any setting this side of utopia.

Wells's Mind of Race—and his utopias—lack soul.

Two Ways of Thinking About Wells;
Two Ways of Wells's Thinking

Among his peers Arnold Bennett was Wells's closest friend, and that friendship allowed candor between them about their own writings that was denied Wells in his exchanges with James and Conrad. When Wells accused Bennett of being preoccupied with mundane considerations, Bennett retaliated by charging Wells with complete disregard for all "surface values" because he was intent only on his thesis of the moment. Bennett observes that anti-Wellsians were complaining of a lack of individual interest in the scientific novels and he regrets "that these persons cannot perceive the 'concerted' effort of your 'scientific' novels. You are not really interested in individual humanity. And when you write a 'non-scientific' novel you always recur to a variation of the same type of hero, and you always will, because your curiosity about individualities won't lead you further."[8] This is perceptive and sympathetic of Bennett. If, as Leonard Woolf observed, Wells *thought* with his imaginaton, it is also true that with the scientific romances readers *read* with theirs. Whether it was because the writing came easier or that their instant acceptance made him feel freer to let himself go, even the most cursory study of Wells's critical readership will reveal that blasts have been seldom leveled at the scientific romances. Roslynn Hayes writes that it is not superiority of craftsmanship that accounts for this but rather their less contentious nature. She continues: "It was only when he invaded the territory of the realistic novel that he fell foul of those who saw the character novels of the nineteenth century as representing the only valid line of development. Science fantasy was acknowledged to be a peculiarly intellectual literary form, but *the novel* was, for James, Conrad, and Bennett, primarily an exploration of sensuous and emotional levels of experience."[9] This raises a further point about readers— and the reading—of Wells's first works. If, in them, there is a less profound exploration of "sensuous and emotional levels of experience," there is a correspondingly more intense *engagement* of the reader's sensuous and emotional levels of receptivity. The fabulism that Borges finds in the early Wells is the product of a certain way of thinking that worked emotively in one kind of writing but did not in another.

Until recently critical scholarship concentrated on various splits in Wells—world planner and dystopian, artist and journalist, philosopher and propagandist, being and becoming, evolution and ethics, optimism and pessimism. In a new book John Huntington has evolved a further split that is so useful in approaching Wells as to promise to subsume the others.

The split between forecast and fantasy represents a distinction between two kinds of thought process which late in his career Wells would neatly define as that between "directed thought," which enters philosophy with Plato and defines the scientific aspect of modern civilization, and "undirected thought," which is basic to primitive nontechnical civilization. "Undirected thought" is "imaginative play" checked by experience and thus close to but different from mere dreaming. "Directed thought" is purposeful and conscious; it arrives at conclusions; it leads to actions and exclusions. [10]

Huntington develops his dialectic slowly, comparing at the outset excerpts from Wells's earliest scientific papers with his final dark testament of *Mind at the End of Its Tether*. He traces the evolution of Wells's thinking from the relatively spontaneous, mythopoeic visions of the earliest scientific romances to the directed thinking of his first explicit forecasts in *Anticipations* just after the turn of the century. He cites key passages from a chapter of one of his late-career outline-books, "How Man Has Learnt to Think Systematically and Gain a Mastery over Force and Matter." Such ratiocinative formulas lead only to "directed thinking," which lends itself to the laboratory, the boardroom, the controlled forecast. The problem with directed thought, he adds, "is that it strives to reduce complexity. It generates results, but at a sacrifice. Insofar as it constitutes a genuine category of thought, its quality depends, not on the sensitivity, accuracy, intricacy, or truth of the process of thought, but on the validity and usefulness of the conclusions. One can catalogue and evaluate such thought according to its "ideas." Directed thought lends itself to practical evaluation: at its purest it is either right or wrong, productive or dead-ended." [11]

Roslynn Haynes would use other words. For her, directed thought would become "scientific methodology," and undirected thought would be "rendering of impressions." But both Haynes and Huntington extend the tension they find at the heart of Wells between forecast and fantasy and between writing that is scientifically oriented and that which is conceived out of disorder—cosmic and private.

The early fictional landscape of H. G. Wells is a canvas by Brueghel. One glimpses, along with the first sight of the spearhead ship of an invasion from Mars, a group of village urchins tossing stones at the cylinder that has fallen from the sky. One hears the bark of a cart-driver as he pulls up at Iping Village with the luggage of the Invisible Man. One follows Mr. Polly into a roomful of similarly dispossessed tradesmen after his "bit of arson" has destroyed the Fishbourne Hotel, but has also made a lion of him for rescuing his landlord's brother-in-law. One smells horse manure and beer and hears, in V. S. Pritchett's description, the accent of the lower middle class from which Wells sprung—"despairing, narrow-voweled yet truculent, with something of the cheapjack and Sunday League in it."[12]

Pritchett's essay is often quoted, a seminal and early—1947—dissenting vote against the critical consensus that cast Wells into oblivion. It notes that "there are always fistfights and fires in the early Wells, above all, there are fires." Huntington also notes the fights and fires—all, for him, discordant and extravagant descriptions "that offset gestures in the opposite direction." These images of violence stand apart from the "other " Wells of utopia, Mind of Race, world state. They are the "lungings . . . of rational consciousness feeling out the possibilities of the intellectual space . . . a way of thinking."[13]

Huntington, not satisfied to write off everything of Wells after a certain date, chronicles the *whole* performance. He sees a movement from the undirected thought of the scientific romances to the directed thought of most of the later work. He views T. H. Huxley's dialectic between evolution and ethics as the theme of Wells's life and one to which only the "undirected" side could do justice.

Almost from the start, Wells honored science, but in doing so he committed it—and himself—to a kind of double-exposure. In "The Rediscovery of the Unique," which, written in 1891 before he was twenty-five, contains all the seeds that would germinate into fantasy and forecast alike, Wells visions science as a match

that man has just got alight. He thought he was in a room—in moments of devotion, a temple—and that his light would be reflected from and display walls inscribed with wonderful secrets and pillars carved with philosophical systems wrought into harmony. It is a curious sensation, now that the preliminary splutter is over and the flame burns up clear, to see his hands lit and just a glimpse of himself and the patch he stands on visible, and around him, in place of all that human comfort and beauty he anticipated—darkness still.[14]

The clearing away of that darkness, which claimed his father, his brothers, and almost himself as victims, proved to be his lifelong mission. Since the means to this end was a science student's ticket from the Home Counties to South Kensington, it was no wonder that scientific knowledge, invention, and—above all—*thinking* became for H. G. Wells the only keys to leaving Victorian opacity—any opacity—in the shadows behind him.

Chapter Nine

Wells at the End
of His Tether: World State
and the State of the World

One can well imagine the perplexity of even sympathetic watchers of Wells
in his heyday trying to reconcile all those New Republics, Open Conspir-
acies, Collective Minds of Race, Universal Citizenrys. The writing of *The
Undying Fire* (1919), the last of a four-book sequence, closed out not only
a brief "theocratic phase" (*E*, 575), but his "middle period" as well. These
years might better be called the "muddle years." Wells's strivings to close
a gap left by the previous book—somehow to make right in the next book
the folly of those "moments of leaping ignorance" of the last—brought
forth too many books too quickly. Out of them it is easy to agree with
Kingsley Martin that utopia was the obsession to which he sacrificed everything.[1] That passion, as has been shown, remained inseparable from another which lay at the heart of the seer who would be the messiah: the Future.

Brave New Worlder:
The Sleeper Awakes (1899)

His earliest views of the future were dark. Had Wells succumbed to any
of the serious illnesses that beset him before 1900 and written only *The
Time Machine, The Island of Dr. Moreau, The Invisible Man, The War of the
Worlds,* and, especially, *The Sleeper Awakes* and "A Story of Days to Come,"
he and not Aldous Huxley or George Orwell or Eugene Zamyatin would
have been accorded the distinction of being the father of the inverted utopia, the first of the major dystopians.[2] Ostrog, the head of the supercor-
poration's governing body in *The Sleeper,* is, as Anthony West notes, the
Wellsian equivalent of George Orwell's Big Brother.[3] The sleeper, a kind
of utopian Rip Van Winkle, awakens four generations after he has inexpli-
cably fallen asleep. He finds himself a master capitalist, owner of half the
world, a world where capital and labor—the symbolic Eloi and the Mor-

locks of *the Time Machine*—have irrevocably destroyed all possibilities of a constructively planned society. The sleeper, Graham, and the dictator, Ostrog, carry on innumerable colloquies about how his mindless capital came to rule the world and reduce men to automatons:

"In the old days [said Graham] we dreamt of a wonderful democratic life, of a time when all men would be equal and happy."

Ostrog looked at him steadfastly. "The day of democracy is past. . . . That day . . . ended when marching infantry, when common men in masses ceased to win the battles of the world, when costly cannon, great ironclads, and strategic railways became the means of power. To-day is the day of wealth. Wealth now is power as it never was power before—it commands earth and sea and sky. All power is for those who can handle wealth. . . ."

Graham did not answer immediately. He stood lost in sombre preoccupations.

"No," said Ostrog. "The day of the common man is past. On the open countryside one man is as good as another. . . . The earlier aristocracy had a precarious tenure of strength and audacity. . . . There were insurrections, duels, riots. The first real aristocracy, the first permanent aristocracy, came in with castles and armour, and vanished before the musket and bow. But this is the second aristocracy. The real one. Those days of gunpowder and democracy were only an eddy in the stream. The common man now is a helpless unit. In these days we have this great machine of the city, and an organization complex beyond his understanding." (*W*, 2:393–94)

I quote at length from this early work because it is very likely the first novel of any literary merit to question the present-day concept of "progress." The Machine, as Wells feared in 1899, exploits human inertia and weakness. It parrots Boss Ostrog's every whim. Children of the laboring class are converted from any inclination to nonconformity into trustworthy machine-minders. A Pleasure City is set aside for Graham, but the rank and file have sallow faces and dull eyes and wear the pale blue canvas uniforms of the Labor Department.

Considering its date of publication, the book must be considered remarkable on another count. It contains a somewhat halting but nonetheless accurate description of aerial warfare fifteen years before World War I; four years before the Wright brothers made their first successful Kitty Hawk flight in 1903; and nine years before Bleriot flew across the Channel. Wells was later to make extended use of what was then called aeronautics in *Tono-Bungay* and to depict a full-scale aerial battle in *The War in the Air*, both extremely avant-garde subjects for 1908, let alone 1899. For other inventions, Wells draws on Edward Bellamy's *Looking Backward:*

enormous automatic restaurants that have replaced dining rooms, modern methods of heating and lighting, television to enable people to witness the news, and the replacement of reading and writing by mechanical devices.[4]

Writing at the time of Wells's death in 1946, George Orwell, when his mind may have been dogged by the fears that would culminate in 1984, was unstinting in his praise for the novel: "In [*The Sleeper Awakes*] . . . Wells drops all traces of optimism and forecasts a highly organized totalitarian society based quite frankly upon slave labor. In some ways it comes extremely close to what is actually happening [1946], or appears to be happening, in the modern world, and it is in any case an astonishing feat of detailed imaginative construction [and] . . . the extent to which it anticipates Aldous Huxley's *Brave New World* and other pessimistic Utopia books has not been generally recognized."[5]

Orwell's tribute is not without irony, for the anti-utopians generally and Aldous Huxley particularly have erected grave-markers over the spiritual locus where Wells's midcareer wishful thinking took him: the World State. Shortly before his death Huxley told a *Paris Review* interviewer that *Brave New World* was begun as a satire of Wells's *Men Like Gods* (1923).[6] As Wagar points out, Wells frequently appears in fictional guise among twentieth-century counter-utopographers. No reader of Wells, for example, can read the early pages of C. S. Lewis's *Out of the Silent Planet* without recognizing that writer's respectful chiding of Wells and his apostasy. As E. F. Bleiler notes, it must not be forgotten that Wells was spiritual godfather to the Huxleys, Orwells, Zamyatins—to the E. M. Forster who wrote "The Machine Stops." "Wells heard the voice in the wilderness before they, and wrote its message before they, sometimes in the same symbols."[7]

Anticipations (1901) and *A Modern Utopia* (1905)

Wells has described *Anticipations* as the main arch of his work, the reasonable expectations he drew from an exceptionally rich creative imagination. *A Modern Utopia* is more speculative: a presentation, not so much of expectations, as of desires. The two books represent a change of stance from trepidation to confidence, and set forth in general that body of ideas that can be called Wellsian. In *Anticipations*, Wells extols the virtues of functional men—men, like himself, trained in science—and calls them "New Republicans." They will be managerial and technical people; no effete talkers will be allowed. Only this scientist elite will be equipped to build from the destruction of the old order a technologically organized world society.

Henry Straker is an embryo creation by George Bernard Shaw who, in *Man and Superman*, written the year *Anticipations* was published, saw with his piercing wit the flaw of depending on the emergence of an elite to rule the world scientifically. In the play, Tanner, the kind of jabberer-intellectual Wells's New Republicans would purge, baits the cockney unmercifully for his pride in dropping his "aitches" and for his bourgeois attitudes that are moored to a fetish for efficiency. In one exchange, Tanner goads Straker into an innocent praise of the "Polytechnic." Oxford, for the latter, is where "they teach you to be a gentleman. In the Polytechnic they teach you to be an engineer or such like. See?" Tanner sees only too well. It is into Henry's soul that he looks. What he sees there, Shavianly, is Henry's prideful arrogance in being an engineer who positively wants the machine to break down to bring out the gentlemanly helplessness of his "betters" and his own skill and resourcefulness. He is moved to define his—and the Polytechnic's—business as doing away with labor ("You'll get more out of me and a machine than you will out of twenty laborers"). Perhaps as commentary against socialist dilettantes of all stripes, Tanner gets in the last word to his friend Octavius: "Don't start Straker on political economy. He knows all about it; and we don't. You're a poetic Socialist; he's a scientific one."[8]

The writing of *Anticipations* corresponded approximately to Wells's coming under the wing of the Fabians. *Man and Superman* shows certain objections to Wells's efficient-engineer New Republican from Shaw, a representative Fabian and a man with no illusions about the adaptability of the Henry Strakers to a new world order. Sidney and Beatrice Webb criticized *Anticipations* because of Wells's failure to recognize the need and probability of a specialized governing class. Like them, Shaw saw the insufficiency of the managerial-technical breed to head the new republic.

Perhaps there is more wisdom in Wells's old friend Frank Swinnerton than in either himself or in Shaw or the Webbs. To Swinnerton, there would be no room for Wells and his natural affection for individuals in any of his utopias stemming from *Anticipations* because "he would either be put to death by the mandarins for being intractable or would clamor for the restoration of our imperfect, greedy, acquisitive, and amusing society, in which a man could breathe without first obtaining a license to do so. It is no wonder that he loathes bureaucrats and drill-sergeants; his true passion is for liberty."[9] Or, as Max Beerbohm put it: "So this is Utopia, is it? Well / I beg your pardon, I thought it was Hell."[10]

By a curious accident in time—a phenomenon unlikely in any other author—*A Modern Utopia*, Wells's clarion call for a ruling hierarchy to make his New Republic hum, and *Kipps,* the author's imperishable monument to inferior, second-class human material, appeared in the same year, 1905. That the two warring tendencies gnawing at Wells's artistic soul should see the light of day within six months of each other is ample testament to the control, at least at this early stage, under which Wells held the demands of artist and polemicist. *A Modern Utopia* crystallizes Wells's mounting inclination to think less and less in terms of individualities like Kipps. "No less than a planet will serve the purpose of a modern Utopia," he writes near the beginning of *A Modern Utopia.* "A state powerful enough to keep isolated under modern conditions would be powerful enough to rule the world. . . . World-state, therefore, it must be" (*W,* 9:13).

However questionable as a work of literary art, *A Modern Utopia* falls definitely in the classic tradition of speculative utopias. Wells's rough equivalents of Plato's guardians are the Samurai, a superior class that by intelligence and good will may be made a ruler caste. The Samurai, drawn from the Japanese word for military knighthood (the Russo-Japanese War had made the term familiar to the English-speaking public), would wear distinctive dress, have a bible of their own selected from the inspiring literature of all ages, and spend at least a week of every year in absolute solitude in the wilderness as a sort of restorative of Emersonian self-reliance (as noted in chapter 6, Trafford and his wife Marjorie were to extend in *Marriage* the Samurai ideal to a year in a Labrador tent).

Wells's utopia is a far cry from Thomas More's virtue and moderation or William Morris's poetic unrestraint made workable by invariable right will. Wells's vision of attainable perfection is always slightly jarred by the inevitable perspective of heroes like Benham in *The Research Magnificent* whose unworldly idealism is defeated by worldly circumstances. Thus Wells departs from belief in man as essentially noble and rational and finds refuge in knowledge and science, organization and management—in George Ponderevo's trust in his battleship at the end of *Tono-Bungay.*

The enfranchising of a head-man species remained, for better or worse, the permanent hope of Wells. The Samurai loom not only as the instruments for his utopian blueprint but are the major inhabitants of all his novels after *Tono-Bungay.* Remington, Capes, Trafford—he, especially—Britling, and Clissold are, each in his way, human projections of the ideals generalized in the Samurai. With the exception of Britling, whose characterization benefits from the empathy a war provides among all concerned in it, none of these personages ever emerges as anything but a spokesman for the idea so dear to Wells's heart: "being" is nothing; "becoming," everything.

No effort would be needed to show how the idealized Trafford of *Marriage*—"the portrait," according to Maugham, "of the man H. G. thought he was, added to the man he would have liked to be"[11]—arose from the underfed poet in Mr. Polly; or, with Wells himself, how the New Republican Samurai caught hold of the imagination of the man who almost lived out his life as a tradesman. Wells endowed his Samurai with the absolute in personal efficiency and orderliness. They are antiseptic, quite without credibility. In assuring that they were innocent of the quality Wells disliked most of all—muddle—he drained them of life. If the Samurai of *A Modern Utopia* provide a logical stepping-stone from the fumblingly real world of Artie Kipps and Mr. Polly to the neatly tiered world of Remington and Trafford, there is an irony lurking behind the transformation. The Samurai of the later novels become dogged by problems, not so much of mankind but of men. Remington's political career is destroyed when he leaves his wife for a more congenial attachment; Stratton in *The Passionate Friends* carries on a doomed romance with a married woman.

The fictional personifications of the utopian supermen are *of* the world in their problems, if not in Wells's delineation of them. But, in his zeal to imagine what the world *ought* to be, Wells deliberately blinds himself to what it *is*. The society forecast in *A Modern Utopia* is unreal. Although Wells is nowhere more visionary and although his vision is a noble belief, André Maurois holds that "the world of flesh and blood, the world of soil and stone is not like that. . . . Plans beyond numbering are applicable in Utopia; on earth, we must live day to day. Equilibrium could only be a stopping-place. Such is the lot of humanity."[12]

The World Set Free (1914)

As early as 1905, then, an insistent part of Wells's mind was firmly committed to world statism. He adamantly refused to concede anything to the other part which had produced the dread intimations of the scientific romances and was even then germinating such novels as *The New Machiavelli, Marriage,* and *The Passionate Friends,* books in which such Wellsian alter egos as Remington, Trafford, and Stratton came to grief because of human egotism and passion.

Just before the outbreak of World War I, Wells published an astoundingly prophetic though badly disjointed utopian work called *The World Set Free.* Not the first novel in which Wells recorded a disastrous world war, the conflict differs in degree if not in kind from *The War in the Air* in that it liberates the race from all obsessions and entanglements that impede moral and material growth. The artisan of world reconstruction is a kind of Albert Schweitzer with portfolio, a prominent member of the World Education Committee named Marcus Karenin. Karenin, like so many of those who have tasted of Wells's food of the gods, expires at the end of the novel but not before he, with a wave of his hand "toward the dark sky above the mountain crests," forecasts the end of human travail by an infinite modification of man to eliminate "the obstinacy of egotism."

The World Set Free might not be worth more than passing mention except for its astonishly accurate forecast of an atomic Armageddon. The war, recorded in a mythical autobiographical novel, dated 1970, as having occurred during "the middle decades of the twentieth century," becomes worldwide. Paris, Berlin, East London, Chicago, and other great cities are made uninhabitable by the dropping of atomic bombs. Earlier, Wells conceived of splitting the atoms of a rare, little-known metal. Karenin, the scientist-teacher so dear to Wells's heart, holds before his unbelieving class a flask containing fourteen ounces of uranium oxide and says: "If at a word in one instant I could suddenly release the energy of the atoms in this bottle it would blow us and everything about us to fragments; if I could turn it into the machinery that lights this city it could keep Edinburgh brightly lit for a week" (*W*, 21:23). A few pages later comes this near-direct hit: "It was in 1953 when the first atomic energy induced radioactivity into the sphere of industrial machinery, and its first general use was to replace the steam engine in electrical generating stations" (*W*, 21:37).

Wells held no illusions about the salutary effect of atomic power on humans: "In the year 1955 the suicide rate for the United States of America quadrupled any previous record. There was an enormous increase also in violent crime throughout the world. The thing had come upon an unprepared humanity; it seemed as though human society was to be smashed by its own magnificent gains" (*W*, 21:41).

There is an interesting postscript to this novel that came to light in 1968, more than a half-century after original publication. Wells's dramatized concept of using atomic degeneration to provide nuclear power, of the possible uses of this power, and of the details of the process, elicited in his memoirs a tribute from the distinguished physicist Leo Szilard, who acknowledges a practical debt to Wells, as though to a fellow scientist. Long after reading the book in 1932 ("It made a very great impression on me, but I didn't regard it as anything but fiction"), Szilard realized how a chain nuclear reaction could be set up, and hastily applied for a patent to cover his invention because, he writes, "knowing what this would mean—

and I knew it because I had read H. G. Wells,—I did not want this patent to become public."[13]

It should be pointed out here, as Warren W. Wagar and Anthony West have stated, that the long-range benevolence of science as viewed in *The World Set Free* is strongly diluted by Wells in subsequent utopist books. He never forgot the limitations of the scientific imagination as he had depicted it in a number of early short stories about absent-minded scientists: in *The Invisible Man*, Griffin turns into a murderer; in *The Island of Dr. Moreau*, Moreau's megalomania threatens the order of the natural world; and in *The First Men in the Moon*, Cavor knows how to resist gravity but presents war to the Grand Lunar as a possible solution to earthly problems. In perhaps Wells's finest idea-novel, *The Undying Fire*, Job Huss monologizes endlessly against the supremacy of old-fashioned rationalism as he argues that science solves nothing among men who have failed in their responsibilities in the ethical sphere.

Men Like Gods (1923)

By far the most sanguine, at least in appearance, of all Wells's utopian novels is *Men Like Gods*, the last to be discussed in detail. If Wells's one-hundred-plus volumes were to be arranged in left-to-right order—from funeral dirge to spritely pastorale—the work on the far right would undoubtedly be *Men Like Gods*. Antonina Vallentin goes so far as to call the novel "a fairy story that Wells told himself on paper."[14] Mr. Barnstaple, the invariable Wellsian, has reached a point of no return. To avoid a nervous breakdown, he slips away from home and family. Suddenly he finds himself in the center of Utopia, a paradise even beyond the expectations of the man who had created a modern utopia two decades earlier. The new Eden makes no concessions to a hierarchy; there are no Samurai to guide the new order. Barnstaple encounters a world of wise, beautiful people, who live in perfect harmony with nature and their fellowmen. They possess unabashed innocence, too, as shown by their clothing—nature's own—a factor that, according to Vallentin, gave much trouble to the illustrator appointed by the Hearst press, which bought the serial rights.

The intrusion of earth dwellers causes near panic in Utopia. At times the book becomes wildly comic, yet always with an underlying note of melancholy. The book had its roman-à-clef undertones, for it was a rare Wells novel during his middle period that did not carry real-life counterparts of the main characters.

Wells takes a page from his Martian invasion. Like the invaders of *The*

War of the Worlds, the Utopians have no acquired resistance to the illnesses that earth-bred microbes are likely to cause. The mortals—intruders in Utopia—are placed in quarantine. Thereupon, the reckless statesman, dreaming of a universal empire, declares war on the Utopians. Warned by Barnstaple, the only earthling who appreciates their noble world, the Utopians crush the revolt; and, by repeating the atomic experiment that has put them into contact with another universe, they send the mortals back to earth. Barnstaple alone grieves at the loss of Eden—a place where such things as constraints, supreme authority, and police methods are unknown.

Wagar concludes that it was H. G. Wells's persistent use of the utopian device, even after civilization had been jolted by World War I, that drew the critics' fire. [15] The majority of the intellectuals scoffed at what they took to be Wells's rose-colored glasses through which he saw, as his shape of things to come, men becoming like gods. Aldous Huxley, grandson of Wells's great mentor, began *Brave New World* as a short-story parody of *Men Like Gods.*

However, Anthony West demurs from this verdict against his father. Wells's detractors, he avers, have missed the supreme irony of *Men Like Gods.* This irony is subtly implicit in the explanation of how Mr. Barnstaple could encounter another universe simply by taking a turn off a familiar road:

> Wonder took possession of Mr. Barnstaple's mind. That dear world of honesty and health was beyond the utmost boundaries of our space, utterly inaccessible to him now for ever more; and yet as he had been told it was but one of countless universes that move together in time, that lie against one another, endlessly, like the leaves of a book. And all of them are as nothing in the endless multitudes of systems and dimensions that surround them. "Could I but rotate my arm out of the limits set to it," one of the Utopians had said to him, "I could thrust it into a thousand universes." [16]

The Utopia where men are like gods is, West asserts, but another play in Wells's fifty-year lark with the Fourth Dimension. The earth and Utopia, in terms of a time scheme are out of joint with one another. The fairy-story aspect of *Men Like Gods* is deliberate on Wells's part: life, as Barnstaple and the other earthlings encounter it, is, in reality, a vacation from life; the novel poses a clash between the human condition and an impossible ideal. "The Utopians are special creations . . . designed simply to evade the truth about human nature," writes Anthony West. "Their triumphs take place in a meaningless free zone in which all reality with which men have to deal is absent. This Utopia could exist for human beings only if the intellect could change the essential nature of reality."[17]

Wells, in what is virtually his last utopian satire, is at the same point he had been in his first one a quarter-century before. Two English monarchs had intervened since he wrote *The Sleeper Awakes* two years before the death of Victoria. However, his message had not really changed: any valid prospectus that does not take into account humanity as it is—fallible, capable of kindness and courage, folly and cruelty—remains, for all its nobility of vision, an empty dream. The overplanning that had dried up civilization in a desert of machinery in *The Sleeper* can no more save a civilization of men, as the Wells of *Tono-Bungay* and *The New Machiavelli* knew it, than the rose-colored glasses that had enabled a world of godlike men to be seen, but never for a moment believed in Wells's valedictory utopia.

The Outline of History (1920)

Although everything about Wells's thinking, especially after World War I, bears the stamp of utopism, the urgency of twentieth-century affairs increasingly obsessed him. "Modern civilization is like an aeroplane in mid-air," he has his autobiographical protagonist in *The World of William Clissold* declare, "an aeroplane with one sole, imperfect engine which is popping and showing many signs of distress." There was little time to make the aerodrome. As he wrote in his seventy-second year—in 1937—"in the race between education and catastrophe, catastrophe is winning."[18] At one point in *Men Like Gods,* Mr. Barnstaple looks pityingly at one of the invaders of Utopia and exhorts him, "Given decent ideas you might have been very different from what you are. If I had been your schoolmaster—But it's too late now" (*M, 219*).

Perhaps the world has not seen so colossal a one-man effort in behalf of popular propagandizing toward a private goal as that embodied by Wells in *The Outline of History*. Carl Becker, in his profoundly fair appraisal of *The Outline,* observes that, in striving to produce a mass awareness to the force of history, the book may well turn out to be, if not history, an action that has helped to make history. He places Wells in the company of Voltaire, and he defines their kinship by quoting a letter written by Diderot in 1760 to Voltaire apropos of the latter's *Essai sur les Moeurs:*[19] "Other historians relate facts to inform us of facts. You relate them in order to excite in our hearts a profound hatred of lying, ignorance, hypocrisy, superstition, fanaticism, tyranny; and this anger remains, even after the memory of the facts has disappeared."

As Wells grew older, he increasingly relied on generalization and synthesis; and he discarded altogether isolated events and disconnected details. It was this characteristic that made of Wells a species of higher journalist who wisely understood, at the opposite pole from the day-to-day "glut of occurrences" of newspapers, what the Present really meant. He made some mistakes—especially, as Orwell has complained, with modern dictators—but, for the most part, his disregard of all those puffed-up "moments of destiny" and their protagonists gave him a wider grasp. He tried to look at Today from the viewpoints of Yesterday and Tomorrow. In that spirit he essayed the heady summit of world history. What started as an essay on the sources and vicissitudes of the idea of European unity since the Caesars grew entirely out of hand into a universal history of prodigious proportions. Wells buttressed his own expanded notes by calling in a corps of specialists to be advisers on his reading and sources of information.

As might be expected of the author of biology texts, of a story like *The Island of Dr. Moreau,* and of a bookshelf of scientific romances, H. G. Wells was most at home writing of prehistory. The same genius that evoked the unforgettable dawn on the moon or the vision of the year thirty million in *The Time Machine* served him well in dealing with pristine eras. A few years later, in his fictional counterpart of *The Outline,* the cumbersome but worthwhile *World of William Clissold* (1926), Wells acknowledged his predilection for writing prehistory. Clissold confesses that "No other part of history so interests me as the opening chapter before the documents begin. There is no excessive presentation of persons and personal names; egotism has left nothing of persons and personal names; egotism has left nothing but defaced monuments and disconnected boats, and we seem to come nearer to the realities of human life than we do in a later age when kings and princes and their policies monopolize the foreground."[20]

Until a recent objection was registered to the prehistory chapters by novelist William Golding, whose debt to Wells's *Island of Dr. Moreau* was noted in chapter 2, most critics of *The Outline* have been willing to accept the first seven chapters, which covered the origins of life through the development of early man to the invention of language, as, in the words of Professor Becker, "the account . . . of a man who has mastered the subject well enough to understand the evidence [who] . . . in the spirit of the scientist . . . with no special thesis to defend and no practical aims to further . . . approaches his subject [in the first chapters]."[21] The Golding demurrer will be discussed in the next chapter.

Wells's history— with its insights, the broad sweep of a superiorly equipped overseer, and its felicity of style—is an unparalleled work until the point where Wells-with-a-mission gets ahead of the Wells-with-a-story. When he leaves the safely remote civilizations and the early steps in the advancement of the science of learning; when he approaches political history—with conquerors, kings and statesmen on center stage; when his narrative touches on events still relatively close to the immediate past, especially the cataclysmic war just ended, then the loving patience of the guidepost builder succumbs to the exasperation of a partisan spectator.

It is not within the province of this study to detail the storm of criticism that accompanied popular acceptance of *The Outline*. Certainly the long, heated diatribes that Wells and his old Anglo-Catholic adversary Hilaire Belloc exchanged over *The Outline*'s interpretation of the origins of Christianity have no place here. In the United States, at that time undergoing sweeping proposals for revitalizing the teaching of history, such New Historians as Professors Becker, J. Salwyn Schapiro, and Carlton J. H. Hayes reviewed the book more conscientiously than their English brethren who either ignored it or discounted it with faint mention. The New Historians, according to an exhaustive investigation of American reviews by Wagar, "all found serious fault with Wells's methods, sources, and content but applauded his scale of objections and his objectives."[22] Hayes spoke for most when he wrote that Wells "was making the world safe for historians. Henceforth professors will not fear to walk where Mr. Wells has leaped, and eventually one of them or a group of them will produce a history of man in the universe that will be as sound and reliable as the 'Outline' before us is inaccurate and impressionistic." His old friends from the Fabian days, Bernard Shaw and Graham Wallas, liked *The Outline;* and Harold Laski called it "the greatest public service the universities have been rendered in a generation."[23]

The book, as noted in an earlier connection, fortified Wells's popular reputation—made his a household name with people younger than the generation that matured during World War I. Although Wells noted in his autobiography that "over two million copies . . . have been sold since 1919" (*E,* 615), the commercial success of the *Outline* has been far out of proportion to its probable influence. Aldous Huxley's view that the work reached the wrong people for it to be lastingly influential is well known.

Most libraries contain the black-jacketed early edition of *The Outline* or possibly the three-volumed edition that brought the story up to the start of World War II. The book, according to Wagar, "became oppressively fashionable in the middle class [but] in mid-century [it] is mostly a dust-collector."[24]

Wells's didactic instinct aside—the fact that, as Hartley Grattan rightly observes, he proposed to rewrite history as propaganda for his world state—*The Outline of History* is undoubtedly a tremendously effective piece of public education in behalf of the plea to read history as a testament to the necessity of Oneness:

> One cannot foretell the surprises or disappointments the future has in store. Before this chapter of the World State can begin fairly in our histories, other chapters as yet unsuspected may still need to be written, as long and as full of conflict as our account of the growth and rivalries of the Great Powers and the insurrection of gangster totalitarianism. . . . Human history becomes more and more a race between education and catastrophe. . . .
> Life begins perpetually. Gathered together at last under the leadership of man, the student-teacher of the universe, unified, disciplined, armed with the secret powers of the atom, and with knowledge as yet beyond dreaming, Life, for ever dying to be born afresh, for ever young and eager, will presently stand upon earth as upon a footstool, and stretch out its realm against the stars.[25]

The writer of those words may have been without all spiritual values, as one of his severest critics asserts; but he was not without a faith. What makes declarations such as these closing words from his best-known work appear so shallow to scoffing intellectuals is that they stem from the soul, not of the artist, but of the pamphleteer—albeit the inspired pamphleteer of a commendable pamphlet. In his seventies, while still writing pamphlets for world statism and when visiting Somerset Maugham at his Riviera villa, Wells ran his thumb down the long ranks of his books. When Wells spoke, the words were as candid as any he had ever uttered: "All dead," he said. "Dead as mutton."[26]

Public Educator

Wells added *The Science of Life* (assisted by Julian Huxley and G. P. Wells, his biologist son) and *The Work, Wealth & Happiness of Mankind* to *The Outline of History*. In the first he sought to provide the nonspecialist with all he could want to know about biological discovery, about his body, about the origins of life. The second was "the first comprehensive summary of the whole of mankind working or playing or unemployed . . . to supersede the vague generalizations on which Marxism rests and to concentrate and synthesize all those confused socialist and individualist theorizings of the nineteenth century which still remain as the unstable basis of our economic needs." This vast trilogy alone, according to Sir Arthur Salter, "would have justified Wells's title to be the greatest public teacher of our time."[27]

It was to this task of educating the public that, for the last twenty-five years of his life, Wells subordinated every other purpose in life. *Joan and Peter* (1918) and *The Undying Fire* (1919) are the last of his novels to pledge even token allegiance to nondoctrinaire art. The first, a book Wells thought much superior to *Mr. Britling,* joins almost successfully its author's increasing preoccupation with education and that attention to characterization with which the creator of Kipps could still clothe a novel. Joan and Peter, two orphans brought up by an empire-builder uncle named Oswald, are thoroughly believable as children; but the feeling persists that Wells regards them more as laboratory specimens than as humans. Wells's central concern is how young people, miseducated by formal education in preparatory schools ("like trying to graft mummy-steak on living flesh . . . boiling fossils for soup"), can adjust themselves to the great war and to adulthood and marriage. The tragedy, as Uncle Oswald (and Wells) saw it, was that young people under King Edward, without clear aims or a sense of responsibilities in a shrinking world, should have been brought face to face with a war.

The Undying Fire, the most spiritual of all Wells's novels, has already been discussed. Job Huss was the dedicated schoolmaster of the "advanced" type school from which Joan and Peter were abducted by a Victorian fossil of an aunt. R. W. Sanderson, the headmaster of Oundle, to whom Wells sent his sons at the outbreak of war, was the living embodiment of Job Huss and virtually the only teacher who escaped Wells's wrath. In *The Story of a Great Schoolmaster* (1924), Wells paid tribute to him.

The World of William Clissold (1926) is, as the modern existentialist Colin Wilson observes, well worth reading,[28] but it is not a novel. Clissold is a tapestry woven from strands of Trafford—the pure scientist who deserted science for business; of Teddy Ponderevo, for Clissold has become wealthy; but, above all, of H. G. Wells, who had himself settled with a mistress in the South of France. Like Remington in *The New Machiavelli,* Clissold has come to rest after a vigorous period that included a scandal. However, fifteen years have elapsed between Remington and Clissold. Wells is no longer concerned with the effects of human irrationality. Clissold is doing nothing less than planning the Open Conspiracy that will bring World State out of present confusions. The book compounds the tendencies of *Mr. Britling,* written a decade earlier. Contemporary names are cited in profusion. In fact, were the book cast as a memoir of Wells at sixty, it might be considered an invaluable record of where, to the spokesman for faith in a progressively scientific future, the world was heading between the two great wars. "Indeed, it is possible to open it anywhere and be stimulated by the brilliant journalism," writes Norman Nicholson, who cites a short biography of Lord Northcliffe; an essay on the development of advertising in England; and, naturally, a dissertation on public schools.

D. H. Lawrence, with whom Wells got along better than most of Lawrence's contemporaries, recognized more forcefully than anyone of comparable stature that Clissold buried Wells as a novelist.[29] The book interested Shaw for another reason. For him, it proved Wells had at last come to know what "gentry" means.[30] But Wells could not, or would not, Shaw said, act the part. This observation, one he never elaborated on, is much more perceptive than even Shaw knew. The Wellsian persona that inhabits all the novels after *Clissold* is a man who finds no peace despite enormous material success; like Sir Richmond in *Secret Places of the Heart* (1922), this man is "entirely capable of being faithful to an idea, and entirely incapable of being faithful to his wife." World planners like Clissold are unable to resolve the chaos of their personal life. Promiscuous living involves for such as Sir Richmond (and Wells) no detriment to social standing or career as it did in the days of Remington's fall. Richmond (and Wells) availed himself of the conventional ways of getting around social conventions—the ways of gentry; he had an artist girlfriend whom he referred to as "my mistress," a far cry from the earlier Wellsian heroes and heroines who regarded marriage as a pact which, if broken, could destroy a career (Remington in *The New Machiavelli*) or bring suicide (Lady Mary Justin in *The Passionate Friends*).

Despair at Sixty

With the death in 1927 of his wife, Jane, Wells's personal problems all but inundated him. The reflection of a worsening private condition is seen in novel after novel in which the protagonist expresses the idea of being squeezed by a muddled world. Invariably, each hero bears a replica of part of Wells's own moral history. In *Clissold,* the scientist hero, like Wells, is sixty and distressed by the idea of death: "I do not want to go yet. I am sorry to have so little time before me. I wish before the ebb carries me right out of things that I could know more—and know better. I came into the world with a clutter of protest; my mind is still haunted by protesting questions too vague for me to put into any form that would admit of an answer" (*C,* 1:29–30).

In *Apropos of Dolores* (1938), the hero tells of contemplating suicide: "I saw my life as an inextricable muddle, and I repudiated suicide perhaps because it presented itself as an effort too troublesome to attempt or . . . because I was under obligation to various people . . . not to confess that the life they had thought worthwhile and found some comfort in, was a failure."[31] In *Brynhild* (1937), the hero, Mr. Rowland Place, awakens to "a world of cheerless realities, persistent and inexorable" in which "like so many men who make their way to positions of importance in the world of thought and letters [he] was a man of acute sensibilities and incessant anxieties."[32]

The mood became so overwhelming that by 1932, when Wells began a prelude to his autobiography, he revealed the tissue of despair his life had become:

I need freedom of mind. I want peace for work. I am distressed by immediate circumstances. My thoughts and work are encumbered by claims and vexations and I cannot see any hope of release from them; any hope of a period of serene and beneficent activity, before I am overtaken altogether by infirmity and death. I am in a phase of fatigue and of that discouragement which is a concomitant of fatigue, the petty things of to-morrow skirmish in my wakeful brain, and I find it difficult to assemble my forces to confront this problem which paralyses the proper use of myself. (*E*, 1)

This despair is more than that of an old man. Wells, throughout his sixties, was in more robust health than during his youth and early manhood. Partly in tribute to one of his all-time favorite books—*The Anatomy of Melancholy*—and partly as a contemporary reflection of it, Wells created in the person—or, rather, the posthumousness—of William Burroughs Steele a modern Robert Burton. *The Anatomy of Frustration* (1936) serves as a fine introduction to the last—the fully "directed"—Wells. Doctrinally, what is frustrating is Steele's balked idealism about the Collective Mind of Race, his sense that it, along with the World State, is an impossibility. Concern for mankind as a whole has no chance in a world where "partials"—individual communities, individual creeds—dominate the collective. Humanly, Wells is visioning his own frustration: mortality. He must contrive a buffer against death—a "merger-immortality": "This Undying Man, this Awakening Spirit in Life, with whom we have to identify ourselves, is not the Crowd or any sort of crowd. . . . Man . . . means not the aggregation but the quintessence of human life."[33]

If Beethoven were living in 1936, Steele's manuscript says, he would not crown his Ninth Symphony with stupendous choral effects—the

expression of an age. There would be no culminating brawling multitudi-
nousness of music: "now the theme would be the clear greatness of the
human mind, fearless and masterful. . . ."[34] It need hardly be added, in
Wells's late mood, that his man Steele, though ambiguously, took an over-
dose, his writings unpublished.

Three other hybrid works of this period, all published in 1937, testify
to Wells's sense that there is to be neither revolution nor favorable evolution—only backsliding into the vagaries of individual human (and national) natures. The gloomiest version is in *The Croquet Player,* in which the
player, George Frobisher, hearing a call for the Mind of Man to arise, declares himself unwilling to have to think about the future. If the sunset of
civilization has come, so be it [but] "I am going to play croquet with my
aunt at half-past twelve today." In *The Camford Visitation,* Trumber recognizes no progress that does not contain the modifier "so-called"; he lives for
revivals and restorations. In *Star-Begotten,* a character pinpoints the dilemma with a domestic metaphor: "But bringing a human mind up against
the living idea of progress is like bringing a badly trained dog into a house;
its first impulse is to defile the furniture."

In these books there is evident a reaction against the notion that absolute self-enjoyment is the aim of life. Wells had stressed this goal in *Men
Like Gods.* In his later testamental novels—and especially in his autobiography—he is a man full of doubt about the Machine as a purveyor of happiness and about material comfort as contributing anything to the creative
will. A passage like the following could only have been written by one
dubious of the efficacy of human effort to find an Elysium of intellectual
activity as opposed to the tiresome necessities of everyday:

Our lives are threaded with [a] desperate effort to disentangle ourselves, to get a
Great Good place of our own, and work freely.
    None of us really get there, perhaps there is no *there* anywhere to get to. . . .
We never do the work that we imagine to be in us. . . . Some of us . . . let
everything else slide, live in garrets and hovels, borrow money unscrupulously,
live on women. . . . exploit patronage, accept pensions. But even the careless life
will not stay careless. It has its own frustrations and chagrins. (*E,* 6)

This speaker is not the incurable optimist, ever confident of the eventual
triumph of common sense. It is a man full of existentialist forebodings
who, in a host of novels and tracts after World War I, refused to look fully
at his world and, by deepening his vision, create books in which his valedictory effort, *Mind at the End of Its Tether* (1945) could rest rather than, as
is the case, fall harshly.

Thus the gradual return of Wells to the pessimism of his creative period can easily be seen even in an idea-novel like *William Clissold* and his massive autobiography. Anthony West, in perhaps the most moving personal memoir ever built around the aging Wells, discusses the impossibility of reconciling the dark world that his father actually inhabited with the place that his bubbling forecasts and avuncular image as apostle of progress seemed to promise.[35] The manner of nearly all Wells's journalism—and that includes the three massive outlines—was best described by Cyril Connolly as "button-holing." The tone is invariably evangelical. The spirit is that of "the hard-sell," and the thing being sold is usually some current enthusiasm of today which will be replaced or repudiated tomorrow.

This study can but touch on the undeniable violence that Wells's strivings to obviate the Shavian "time-lag" did to his work. He once chided Julian Huxley on his failure to produce copy for *The Science of Life* at deadline.[36] It is doubtful if Wells ever missed a deadline in that private schema which he, after the manner of his earliest alter ego, Mr. Lewisham, formulated. It called for every accord and discord to produce a book. If it was a tenet of philosophy—his World State, for example—it could produce several dozen books, as that overriding ideology assuredly did. The production of a superjournalist thus driven can be, as it was with Wells, unparalleled; but it is not the method of the writer of books that last beyond their original impulse.

Dictators, Not Samurai

The last ten years of Wells's life need be mentioned only in passing. In 1935, he wrote a scenario based on his utopian novel *The Shape of Things to Come*. The film, *Things to Come*, was produced by Alexander Korda and starred Raymond Massey and Cedric Hardwicke. It provided millions of young filmgoers who had never read him with a celluloid version of the popular image of Wells as architect of the mechanized, scientifically planned order that would follow the Armageddon depicted in the novel. The man who had "invented" tanks, aerial warfare, and the atomic bomb portrayed white-suited air-borne Samurai who would be custodians of the automated world to come. In Germany, even as Wells prepared his scenario, Hitler was writing one of his own; and the Western World was plunging to its own Armageddon.

That Wells knew that disaster was close at hand is indicated by the wry, semicomic irony of a trio of novels written during the decade before Germany invaded Poland. *Mr. Blettsworthy on Rampole Island* (1928), written as "a caricature of the entire world of humanity," introduces a note of cruelty not found in Wells since *Dr. Moreau;* and it comments also on the Sacco-Vanzetti case. The shipwrecked Blettsworthy is washed up on Rampole Island among cannibals who intrude on the imagination as blatantly as the beasts that Dr. Moreau tried to transform into men. Blettsworthy lives among the savages as a sacred lunatic, like the leaders of the world who sorely disappointed Wells with their immunity from responsibility to forge a world order.

The Autocracy of Mr. Parham (1930) and *The Holy Terror* (1939) are about dictatorship and reveal once again how events serve to outstep Wells's fiction. Parham is a flamboyant cartoon of the British imperialist who fears Russia but idolizes Mussolini. In a dream, Parham sees himself as dictator of England. He summons his followers to a mass meeting at Albert Hall and harangues an excited crowd in the manner of Il Duce's "i-popoli-d'-Italia" speeches of the time. Four years after *Mr. Parham,* Oswald Mosley held a meeting of his black shirts in the same Albert Hall.

Young Rudolf (rhymes with Adolph) in *The Holy Terror* is a tiresome, bad-tempered boy, a fugitive from *Joan and Peter,* who could not overcome his miseducation (as his creator had done). He becomes Rud the dictator. The novel, one of Wells's poorest, has a certain academic interest for the evolution of the Wellsian rebels it tokened. Dr. Moreau, Griffin, Trafford—Wells's early scientists—were exceptional men who drew their fire from a sense of mission stemming from a Huxleyan scientific education. Rudolf's strength lies in his failings. Far from being a member of any elite—Samurai or New Republican—Rud draws his breath in an atmosphere of ignorance, laziness, vulgarity. He becomes "a holy terror" of a megalomaniac by exploiting all that is basest and vile in human nature. When Wells wrote his first books, vengeance—his own as well as those of his fictional alter egos—could still be a virtuoso matter. Griffin ranged the Woking countryside—but alone. In the days of Hitler and Mussolini, the avenger raises armies.

Babes in the Darkling Woods (1940)

On the eve of World War II, Wells tried to repeat the success of *Mr. Britling* with the novel *Babes in the Darkling Wood.* Then in his seventy-fifth year, he was disenchanted by a world that had failed to heed his counsels. He had watched with stern vigilance the world move farther away from the one active order he had always envisaged. In 1939, Wells's panic at the onset of world war had moved him to revise his most famous short story, "The Country of the Blind," after a third of a century. Then in 1940 he wrote a three-decker novel to assuage the urgency in his heart and mind. *Babes in the Darkling Wood* is the poorest work of fiction Wells ever wrote. Instead of some reassuring dedication, such as the kind Maugham was prone to append to his own potboilers of this period, Wells wrote a long justification for the "dialogue novel" which appeared as a foreword to *Babes;* he rehashed his *Fortnightly Review* article of 1911 and added a bitter inveighing against the critics for slighting him.

The novel is not discounted by its form but by its execution. Stripped of its flimsy framework of plot, the book tends in the direction of reporting and of lightly diluted interview technique. Wells takes many subjects— education, sex, religion, schools of psychology, communism—and contrives situations in which "experts" in these fields are able to expound articulately. The novel is best dissected by division into interviews in which characters do not so much move about and function as they talk incessantly. In an unintentional parody of Plato's Socratic dialogues—a form for which Wells, not surprisingly, expresses great admiration—character after character is produced to state his views in long interviews with an interlocutor.

The two principals—an intellectual young couple who do not talk like young people but as an old man thinks young people talk—discuss in page after page set between quotation marks the need for a mass of human beings to shape the world under a single authority. Then the pair—Stella and Gemini—"interview" a free-lance journalist, a clergyman, a psychotherapist, and finally an omniscient being who seems created in the image of the aging Open Conspirator himself.

Wells once wrote a justification to Frank Swinnerton for assembling an unlikely group for the purpose of airing viewpoints. Whatever his success in earlier novels—*Mr. Britling* and *Clissold* come to mind as books that survived such a contrivance—*Babes in the Darkling Wood* does not. One almost hears the creaking of furniture as Wells "stages" his interviews. These noises mute entirely the ring of reality necessary to the novel. At many points in the dialogue, Wells encounters difficulties experienced by the journalist writing up an interview report. Often the weight of the ideas expressed are such that quotes—or, using Wells's term, "monologues"— cannot carry them adequately. The newswriter resorts to exposition and narrative instead of question and answer. In the interview between Gemini Twain and the clergyman, one finds Wells breaking in to give expositorily the substance of the argument: "And Gemini proceeded to argue, with all the confidence and ready fullness of a brilliant student fresh from his preparation, that the false dichotomy implied in the opposition of material and spiritual was being kept alive by the organized religions in spite of advancing human thought, and it encumbered that advance, and this was the chief cause of the stupefaction of civilization in the present crisis" (B, 39). When this interview is nearly over, Wells makes the vicar summarize. He gives to the clergyman words that a newspaper journalist, writing his article "straight," would work into his first paragraph. The novel, the next to last he wrote, is the skeleton of thirty years' decomposition of the novelist's art.

The Last Books

Curiously enough, a year later, Wells returned in *You Can't Be Too Careful* (1941) to the characterization of the social misfits—the Kippses and Pollys—he had portrayed in his golden period as novelist. His Edward Albert Tewler is as spiritually starved as Albert Polly, but he does not have Mr. Polly's determination to impose change on his life. Also a victim of dishonest education, Tewler lacks George Ponderevo's zeal to force a link to the Mind of the Race; he deliberately chooses to withdraw into mediocrity. The post-Victorian world creaked under the strain of many tiny rebellions; the world at mid-century walls up the Tewlers in a cage of security: one cannot be too careful. This last of Wells's novels carries the same shrill note of warning as his first book a half-century earlier. Wells describes a state of mind that existed on the eve of World War II. "A solid mass of Homo Tewler," writes Madame Vallentin, "was still blocking up all paths toward the future, an impenetrable mass, which perhaps would never awaken to that idea of the cosmopolis that alone could save mankind."[37]

You Can't Be Too Careful came without any preparation just after his unintentional parody of the idea-novel devices he had worked to death for so long and just before he was to give vent to total despair in *Mind at the End of Its Tether*. In the story of Edward Albert Tewler, Wells saw in the flash of a double-take the quality of the raw material that would have to man the wheel of destiny. The novel proved the last time that H. G. Wells would see the human condition clearly.

Wells lived through the blitz in the middle of a London under bombardment. He refused to leave his home in Hanover Terrace—the one he had purchased in 1935 from Alfred Noyes—and the world press's last pictures of him are those of an adamant Britisher shaking his fist at the invading planes. Elizabeth Bowen tells of calling on Wells late at night at the height of the blitz. A trembling Wells came to the door. "But you shouldn't be frightened at all this," Miss Bowen remarked. "After all you invented it all." Wells looked at her and said: "It's not the bombs, it's the dark. I've been afraid of darkness all my life."[38] Wells suffered a physical breakdown in 1942, from which he never recovered. It was spiritual as well. He lived to see World War II concluded by an atomic blast he had predicted in 1913.

If *You Can't Be Too Careful* had been the final published work of H. G. Wells, there would have been a kind of divine justice about the return of a wayward artist to homeport. Instead, his body racked and weakened by a damaged kidney, diabetes, weak heart, and catarrh, he wrote almost until the end. In his seventy-ninth year he published a curious, misanthropic, and disorganized little book which, in its thirty-seven pages, repudiated all he had ever stood for as a writer. A modern existentialist like Colin Wilson places the pamphlet, *Mind at the End of Its Tether*, beside T. S. Eliot's *Hollow Men* as "the most pessimistic single utterance in modern literature."[39] Wells wrote:

> Our universe is not merely bankrupt; there remains no dividend at all; it has not simply liquidated; it is going clean out of existence, leaving not a wrack behind. . . .
> The writer sees the world as a jaded world devoid of recuperative power. In the past he has liked to think that man could pull out of his entanglements and start a new creative phase of human living. In the face of our universal inadequacy, that optimism has given place to a stoical cynicism. . . . Ordinary man is at the end of his tether. Only a small, highly adaptable minority of the species can possibly survive. . . .[40]

Wells repudiated his penultimate volume, *'42 to '44*, which contained a doctoral thesis submitted in the twilight of his career to London University. This book had sought to do in World War II what his pamphleteering during the previous war had done: find some reassurance against disaster. But in *Tether* Wells compared those hopes to "the remembered shouts of angry people in a train that has passed and gone forever." In perhaps the most revealing section of his melancholy tract, he turns to deal with the individual, the single human soul he had neglected during his long period of sterility as a novelist:

> Whatever dismaying realities our limited reasoning unfolds before us, our normal life is happily one of personal ambitions, affections, generosities, a mixture in nearly every individual of the narrowest prejudices, hates, competitiveness and jealousies with impulses of the most unselfish and endearing quality, bright

friendliness, unasked helpfulness; and this, the everyday foreground of our thought will always be sufficiently vivid to outshine any sustained intellectual persuasion. . . . *We live in reference to past experience and not to future events, however inevitable.*[41]

Here Wells seemed to be reducing the fountainhead idea of his life— that *becoming* not *being* is important—to rubble. Elsewhere in the essay Wells constrains readers to regard his final testament as based on scientific fact, objective reality. The grain of all of Wells's major fiction (and even a bad book like *Babes in the Darkling Wood* has a significant whimpering amid the brave trumpetings) is strongly skeptical of the forging of any sustained rational program on a large scale when the raw material it would have to deal with is malleable to the point of chaos. Only the single-minded intensity of *Mind at the End of Its Tether*—the degree of its despair—can be taken as surprising. And this new dimension may be said to stem from the urgency of a man under sentence of death.

Chapter Ten

Wells and the Critics

Art and Journalism:
The Celebrity Fallacy

H. G. Wells became during the first third of this century more than the writer of such-and-such a book; he took on the guise of a "term." One disillusioned former disciple hints—another comes out with it directly—that those years could with justice be called "The Age of H. G. Wells."[1] The starting-point of this examination of the ebb and flow of his critical standing might well be the perils—in his time and since—of fame itself.

Jessie Chambers, in her revealing memoir entitled *D.H. Lawrence: A Personal Record,* recalls her lover's sense of "despair about himself" when he read *Tono-Bungay.* "Most authors write out of their own personality," Lawrence, then twenty-three and on the threshold of fame, told her. "Wells does, of course. But I'm not sure that I've got a big enough personality to write out of."[2] During Wells's life most of his critics, whether enthusiastic or hostile, were so much taken over by what we could now call his *image*—its sheer bigness—that few cared to regard his work as literature. One thinks of Chesterton's experience of waking up at night and hearing Wells grow.

The distinction between assessments of Wells as pundit/prophet and as imaginative writer can be illustrated by the contrasting responses to Wells by Rebecca West and E. M. Forster. Reviewing *The Research Magnificent* in 1915, a year after she had borne a son by its author, West found in the Wells of that period "a temple for our homeless faiths, a place of beauty where we can satisfy the human instinct for high endeavors, a place of power where we can compromise our ambition, the leadership of the world."[3] Forster is appalled by the world planner: "Each time Mr. Wells and my other architectural friends anticipate a great outburst of post-war activity and world planning my heart contracts."[4] As to novelist Wells, he became for West one of her "literary uncles"; in that sphere, her real interests were in Joyce and Proust. Forster was one of the relatively few to defend Wells's position against Henry James, in whose novels he found "maimed creatures can alone breathe . . .—maimed yet specialized."[5]

Evelyn Waugh finds himself surprised that a memorable passage should have come from "The Door in the Wall" and from Wells.

Late in Wells's life, we still find T. S. Eliot returning to the matter of size. "As for the men of my time who have been able to capture a large audience . . . they are all, by comparison with Mr. Wells, pygmies."[6] The time is 1940, and Wells has just initiated still another of his discussions of the Rights of Man to the accompaniment of catastrophic headlines. Eliot finds such manifestos unreassuring. Not unlike that temporary theist Mr. Britling in the earlier war, he calls for something more spiritual to fend off despair and keep alive human aspirations in a time of calamity.[7]

That his imaginative appeal gradually was neutralized in the glare of this largeness becomes a fact of life in any examination of his critical standing. As for the imaginative side, it may not be entirely idle to wonder how different would have been Wells's lapsed progress from the author-as-god stronghold of the late Victorian/Edwardian novel to post-1910 modernism if just one man had never lived. Undoubtedly Henry James's formalist legacy—determinedly New Critical a generation before New Criticism's vogue—made it fashionable to disqualify self-revelatory fiction like Wells's and to welcome elaborately evasive narratives in the manner of Joseph Conrad and James and their Georgian successors. Parrinder puts the matter well: "In the long run, the growth of modernism in the arts after 1912, with the emergence of Joyce, Lawrence and Virginia Woolf as novelists, was the major force which led to the repudiation of Wells's methods and influence. As the 'modern' with its cultivation of dissonance, subjectivity and technical experimentation, replaced the 'contemporary,' Wells came to be seen as an artistic reactionary."[8]

Posterity's wishes, as codified in book-review literature, always disdain artists who do not hold *art* and *artist* up for special honors. Such a one as Wells, goaded by the mandarins of literary taste into overreacting in his preference to be called journalist over artist, was unlikely to be forgiven.

Edwardian Salvage Operations: The Rescue of Wells

Frank Swinnerton wrote in 1935 that *Edwardian* in the 1920s was a term of abuse to suggest that Shaw, Wells, Conrad, and Bennett were out-of-date.[9] The oldest and almost last of that era's literary tribe, Swinnerton died in late fall of 1982 at the age of ninety-eight. Had he been well enough to read during his final months, he would have surely noted the names of many departed friends in the review pages of the *London Times*. As one who had helped keep the memory of the Edwardians alive with his memoirs, "Swinny" could not help but have observed an outpouring of books with Edwardian perspectives. It was as if the period from the death of Victoria through the end of the Great War has "settled" so as to be perceptible anew. It is beyond the scope of this book to review this literature in detail, but several volumes merit consideration because of their part in the revisionism on Wells.

Jefferson Hunter's *Edwardian Fiction* and John Batchelor's *Edwardian Novelists,* both published in 1982, view the decade before 1914 as one that confronted British writers with a knocking away of props. Hunter provides a lucid and careful reassessment, finding the attentions of writers moving from the setting sun of empire to the muddle of life at home. Batchelor is comfortable with "epistemological crisis" as his umbrella for a period whose time frame he wisely leaves inexact: an "abyss" of "contracting moral horizons . . . [eroding] of the old certainties leaving Edwardian man with the self and nothing beyond." The corollary of this apocalyptic impulse, for Batchelor, is that the principal Edwardians—Conrad, Wells, Ford, Bennett, Galsworthy and Forster—write "within a received convention from which a central force . . . is missing [and whose heroes] must behave as though the old world of established certainties still exists since that world has determined the dramatic shape with which these writers are working."[10] Samuel Hynes had already sounded these notes in *The Edwardian Turn of Mind* (1968). He sees the Great War as delaying the modern movement. When it did flower, artists in all fields were determined to reject everything that could be identified with prewar England.

Batchelor echoes Hynes and others in concentrating on his six writers "between acts," novelists in a relatively stable yet uneasy culture that displays a lack of connection between moral conviction and effective action. He links Ford's *Parade's End* with *Tono-Bungay* as among the era's most powerful recognitions of the crisis of modernity. Where the ordinary nineteenth-century novel presents an apparently static society with only an undercurrent of dissatisfaction and turmoil, the modern novel reveals a society whose institutions have been discredited. Wells protrays the disruption of moral values at the hands of a get-rich-quick swindler; Ford depicts the disruption of society in the wake of the war.

Although it was Ford who published *Tono-Bungay* serially in the first issues of his *English Review,* he quarreled openly with Wells from the start. "Mr. Wells," he protested, "is a disciple of no technical school. . . . He trusts to his personality."[11] The dominance of personality over principle—the author as vessel—bothered Ford just as it vexed James. The question remains unresolved today. The first-person novel and its many variations comprise a convention in which fictional autobiographers gather their evidence from self and leave it at that.

Approaching seventy, Wells asserted the primacy of "writing autobiography—all out." A quarter-century earlier he had done just that in *Tono-Bungay*. The resurgence of acclaim for that book exemplifies the "rescue" of Wells to occupy the status of one who once more is being recognized as among the important novelists of the century.

"Other Ways" to Grip the Imagination: *Tono-Bungay*—A Reassessment, 1983

Wells expressed disappointment in the reception accorded *Tono-Bungay* in 1908. He had reason. "It bores me," wrote Beatrice Webb in her diary (24 February 1909), "because its detail is made up, not of real knowledge . . . but of stray bits. . . ."[12] Hubert Bland found the combination of story and essay "irritating, [for] just when one has become interested in a story [he has] to drop it, and read an essay."[13] Webb and Bland were leading activist and founder, respectively, of the Fabians, from which Wells had resigned the year *Tono-Bungay* was published. From a close friend, Arnold Bennett, came unstinting praise. "There are passages toward the close of the book which may fitly be compared with the lyrical freedoms of no matter what epic. . . . *Tono-Bungay*, to my mind, marks the junction of the two paths which the variety of Wells's gift has enabled him to follow simultaneously. . . . It is his most distinguished and powerful book."[14]

The "two paths" comprise socially realistic novels like *Love and Mr. Lewisham* and *Kipps* ("daily verifiable actualism") and the scientific romances ("on the plane of epic poetry"). Wells had reason to expect more readers—professional *and* general—to side with Bennett. He wrote in his preface in the Atlantic Edition that, having planned *Tono-Bungay* with elaborate care," he regarded it "as the finest and most finished novel upon the accepted lines that he has written or is ever likely to write . . . He realized that the fully developed novel, like the fully developed Gothic Cathedral, is a fabric too elaborate for contemporary needs and uses" (*W,* 12:i). The last sentence is the important one. Wells was acknowledging the passing of the four-decker: the chronicle novel after the manner of George Eliot and Trollope, the "life" novel—or bildungsroman—like *Great Expectations*. In such company *Tono-Bungay* shrinks, size-wise—just over 300 pages in the Riverside edition. But the sweep of the book—the *woosh!* and hum of "the great days of tono-bungay"—makes it seem panoramic.

Since 1967 *Tono-Bungay* has been a work big enough to absorb a diverse critical oeuvre comparable to that of any novel published during the Edwardian period, the works of James, Conrad, Joyce, and Lawrence excepted. However, at the time I was writing the first edition of this book—the mid-1960s—there was not a single essay that challenged Mark Schorer's savaging in "Technique as Discovery" (1948).[15] Schorer declared that art will not tolerate the writer who eschews technical refinements to accommodate the private novelistic materials of autobiography, social ideas, and personal passions. That art reverses Gresham's Law—good driving out bad—is proved, for Schorer, by the case of Wells, "whose enormous literary energy included no respect for the techniques of his medium," and by *Tono-Bungay*. Schorer places *Tono-Bungay* at the opposite pole from *A Portrait of the Artist as a Young Man,* which is also autobiographical but which "analyzes its material rigorously [defining] the value and the quality of its experience not by appended comment or moral epithet, but by the texture of the style."

Everything in the essay is well said. Schorer makes his case for technique as the only means a writer has "of discovering, exploring, developing his subject, of conveying its meaning, and, finally, of evaluating it."[16] His literary rogue's gallery includes, besides Wells, the Lawrence of *Sons and Lovers* (thematic unsureness), the Defoe of *Moll Flanders* (inadequate concern for Moll's character), the Thomas Wolfe of *Of Time and the River* (uncontrolled authorial ego), and a list of distinguished postwar American writers who, for Schorer, had not learned their craft.

The indictment against Wells is by far the most serious. He ridicules Wells's pretensions to convey the intellectual and moral history of the era, declaring "that the order of intellect and the order of morality do not exist at all, except as they are organized in the order of art." Rather than art, Schorer charges, Wells makes his own abstract thinking the framework for a novel, which is an unfortunate pastiche of Dickens, Shaw, Conrad, and Verne. Even *Tono-Bungay*'s ending, whose meaning, as will be shown, has been a source of lively commentary in recent years, only fires up Schorer further, for it "denies every value the book has been aiming toward."[17]

Counterattacks on Schorer's position were twenty years in coming, and they were tentative—at first. As early as 1961 Kenneth B. Newell's textual study ("The Structure of H. G. Wells's *Tono-Bungay*") hazarded the conjecture that the novel is quite other than the "agglomeration" narrator George Ponderevo promises on the first page. He notes the persistence of certain images that exemplify the theme of tranformation of reality into illusion.[18] Newell's essay, given credit by both, sparked two others by English critics, both published in 1966.

David Lodge, in "*Tono-Bungay* and the Condition of England," refrains from any direct entanglement with the anti-*Bungay*ists. He is willing to acknowledge, with Arnold Kettle, that there are almost no memorable characters in *Tono-Bungay* (although E. M. Forster opts for Aunt Susan) and, with Walter Allen, that the most extended love scenes Wells ever put into a novel are "sentimentally vulgar." But even Kettle, while rendering a verdict against the novel, will not write off its creator. "Wells is a writer whom one tends to underestimate until one actually returns to his books."[19] Lodge poses an overriding question that provides the key to any reassessment of Wells: "But what if Wells set out to grip the imagination of the reader in *other* ways?"[20] The "other ways" have gone by many names, but Lodge is the first critic since the start of Wells's decline seventy years ago to relocate him at a frontier that has been traditionally closed to him: that of language. He suggests that "if we read *Tono-Bungay* with an open mind, with attention to its language, to the passages where that language becomes most charged with imaginative energy, we shall find that it is an impressive, and certainly coherent, work of art."[21]

Bernard Bergonzi's Riverside introduction is largely a spinoff of Lodge's more comprehensive essay. He agrees with Lodge's demonstration that the book belongs in the condition-of-England tradition, and is much impressed by the web of metaphor that unifies the story. He is especially illuminating on what has always been the novel's most puzzling episode. With Uncle Teddy's fortunes beginning to collapse, George makes a dash by sea to Mordet Island, off the African coast, where there is a large deposit of an extremely valuable radioactive substance called quap. He hopes to bring back enough of it to rescue the Ponderevo enterprises, but the attempt fails. Traditional readings have seen this section, which crosses the Poe of *The Narrative of A. Gordon Pym* with the Conrad of *Heart of Darkness,* as a digression, not untypical of so discursive a writer, or as an afterthought.

Bergonzi hails the quap episode as "brilliant improvisation" and concludes that the greatness of the novel lies in its panorama "where the sociological imagination works through metaphor and symbol to achieve a memorable analysis—and indictment—of a whole social order."[22]

Among a number of strong ones, two essays subsequent to those of Lodge and Bergonzi merit brief mention.

In the more recent, Geoffrey Galt Harpham continues Lodge's thesis that cancer and decay are brilliantly metaphorized throughout. He goes even further, seeing in the novel a portent of apocalypse in which the anarchic dreams of *Kipps* and *Mr. Polly* are fulfilled. "Wells found [anarchy] a wondrously plastic concept," Harpham writes, "suited to any tone from hysteria to outrage to exhilaration."[23]

Lucille Herbert's "*Tono-Bungay*: Tradition and Experiment" takes direct issue with Mark Schorer—and indirect issue with Henry James. She stresses, as I did in the original edition, Wells's profound sense of the illusoriness of "separate individuality." Given such a credo, expounded as his metaphysic in *First and Last Things*, Wells can hardly be expected to have shared the novelist's traditional preoccupation with "individual destiny"—a concern that animates, in an old-fashioned way, a book with superficial similarities to *Tono-Bungay*, that is, *Great Expectations*, and, in a new-fashioned way, *A Portrait of the Artist as a Young Man*. To Schorer's charge that the novel "flounders through a series of literary imitations," Herbert answers that the Wells persona, in its impulse to desert its time frame, cannot be "merely saying what had been said before."

George Ponderevo's "private" story concerns a crisis and conversion that make him attempt to purge [himself] of the delusions and maladies of the existing social order so that, as he writes, he is in the process of *becoming* what Wells would have us believe is a man of the future. . . . Ponderevo borrows some ready-made forms and languages, including those of the "Condition of England novel," religous confession, and fictional autobiography. But the "spirit of truth-telling" in which he writes requires that the controlling perspective . . . be that of his renovated consciousness, and this in turn requires a new language and a new form for which he can find no models. Thus the essential and unifying form of *Tono-Bungay* becomes that of *a search for expression which inheres in the process of composition itself*.[24]

Tono-Bungay, then, is one of those rare novels in which the reader is privy to the cultural change-of-the-guard. It represents H. G. Wells's decoding from inside of the discordant messages he was hearing and a transformation of them into the imagery of social topography even as the old order was changing. The sense of simultaneous witness at the end of one era and the start of another is given to only the greatest of novels.

The Hand of the Master: Influences and Confluences

This final section of my revised study of H. G. Wells began with an implied recognition of the difficulty in getting to the imaginative core of a writer who has become a "term." That F. R. Leavis can use the phrase "crass Wellsianism" in derogatorily linking C. P. Snow with Wells demonstrates further, according to Mark Hillegas, that "most intellectuals have long since rebelled against Wells and the ideas he represented."[25] The important word is the last. Wells came to *represent* all the notions that have come to be associated—at least by its detractors—with progress. Some of these are mechanization and the Machine, planned states and utopia, optimism and the powers of modern science. The list could be extended indefinitely. It is enough to say that their spirit is explicit—even rampant— in Wells's trilogy of compilations, *An Outline of History, The Science of Life,* and *The Work, Wealth, and Happiness of Mankind.* Even the titles are redolent of the Wellsian powers of positive thinking. The opposing view sees the idea of inevitable progress as fallacious, insisting, in Martin Green's words, "on narrow intense knowledge (insights), on the need for personal freedom within the best-planned society, on the dangers of modern science and technology, on the irreducibility of artistic and religious modes."[26]

The decline of H. G. Wells began in the 1920s—the years whose thematic landmark was *The Waste Land.* In 1928 G. Lowes Dickinson praised E. M. Forster's "The Machine Stops" for turning the Shaw-Wells prophecies inside out. In 1937 George Orwell praised Aldous Huxley's *Brave New World* for parodying Wells's vision of utopia. In 1952, Wyndham Lewis described *Nineteen Eighty-Four* as a nightmarish reversal of Wellsian forecasts. And during these same years Edmund Wilson wrote of Eliot's detestation of Wells's "substitute religions."

The confident air of *The Outline of History,* as well as the mass of journalism and idea-novels peripheral to it, has had no appeal for intellectuals since the 1930s. It was, as Frederick J. Hoffman put it, "too easy to believe."[27]

But so is this excessively retouched photograph of Wells. It has been too easy for critics who have read their Eliot, Kafka, and Sartre—who have pondered apocalypse and existential nothingness—to misread Wells. Actually, the fruits of Wells's best period, garnished by storytelling verve, take the form of grave warnings to mankind. It was mainly the repetitious, droning voice of the figure in News Theater that made Wells the scapegoat for a simplistic trust in science.

Well's major works form a catalog of forebodings: the end of intellectual life in *The Time Machine*; the resort to something very like brainwashing in "The Country of the Blind"; moral collapse traceable to the consequences of the Darwinian revolution in *The Island of Dr. Moreau*; the catastrophe of uncontrolled experimentation in *The Invisible Man*; capitalistic charlatanry in *Tono-Bungay*; the development of intelligence at the expense of human sympathy in *The War of the Worlds*; the destructive consequences of irrational impulses in *The New Machiavelli.*

Writing of his father in 1957, novelist-critic Anthony West was the first to protest the relegation of Wells to the purgatory of the "progressive fallacy": "He was by nature a pessimist, and he was doing violence to his intuitions and his rational perceptions alike when he asserted in his middle period that mankind could make a better world for itself by an effort of will."[28] Likewise, Bernard Bergonzi in *The Early H. G. Wells* (1961) demonstrated the affinities of the scientific romances for the mordant impulses of the fin de siècle. The serious defect of these revisionist voices was to thrust Wells into an optimist-or-pessimist bifurcation.

What had been overlooked by my book and all others on Wells until 1967 was the extent to which Wells's most formidable critics—his peers among novelists—despite their quarrel with the roseate side of his vision, have embraced and drawn on the Wellsian imagination. It remained for one book to set the accountability-score straight.

Mark Hillegas's *Future as Nightmare: H. G. Wells and the Anti-Utopians* breaks free of simplistic rebuttals made to simplistic charges. His book is an in-depth catalog of science-fiction writers generally, and anti-utopian novelists in particular, which establishes the Wellsian imagination as a kind of clearinghouse for the imagery of world's end. Hillegas sets himself to chart the ways in which many of the dominant figurations of these writers originally appeared in the mythology of Wells's scientific romances; and to reveal, as a consequence, the likelihood that the works of writers like Huxley, Orwell, Zamyatin, Golding, Vonnegut, and many others are at once extensions of the Wellsian vision and reactions against it. Tirelessly researched and lucidly written, *The Future as Nightmare* locates "Wellsian" as—much more than a term—a mythos in itself—one so compelling as to be continued, reversed, and parodied by "pupils" who have become peers.

Fabulist Takes Issue with Fabulist: Golding, Wells, and the Neanderthals

A crowning example—and a fairly recent one—of the cycle of attraction and recoil that characterizes the influence of Wells among contemporary novelists is presented by William Golding and *The Inheritors* (1955). Golding, who is a writer more like Wells than, say, Orwell, was for most of his adult life a teacher. The force of his best novels and essays lies in a kind of modified didacticism in which he invites the reader to *discover* the truth of elemental matters that he believes has been hidden by scientific popular mythology. Golding possesses some of the same mental equipment, rare in a novelist, that conditioned Wells: a knowledge of science. He has been an

avid amateur paleontologist and anthropologist since his youth. Both writers at their best can be classified as "fabulists," that is, as writers of fables
that carry moral lessons.

If Wells could have lived another ten years and read *The Inheritors*, he
might have been moved by Golding's epigraph—an excerpt from *The Outline of History*[29]—to work his way through the novel. Having done so, he
would surely have been reminded of his own story "The Grisly Folk" (*F*,
595–609), which also chronicles a confrontation between Neanderthal
man and Homo sapiens. Would he, the aging originator, have bristled at
the brash reconstructionist, as Jules Verne did apropos of Wells in 1903?
What Wells might have produced, vis-à-vis *The Inheritors*, would have
been a long list of borrowings from "Grisly Folk" and *The Outline of History*.
What can also be shown is how *The Inheritors* goes as far beyond anything
Wells wrote about *Homo neanderthelensis* as *The First Men in the Moon* went
beyond Verne.

Wells contrasts the "Neanderthalers"—his grisly folk—and the "menfolk" with customary vividness, but he always sides with the latter, whom
he terms "our ancestors." His comparison is always the simple one of "better" or "worse." After several pages of what sounds to be convincing documentation about excavations ("Can these bones live?" begins the story),
Wells comes down hard with an evolutionist bias. We can understand creatures, he writes, who were kept in check by taboos. Not unlike a latter-
day species. He endows the menfolk with judgment to counter violence,
wisdom to moderate lusts and desires. But the grisly folk defy our understanding: "We cannot conceive in our different minds the strange ideas
. . . [of] those queerly-shaped brains. As well might we try to dream and
feel as a gorilla dreams and feels" (*F*, 599).

"The Grisly Folk," in fact, is a gloss for the ten-page seventh chapter
("The Neanderthal Men, an Extinct Race") of *The Outline of History*, which
Wells would write some twenty years later.

And as we realise the want of any close relationship between this ugly, strong,
ungainly, manlike animal and mankind, the less likely it becomes that he had a
naked skin and hair like ours and the more probable that he was different, and
perhaps bristly or hairy in some queer inhuman fashion like the hairy elephant and
the woolly rhinoceros who were his contemporaries. . . . Hairy or grisly, with a
big face like a mask, great brow ridges and no forehead, clutching an enormous
flint, and running like a baboon with his head forward and not, like a man, with
his head up, he must have been a fearsome creature for our forefathers to come
upon. (*F*, 597)

Wells climaxes "The Grisly Folk" with a kind of prehistoric Armageddon, the war "between these men who are not quite men and our men, our ancestors. . . . Until at length the last poor grisly was brought to bay and faced the spears of his pursuers in anger and despair." Throughout, Wells places his bets on humankind to prevail ("One likes to think of a victory for the human side"). However, as Robert O. Evans notes, no one can be sure that the species ever met: "For Wells's speculation there is no evidence at all. Neanderthal Man may simply have starved to death or been unable to adapt to changes in his environment. Or he may have been destroyed through cosmic accident (plague perhaps)."[30]

The possibility provided Wells with his *Outline*'s first heroic narrative— and Golding with an inversion that takes on an aspect of tragic myth. "Wells's *Outline of History* is the rationalist gospel *in excelsis*," Golding told Frank Kermode.[31] He was unwilling to join Wells, his fellow fabulist and a self-admittedly major influence from the start of his career, in equating intelligence with superiority of every kind. In truth, he notes, moral or spiritual superiority is sometimes the province of very simple creatures. In the last half of *The Inheritors*, where he several times shifts the narrative angle from the Neanderthalers to the "New People," Golding's fable reveals that modern man has lost many desirable characteristics.

Although "The Grisly Folk" is not one of Wells's best stories and *The Inheritors* is placed at or near the top of the Golding oeuvre, it becomes impossible not to see the issue as at least as much an aesthetic one as historical/philosophical. When Golding describes as "too neat, too slick" Wells's version of prehistory which would discount the Neanderthalers as ignoble savages, he lodges the same sort of complaint that Henry James had made a generation before about *Marriage*. James accused Wells of ignoring the psychological implications of the first encounter between the lovers. Likewise Golding, unwilling to settle for a merely descriptive account of the Neanderthalers and their encounter with Homo sapiens, starts where Wells left off. Mark Kinhead-Weekes and Ian Gregor put the matter well:

The sensuous texture [of *The Inheritors*] is a direct result of [Golding's] challenge to himself to imagine what it is like to live through sense and instinct, not the mind, breaking the barrier of "modern" consciousness. To turn from this to "The Grisly Folk" is to perceive that the significant difference is not the contrasting ideas of the moral nature of Neanderthal Man. It is that Golding has accepted the challenge to imagine himself into an alien mode of life, as Wells has not. Without imagination there is nothing between scientific data, obviously susceptible to op-posite interpretations, and unsupported fantasy.[32]

The above critique is unfair to Wells to the extent that Golding's impres-sive novel is no less an invention than Wells's story. Wells demonstrated in his best fantasies his capability for imaginative takeoffs on cultural and scientific possibilities. That he could be responsive to a version of John Milton's aesthetic problem in *Paradise Lost* of "likening spiritual to corporal forms" was shown in his undervalued novel *The Undying Fire*. But it is not the "fall" of man that interests Wells in *The Outline of History* and such dramatized predecessors as "The Grisly Folk." He is impatient to demon-strate evolution. For him, Man—with a capital *M*—had to emerge from lesser folk, and the Neanderthalers were his scapegoats. It is hard to believe that an apostle of inevitable progress could have studied under Huxley and written *The Island of Dr. Moreau* and *The Invisible Man*.

William Golding warms, not to the defense of earlier man, but to the challenge. The aesthetic problem is that, without the faculty of speech, his people must be made to live, in a fictionally convincing way, through their senses. Style is the means. It requires not only a denial of all analysis, by himself or his characters, but of the possibilities of dialogue. The People communicate by "sharing Pictures" or imagining simultaneously images of events. These "pictures," explain Kinhead-Weekes and Gregor, "are vi-sualizations not conceptualizations, telepathic snapshots not of an idea but of an entire event."[33]

Thus words are by far the smallest part of the People's resources of inter-change. Lest it be thought that the elimination of the verbal cuts Golding's literary legs from under him, visual reconstruction takes over—ani-mates—our consciousness as readers. What Golding accomplishes in *The Inheritors* might better be paired with the end-of-the-world scenes in *The Time Machine* or the lunar dawn in *The First Men in the Moon*—an extending to their fullest of the resources of the language in which myth is clothed, a reach to something that is never fully possible, a rendered comprehension of worlds no one—neither savant nor scientist—can know.

The Inheritors speaks to "things visible and invisible"—to the moral/eth-ical imperative that inspired T. H. Huxley's view of evolution, a view in which H. G. Wells found his earliest moorings but one that was beginning to founder when he wrote *The Outline of History*. Carlson Yost expresses the belief, in common with other commentators, that Golding likely kept the text of *The Outline* before him as he wrote, a kind of unholy writ:

The whole of *The Inheritors* is in opposition to Wells's statement relative to religion and evolution: "Many individuals dissent from the scientific opinion because they feel it is more seemly to suppose that man has fallen rather than risen. . . . The task of the historian is to deal not with what is seemly but with what is true." Golding implicitly shows us that Wells violates the truth of his second sentence with the question-begging of the first. . . . Wells believed it seemly to view man as the highest point in evolution and cleverly avoided any objection by labelling it "unscientific" to think otherwise.[34]

To go into the reasons that the "scientific" view propounded by Wells arose is clearly beyond the province of this book. It would involve an investigation into the philosophical, cultural, and religious aftermath of new information, especially Darwinism, in the final years of the nineteenth century and the first years of the twentieth. Suffice it to say that the intellectual climate of those years demanded a brutish, inhuman interpretation of Neanderthal fossils.

"Can these bones live?" indeed. They have lived—are living—many "lives"—as fabulists Wells and Golding demonstrate.

The Science Fictionists: *The Time Machine*

New Readings: Darko Suvin. If we seek to determine the causation behind the first Wells, it is, as I have tried to show, to the impulses sparked in him at South Kensington that we have to go. There is a remarkable 150-word sentence from a Royal Institution lecture in which the thirty-year-old Wells poses a question that, for him, was proving academic: why, if geologists can read fossils for clues to the Cambrian waves, shouldn't it be possible, given a knowledge of "operating causes," to direct "a searchlight of inference *forward.* . . .?"[35] Only then, at the start of the new century, did Wells begin to conceive of foreseeing the future in both imaginative and didactic writing—in what Huntington calls his "undirected" and "directed" sides. *Anticipations,* the utopias, and many of the scientific fantasies all stemmed from the thrust to vision future societies—long-range extrapolation—as a prelude to the actual end of Victorianism—short-range extrapolation—as reflected in *Tono-Bungay.*

I tried to show in chapter 2 that Wells's scientific romances, however their creator regarded them, have retained their attractions for almost a century because of the romantic ideas that they brought to a dramatic and timeless realization. At the heart of *The Time Machine* is the ever appealing narrative of a central character marooned in, or transported to, a setting that is always strange, often exotic, and invariably forbidding. Whether of a mountaineer trapped in a valley of the blind, or of an angel fallen from the sky, or of a shipwreck survivor washed ashore on an island inhabited by a mad doctor and his bestial creations, the dilemma connects to fears and aspirations alike. Edward Shanks may have been the first to see these stories as "myth" and Wells as a "mythmaker."[36] Forty years later, Bernard Bergonzi took Shanks's word, added "poetic," which Shanks had declined to use for fear of conveying a false impression, and called the scientific romances "mythopoeic."

Between Shanks and Bergonzi, V. S. Pritchett called *The Time Machine* "poetic social allegory," and Jorge Luis Borges wrote of the "sociological parables" that Wells "bestowed with a lavish hand." Perhaps the last word in the fruitless attempt to pin down to a category the bounty of the early Wells should be Borges's: Wells is "less a man of letters than a literature."[37]

The same folly of specific categorization presents itself in trying to forge a relationship between Wells's scientific romances and modern science fiction. Certainly, as his earliest writing, generally, and his paper, "The Discovery of the Future," specifically, demonstrate, he was the most munificent of practitioners of something that is dear to the hearts of science fictionists: extrapolation. Our world, at once attuned to and fearful of "future shock" and the threat of destruction, may not offer as awed and wide-eyed an audience for futurism and extrapolation as Wells's did; still, I have noticed, based on the books strewn in open carrels, that science-fiction paperbacks clearly dominate the spontaneous reading of undergraduates at every university where I have taught. Science fiction, according to one of its leading scholars, is impossible to define. Yet, in J. P. Vernier's view, Wells's stories remain modern, still pertinent for today's science-fiction writers and readers because

today's circumstances are so similar to Wells's. Space travel does exist, and the spreading of nuclear weapons has turned mass killing and biological mutation from fantastic hypotheses into frightening possibilities. Modern man has at least equalled the Martians in destructive capability. The complacence out of which Wells wanted to shake his contemporaries is still part of everyone's daily life; and the sense of an age coming to its end and opening out into an unknown future, which Wells expressed in his fantasies, is an integral part of today's background.[38]

At their best, the books and articles of the science-fiction critics have done most to reawaken scholarly interest in Wells after its long snooze for twenty years on either side of his death in 1946. The whole issue of whether Wells was an incurable optimist or a closet pessimist—so divisive at the time I was writing this book's original edition in the early 1960s—has been put to rest for more important concerns. While a part of the thrust of these scholar-critics has been to uncover—and often overdo—a kind of palimpsest of ambiguity, the real contribution of both the science-fiction and literature-at-large Wellsians is to accept him *whole* rather than simply to write off everything after an arbitrarily assigned cutoff year.

My debt to these critics is extensive; their work is indispensable for anyone who tries to assess the renewed interest in Wells. I can only in this limited space show in cameo the diverse richness of the rebirth. Except for *Tono-Bungay,* whose revisionist readings are summarized in chapter 5, the most impressive body of new work is that devoted to *The Time Machine.*

Major tributes to this first of the scientific romances are highlighted at the start of chapter 2. To these can now be added Darko Suvin's panegyric: "All significant science fiction since Wells can be said to have come out of his *Time Machine.*"[39] Suvin's two essays in *H. G. Wells and Modern Science Fiction* (1977), which he also edited with Robert M. Philmus, view *The Time Machine* as a masterful narrative; as a work whose "Eloi episode is marked by cognitive hypotheses that run the whole logical gamut of sociological science fiction"; and as a paradigm of the devices, both innovative and derivative, that would appear in subsequent "cosmological" romances and fantasies.[40]

Suvin is one of the few to attempt a serious classification of Wells's science fiction. He goes beyond any mere labeling of Wells as the popular genre's "father" by strongly hinting that Wells's works anticipated all of science fiction's contemporary forms. Suvin's categories are: (1) Wells's early work, that up to 1904, based on the vision of the horrifying novelty, the disruptive "Unique" as the long-range—the extrapolative—outlook for mankind; (2) those works based on shorter-range extrapolation that interweaves "technological novelties such as the airplane and the atom bomb but . . . centrally concerned with the utopian organization of mankind"; and (3) a disparate oeuvre that combines in the later work a little science fantasy with a lot of programmatic utopian thinking transposed with his momentary political biases and hopes.[41]

Suvin, a European who originally encountered Wells in translated editions in his native Yugoslavia, views science fiction as "cognitive by virtue of its affiliation with science and rationality, and estranged by its presentation of a conceptual 'new world' differing from empirical reality." Wells remains for him the "central writer and nodal point" in the tradition of modern science fiction.[42]

New Readings: Patrick Parrinder.   Terminologically, the English critic Patrick Parrinder reaches for the highest plane on which to classify *The Time Machine*. He glorifies it as a "truncated epic" or "epic fable."[43] The qualifying words "truncated" and "fable" represent significant disclaimers, however. Science-fiction writers shy away from the traditional trappings of epic because of the recognition that futurist narratives cannot help but lose credibility the more they are extended. It is difficult to keep future history convincing in detail.

For all of his attempts to lock in *The Time Machine* with epic, the most magisterial of genres, it would appear that Parrinder makes a better case for considering *The Time Machine* a futurist fable, an anticipation of a work like Arthur C. Clarke's *2001: A Space Odyssey*. Clarke's obelisk stands in the same relation to his fable as the "winged sphinx" does at the moment of its appearance when the Time Traveller enters the world of 802701. The statue of the sphinx, for Parrinder, is an embodiment of the awesomeness of the prophetic vision, which the Time Traveller himself experiences as "the full temerity of my voyage." The fable, then, is a product of the confluence of Wells's gift for dramatic myth, which sets the story apart from ordinary futurology, and the "anticipatory and eschatological tendencies" in the scientific thought of Wells's Time.

New Readings: Robert M. Philmus.   Philmus's felicitously written "Logic of 'Prophecy' in *The Time Machine*" avoids trying to classify the story and adheres instead to the claims Wells himself made: a vision of social disintegration as a critique of the end-of-century ideal of comfort and self-satisfaction. What interests Philmus is the Time Traveller's compulsion at the end to resume his journey—even to return to the world of the Eloi and the Morlocks. That Wells has brilliantly fulfilled the "vision" or "prophecy" which is the imaginative frame of the fable constitutes for Philmus an advance in this kind of narrative. He concludes that the Time Traveller "takes his vision literally, that he allows it the same ontological status that he himself has. Hence to dramatize the assertion that he has told the literal truth, he must go back into the Fourth Dimension: since he cannot accept the 'prophecy' as metaphor, he must disappear into the dimension where it 'exists'."[44]

In a related essay, "Borges and Wells and the Labyrinths of Time," Philmus stresses the metaphoric force that he sees in the return of the Time Traveller from the one hundred twenty-first century carrying a wilted flower from the future.[45] For Wells, time is a function of space and, more important, the future—real and prone to catastrophe—is not beyond redemption.

New Readings: John Huntington. Finally, the most recent extended interpretation of *The Time Machine* is John Huntington's from his instructive *Logic of Fantasy: H. G. Wells and Science Fiction*—a reading that sheds light on the seeming coexistence of utopian optimism and cosmic pessimism in Well's writings. Throughout *Logic of Fantasy*, Huntington argues persuasively not only to regard Wells's writings as reflective of undirected and directed thinking but to see in them the "coexistence of opposites" as *the* crucial component, especially of the scientific romances. One is reminded of F. Scott Fitzgerald—himself an admirer of *Kipps* and *The New Machiavelli*—who attributed his crackup to the inability to maintain the saving balance between the sense that although life inevitably defeats, it is still necessary to go on.

It is the combining of these two attitudes in the stance of the Time Traveller that strikes Huntington as being the heart of *The Time Machine:*

> If the Time Traveller's vision of bleak decline is the true one, the narrator argues, "it remains for us to live as though it were not so." He finally settles on an image that echoes the more hellish imagery of the novella itself and also alludes to the image of the feeble light shed by the match of science at the end of "The Rediscovery of the Unique": "But to me the future is still black and blank—is a vast ignorance, lit at a few casual places. . . ."[46]

For Huntington, *The Time Machine* not only balances pessimism and optimism but strikes a more pivotal equilibrium between visions of change and no change: "The horror of the split between the Eloi and the Morlocks lies in the fact that the divisions of modern civilization have not changed. . . . But the other opposition, that between the present and the future, is a vision of change, of entropic decline."[47]

Thus, in viewing the conflict of class—the essential injustice—as unchanging but also the certainty that, for all that humans do, things will change, Wells demonstrates an "antithetical" condition of humankind that, for Huntington, "gives [Wells's] fiction a profundity, based on the ambiguities of human desire and experience, that is rare in thought about the future."[48]

Chapter Eleven
The Way of the Wellsian: An Afterword

He was a great writer who did not always write well. He made his reputation with—and will be longest remembered for—scientific fantasies which he never took seriously. Pushing seventy, he wrote: "It had become a bore doing imaginative books that do not touch imagination." In an auto-obituary,[1] written when he knew he was dying, he discounted the "original freshness" of his romances; they had been destroyed, he wrote, by "the general advance of knowledge." Wells probably intended these words to bear a truth-telling writer's candor. Instead they demonstrate the grain of Wellsian thinking, when it was directed, and the perversity of the Wellsian imagination, when it was undersold. He believed that knowledge, born of the scientific spirit and buttressed by rational faith, would always mark advances and thereby redeem the future. In the same auto-obituary, he half joked about the impairment to his health "by a spell in a concentration camp under the brief Communist dictatorship of 1952." Certainly Bertrand Russell, his old ally with the Coefficients, was right when he speculated that confinement to a place like Buchenwald would have cost Wells his belief in the omnipotence of reason. "To the end of his days," Russell concluded, "Wells could not face the fact that sensible men have no power."

Or that the imagination *has*. Because his studies at South Kensington in biology played like a monitoring palimpsest over the free flow of his imagination, he never credited the arming irony behind such truths as Auden's that poetry makes nothing happen. The coexistence of a glowing imaginative sensibility with a glowering scientific one eventually betrayed their possessor into a crippling messianism.

The moment of crucial ambivalence reveals itself at the end of Wells's best book when George Ponderevo touches the heart of his creator's imaginative side in his recognition of a consciousness capable of thrusting beyond the waste and decay of the old world. But the vehicle—literally, the vessel—for the Wellsian vision is a battleship, a destroyer. Certainly Wells needed a metaphor powerful enough to contain what he would thereafter, in book after book, call the Mind of Race. But in installing mind over matter, in making science his destroyer, Wells unleashes his confidence in an outward-bound, all-powerful force that will mow down everything, including the imaginative side.

The efficacy of Wells, at the top of his form, for the literate, nonspecialist reader lay in the assurance—not necessarily so recognized—that he was being conducted into the ways of the imagination but by a guide who knew that "other" world too. Whether that other world was scientific, romantic, "Kippsian," or a combination, hardly mattered, so magically endowed was the transport.

The magic went out of Wells a lot more gradually than many of his detractors suggest. Except for a "late late" novel like *Babes in the Darkling Wood,* there is rarely a book that lacks a redeeming feature. Arnold Kettle is certainly right when he says that Wells is a writer who is easy to dismiss until you read him. Nevertheless the demise of nearly all of Wells's fiction after *The Undying Fire* cannot, it seems to me, be seriously doubted. The efforts of Wellsians like Robert Bloom, William J. Scheick, R. D. Mullen, and others to show there was still life—even a perceptible aesthetic—in the latter books are often well taken and sometimes impressive. That I am in their debt I have freely acknowledged in these pages. It should be added that exhaustively exegetical studies will become counterproductive in a writer like Wells who rarely concealed his meanings.

The Wells that holds up is the mythopoeic Wells of the scientific romances, which still stand among the supremest of their genre; the poet-fantasist of the short stories for which he has never received full credit; and the extraordinarily ordinary sage of that comic Edwardian trio, Kipps, Polly, and Ponderevo.

In going back to some of them after twenty years, I found the novels of society unreadable except for *The New Machiavelli, Marriage,* a midcareer love story, *The Passionate Friends,* and *Apropos of Dolores,* a revealing and often poignant study of the perils of the self-absorbed Great Man in old age. *Mr. Britling,* as I have tried to show, is more carefully crafted than is generally believed. It and *The World of William Clissold* tell us a good deal about the condition of England in the midst of World War I and the years between the two wars, respectively. *Experiment in Autobiography*—the first half, especially—is a remarkable self-study.

Wells's gifts in the area of psychological probing were minimal. A novelist like Joyce Cary possesses as much vigor as Wells at his best and is capable of a gallery of characters denied his predecessor.

What one wonders, finally, is whether, in an age given to the merchandised best-seller, it is possible for a young reader to come upon a book, like Orwell's George Bowling[2] does *Mr. Polly,* and ask "if you can imagine the effect it had on me, to be brought up as I'd been brought up, . . . and then to come across a book like this." To the spiritually underfed young of post-Victorian days and ones much later, H. G. Wells introduced a priceless ingredient: exhilaration.

Notes and References

For the sake of uniformity, most references to primary sources will be to *The Works of H. G.Wells: Atlantic Edition* (28 volumes [New York, 1924– 27]). The final novel in the Atlantic Edition is *Men Like Gods* (1923). Novels subsequent to that one will be referenced to the standard American editions, all of which are now out of print. Notes on Wells's five major scientific romances are to *Seven Famous Novels of H. G. Wells* (New York, 1934). In chapter 3, which deals with the short fiction, the omnibus *Famous Short Stories of H. G. Wells* (Garden City, N.Y., 1938) is the base volume.

Preface

1. Walter Allen, *As I Walked Down Grub Street* (New York, 1982), 14.
2. David Lodge, "*Tono-Bungay* and the Condition of England," in *Language of Fiction* (New York, 1966), 216.
3. W. Warren Wagar, *H. G. Wells and the World State* (New Haven, 1961).
4. Roslynn D. Haynes, *H. G. Wells: Discoverer of the Future; the Influence of Science on His Thought* (London, 1980), and John Huntington, *The Logic of Fantasy: H. G. Wells and Science Fiction* (New York, 1982).
5. Mark Hillegas, *The Future As Nightmare: H. G. Wells and the Anti-Utopians* (New York, 1967).
6. Kingsley Martin, "Shaw and Wells," in *H. G. Wells: Interviews and Recollections,* ed. J. R. Hammond (London, 1980), 92.
7. Norman and Jeanne MacKenzie, *H. G. Wells: A Biography* (New York, 1973).

Chapter One

1. Quoted by George Catlin, "Prophet of Modernism," *Commonweal,* 27 September 1948, 573.
2. Vincent Brome, *H. G. Wells* (London, 1951), 237–38.
3. Quoted by Edward Mead Earle, "H. G. Wells, British Patriot in Search of a World State," in *Nationalism and Internationalism* (New York: Columbia University Press, 1950), 84.
4. *Experiment in Autobiography* (New York, 1934), 37; hereafter cited in the text as *E.*
5. *The World of H. G. Wells* (New York, 1915), 57.

6. *Tono-Bungay,* in *Works* (New York, 1924–27), 12:63–65; Wells's *Works* are hereafter cited in the text as *W.*

7. Perhaps no other man of letters in this century has been accorded recognition of this kind. While a correspondent for the *London Tribune,* Wells lunched with President Theodore Roosevelt in 1906. He made his second journey to Russia in 1920 and spoke at length with Lenin. Wells returned to the Soviet Union in 1934, a few months after a visit to President Franklin D. Roosevelt. His interview with Stalin that year was widely publicized (for its text see Louis Biancolli, ed., *The Book of Great Conversations* [New York, 1948], 559–60) and set off a long debate with Bernard Shaw (see Vincent Brome, *Six Studies in Quarreling* [London, 1958], 170–80). Wells addressed the German Reichstag on 15 April 1929, and the French Chamber heard him at about the same time.

8. MacKenzie, *H. G. Wells,* 57.

9. Ibid., 55–56.

10. Quoted in Mark R. Hillegas, "Cosmic Pessimism in H. G. Wells's Scientific Romances," *Papers of the Michigan Academy of Sciences, Arts, and Letters* 46 (1961):655–63.

Chapter Two

1. J. P. Vernier, "Evolution as a Literary Theme in H. G. Wells's Science Fiction," in *H. G. Wells and Modern Science Fiction,* ed. Darko Suvin and Robert M. Philmus (Lewisburg, Pa., 1977), 71–2.

2. Robert M. Philmus and David Y. Hughes, eds., *H. G. Wells: Early Writings in Science and Science Fiction* (Berkeley, 1975), 3.

3. Ibid., 4.

4. *The World of William Clissold* (New York, 1926), 1:112–13.

5. Quoted in Godfrey Smith, "Astounding Story! About a Science Fiction Writer!," *New York Times Magazine,* 6 March 1966, 77.

6. Quoted by Hillegas, "Cosmic Pessimism," 658.

7. *The Time Machine,* in *Seven Famous Novels by H. G. Wells* (New York, 1934), 56–57; hereafter cited in the text as *S.*

8. Norman Nicholson, *H. G. Wells* (London, 1950), 28.

9. V. S. Pritchett, "The Scientific Romances," in *The Living Novel* (New York, 1947), 124.

10. Winston Churchill, "H. G. Wells," *London Sunday Dispatch,* 26 August 1946, 25.

11. Pritchett, *Living Novel,* 124.

12. *The Island of Dr. Moreau,* in *Seven Famous Novels,* 105; hereafter cited in the text as *S.*

13. Carl Niemeyer, "The Coral Island Revisited," *College English* 22 (January 1961):241–45.

14. Leo J. Henkin, *Darwinism in the English Novel: 1860–1910 (New York, 1940),* 193.

15. Anthony West, "The Dark World of H. G. Wells," *Harper's* 214 (May 1957):68.

16. Thomas H. Huxley, "Government, Anarchy or Regimentation," in *Method and Results—Essays* (New York, 1894), 423.

17. Review by Chalmers Mitchell, in *Saturday Review* 82 (7 November 1896):498.

18. Introduction to *Creeps by Night,* ed. Dashiell Hammett (New York, 1944).

19. *The Invisible Man,* in *Seven Famous Novels,* 261.

20. *The War of the Worlds,* in ibid., 288–89; hereafter cited in the text as *S.*

21. *George Gissing and H. G. Wells,* ed. Royal Gettmann (Champaign, 1961), 25.

22. Mark Hillegas, "The Cosmic Voyage and the Doctrine of Inhabited Worlds in Nineteenth-Century English Literature" (Ph.D. diss., Columbia University, 1957), 199.

23. Quoted in "Wells's Son Treads the Path of the Moon Men," *London Times,* 19 January 1964, 33.

24. Hillegas, "The Cosmic Voyage," 219.

25. *Arnold Bennett and H. G. Wells,* ed. Harris Wilson (Champaign, 1960), 260–65.

26. "Jules Verne Revisited," *T. P.'s Weekly,* 9 October 1903, 589; also quoted in Bernard Bergonzi, *The Early H. G. Wells* (Toronto, 1961), 157–58.

27. *The First Men in the Moon,* in *Seven Famous Novels,* 393; hereafter cited in the text as *S.*

Chapter Three

1. William Bellamy, *The Novels of Wells, Bennett, and Galsworthy: 1890–1910* (London, 1971), 29–30.

2. Hillegas, "Cosmic Pessimism," 658.

3. Patrick Parrinder and Robert M. Philmus, eds., *H. G. Wells's Literary Criticism* (London, 1980), 249.

4. H. E. Bates, *The Modern Short Story* (Boston, 1941), 110–11.

5. Ingvald Raknem, *H. G. Wells and His Critics* (London, 1962), 341.

6. Bellamy, *Novels of Wells,* 28.

7. Quoted in ibid., 31.

8. Ibid., 32.

9. "The Lord of the Dynamos," in *The Famous Short Stories of H. G. Wells* (Garden City, N.Y., 1938), 277; hereafter *Famous Short Stories* cited in the text as *F.*

10. Thomas H. Huxley, *Evolution and Ethics and Other Essays* (New York, 1904), 16–17.

11. I could find no evidence that Eugene O'Neill had read "The Lord of the Dynamos." Both Yank in *The Hairy Ape* and Azuma-zi in the Wells story are

symbolic of man who has lost his old harmony with nature. Yank worships the engines of the ship because they appear to give him, a stoker, a sense of belonging. Axuma-zi sees the dynamo as an extension of his heathen idols.

12. See Lewis Mumford, "The Revolt of the Demons," *New Yorker,* 23 May 1964, 171.

13. H. G. Wells Archive, Rare Books Room, University Library, University of Illinois at Urbana-Champaign, contains the letter of rejection.

14. Wilson, ed. *Arnold Bennett,* 59.

15. See Reginald Pound, *Arnold Bennett: A Biography* (London, 1952), 114.

16. Bergonzi, *Early H. G. Wells,* 88.

17. Ibid., 81.

18. The Wells Archive contains one of the 280 numbered copies of the Golden Cockerell Edition.

19. See *Mind at the End of Its Tether* (New York, 1946), 17.

Chapter Four

1. Richard Rees, in *George Orwell: Fugitive from the Camp of Victory* ([London, 1961] 18–19, 130–31) is especially illuminating on Wells as an Angry Young Man. And Winston Churchill, in the *London Sunday Dispatch* obituary tribute to Wells cited above (chap. 2, n. 10), wrote that Wells nursed a grievance against the British Empire, the United Kingdom, and, in particular, against England, which, like an "uncomfortable and querulous baby . . . he has to carry with him everywhere."

2. E. M. Forster, *Aspects of the Novel* (New York, 1927), 110–11.

3. Nicholson, *H. G. Wells,* 55.

4. Quoted in Raknem, *H. G. Wells,* 69.

5. C. E. M. Joad, "The Most Ordinary of Great Men," *London Evening Standard,* 14 August 1946, 6.

6. Quoted in Wells, *The Wealth of Mr. Waddy,* ed. Harris Wilson (Carbondale, 1969), x.

7. Brome, *H. G. Wells,* 110.

8. Sinclair Lewis, foreword to *The History of Mr. Polly* (New York, 1941), vii.

9. Sidney Dark, *Outline of Wells* (New York, 1922), 121.

Chapter Five

1. C. Hartley Grattan, "Good-Bye to H. G. Wells!," *Outlook* 157 (4 February 1931):178.

2. See *Boon,* in *Works,* 13:455.

3. MacKenzie, *H. G. Wells,* 170.

4. Martin, "Shaw and Wells," 92.

5. See Edward R. Pease, *The History of the Fabian Society* (New York, 1916), chap. 9, "The Episode of Mr. Wells."

6. George Bernard Shaw, "The Man I Knew," *New Statesman and Nation,* 17 August 1946, 115.
7. Leonard Woolf, "Some Portraits," *Encounter* 22 (May 1964):80. Woolf credits the words to A. L. Rowse.
8. See "The Contemporary Novel," in *Works,* 9:379.
9. William C. Frierson, *The English Novel in Transition* (Norman, 1942), 131–35.
10. David Daiches, *A Critical History of the English Novel* (New York, 1958), 35.
11. David Lodge, "*Tono-Bungay* and the Condition of England," in *H. G. Wells,* ed. Bernard Bergonzi (Englewood Cliffs, N.J., 1976), 111. This seminal essay was originally published in Lodge's *Language of Fiction,* 214–42.
12. Wells was a connoisseur of outsiders, writes John Raymond ("Alive and Kicking," *New Statesman,* 10 January 1959, 46), an acute paralleling of the roles of Wells and Lloyd George. Wells always thought adventurous outsiders are inevitable in periods of obsolete educational ideas and decaying social conditions. He included himself as one (see *Experiment,* 439).
13. Foreword to *Tono-Bungay* (New York, 1960), xii.
14. Geoffrey West, *H. G. Wells: A Sketch for a Portrait* (New York, 1930), 237.
15. John Fowles, *The French Lieutenant's Woman* (New York: New American Library, 1969), 364.

Chapter Six

1. MacKenzie, *H. G. Wells,* 256.
2. Ibid., 205–6.
3. Gordon N. Ray, *H. G. Wells and Rebecca West* (New Haven, 1974), 13.
4. Ibid., 36.
5. Ibid., 69.
6. Ibid., 193.
7. Raknem, *H. G. Wells,* 95.
8. *The New Machiavelli,* in *Works,* 14:ix.
9. See Pound, *Arnold Bennett,* 262.
10. André Maurois, *Prophets and Poets* (New York, 1935), 87.
11. Montgomery Belgion, *H. G. Wells* (London, 1953), 23.
12. Kenneth Rexroth, "The Screw Turns on Mr. James," *Nation,* 16 August 1958, 76.
13. *A Modern Utopia,* in *Works,* 9:261.
14. Brome, *H. G. Wells,* 112.
15. Wells expressed his debt to the liberating spirit of Shelley's poems throughout his autobiography and in many of his novels. For Edmund Wilson, in personal conversation with me, the influence of Wells and Shaw on his (Wilson's) generation may have been, in the final analysis, damaging: "They were too Rou-

seauvian—Wells and Shaw—and their novels and plays never go on to trace the outcome of the polygamous situations they herald. Many men and women of my generation saw in these books carte blanche for license and were irreparably injured" (see Richard H. Costa, *Edmund Wilson: Our Neighbor from Talcottville* [Syracuse, 1980], 77).

16. Brome, *H. G. Wells*, 110.

17. Odette Keun, "H. G. Wells—The Player," *Time and Tide* 15 (20 October 1934):1307.

18. Patrick Parrinder, ed., *H. G. Wells: The Critical Heritage* (London, 1972), 170–71.

19. Brome, *H. G. Wells*, 112.

20. Edwin E. Slosson, *Six Major Prophets* (Boston, 1917), 113.

21. See Nicholson, *H. G. Wells*, 72.

22. *Marriage*, in *Works*, 15:531.

23. See Edmund Wilson, "T. S. Eliot and the Church of England," in *A Literary Chronicle: 1920–1950* (Garden City, N.Y., 1956), 135.

24. Vladimir Nabokov, "Reputations Revisited," *London Times Literary Supplement*, 21 January 1977. Nabokov expresses admiration for Wells's handling of the aftermath of a "supervised" last meeting between Stratton and Mary, illicit lover, calling it "genius denied Conrad and Lawrence."

25. Peter Kemp, *H. G. Wells and the Culminating Ape* (New York, 1982), 115.

26. Ibid., 115.

27. Freda Kirchway, "A Private Letter to H. G. Wells," in *H. G. Wells*, ed. Parrinder, 309.

28. Martin, "Shaw and Wells," 92.

29. Quoted in John R. Reed, *The Natural History of H. G. Wells* (Athens, Ohio, 1982), 58.

30. See ibid., 58.

31. Ibid.

32. Ibid., 57–58.

33. Kemp, *H. G. Wells*, 5–6.

34. See ibid., 80.

35. Ibid., 88.

36. Ibid.

Chapter Seven

1. Virginia Woolf, "Mr. Bennett and Mrs. Brown," in *Reading I've Liked*, ed. Clifton Fadiman (New York, 1941), 361–79. Mrs. Woolf's essay was originally presented as a lecture to the Heretics Club at Cambridge (18 May 1924).

2. Stanley Kauffmann, "Wells and the New Generation: The Decline of a

Leader of Youth," *College English* 1 (April 1940):574.

3. See Leon Edel and Gordon N. Ray, eds., *Henry James and H. G. Wells* (Champaign, 1958), 67.

4. Ibid., 16.

5. Ibid., 27.

6. Michael Swan, "Henry James and H. G. Wells: A Study of Their Friendship Based on Their Unpublished Correspondence," *Cornhill* 997 (Autumn 1953):43.

7. Edel and Ray, eds., *Henry James, 105*.

8. Ibid., 123.

9. Ibid., 128.

10. Ibid., 168.

11. Ibid., 27.

12. Wells provides a perceptive account of popular taste in the Edwardian days in a preface to an omnibus volume, *Stories of Men and Women in Love* (London, 1933), which contains *Love and Mr. Lewisham, Secret Places of the Heart, The Passionate Friends,* and *The Wife of Sir Isaac Harman.*

13. Edel and Ray, eds., *Henry James, 32.*

14. Henry James, "The New Novel," in *Notes on Novelists, with Some Other Notes* (New York, 1914), 319.

15. Ibid., 334.

16. Edel and Ray, eds., *Henry James, 266.*

17. Ibid., 267.

18. Ibid., 267, n.

19. See Robert E. Scholes and Eric S. Rabkin, *Science Fiction: History, Science, Vision* (New York, 1977), 23.

20. Dark, *Outline of Wells, 98.*

21. Henry James, *The Art of the Novel: Critical Prefaces,* ed. R. P. Blackmur (New York, 1962), 321.

22. For a concise explanation of Henry James's use of *ficelle,* see Wayne Booth, *The Rhetoric of Fiction* (Chicago, 1961), 115.

23. Ian Watt, "The First Paragraph of *The Ambassadors:* An Explication," in *Rhetorical Analyses of Literary Works,* ed. Edward P. J. Corbett (New York, 1969), 192.

24. Raknem, *H. G. Wells, 136.*

25. Brome, *H. G. Wells, 232–33.*

26. Wells's letter to Swinnerton, 24 August 1932; in the Wells Archive. It was part of a criticism of Swinnerton's novel, *The Georgian House* (1932).

27. John Milton, *Complete Poems and Major Prose,* ed. Merritt Y. Hughes (New York, 1957), 315 (*Paradise Lost,* book 5, lines 564–74).

28. Ibid., lines 574–76.

29. See *Babes in the Darkling Wood* (New York, 1940), xii; hereafter cited in the text as *B.*

Chapter Eight

1. Haynes, *H. G. Wells,* 251.
2. Ibid., 39.
3. Ibid., 209.
4. Ibid., 210.
5. Ibid., 212.
6. Ibid.
7. See Costa, *Edmund Wilson,* 43.
8. Quoted in Haynes, *H. G. Wells,* 248.
9. Ibid.
10. Huntington, *The Logic of Fantasy,* 2.
11. Ibid.
12. Pritchett, *Living Novel,* 122.
13. Huntington, *Logic of Fantasy,* ix–x.
14. Quoted in ibid., 3.

Chapter Nine

1. Martin, "Shaw and Wells," 91, 96.
2. This is not to suggest that either Orwell, Huxley, or Zamyatin merits the distinction. *Brave New World* (1932) certainly was an effective rebuttal to Wells's *Men Like Gods* (1923) and a work that is imprinted in the popular mind as the first book which looked at the future of civilization darkly. However, as George Orwell has pointed out, Huxley owes a great deal to Wells's *The Sleeper Awakes.* He also finds *Brave New World* derives partly from a book by Zamyatin, which he (Orwell) read in a French translation, *Nous Autres.* Writing in 1946, Orwell noted that both the Huxley novel and the one written in 1923 by Zamyatin deal with the rebellion of the primitive human spirit against a rationalized, mechanized, painless world and both are supposed to take place six hundred years hence. Orwell's tribute to Zamyatin and his dystopian work—English title, *We*— is well worth reading (Orwell, "Freedom and Happiness," *London Tribune,* 4 January 1946, 15). Orwell's own *Nineteen Eighty-Four* also bears the unmistakable influence of *We.* Mark Hillegas is illuminating on Zamyatin's debt to Wells, generally, and to *The Sleeper Awakes,* particularly (see *The Future as Nightmare,* esp. 99–109). The Russian expressed admiration for Wells in a little-known book, *Herbert Wells* (1922), which was a by-product of his editorial supervision of a series of Wells translations in the Soviet Union between 1918 and 1926.
3. Anthony West, "H. G. Wells," *Encounter* 8 (1957):55.
4. See Sylvia Bowman et al., *Edward Bellamy Abroad* (New York, 1962), 116.
5. George Orwell, "The True Pattern of H. G. Wells," *Manchester Evening News,* 14 August 1946, 10.
6. See *Writers at Work: "Paris Review" Interviews,* 2d ser. (New York, 1963), 198.

7. E. F. Bleiler, Introduction to *Three Science-Fiction Novels of H. G. Wells* (New York, 1960), ix–x.

8. George Bernard Shaw, *Man and Superman* (New York, 1962), 564–65.

9. Frank Swinnerton, *Swinnerton: An Autobiography* (London, 1937), 198.

10. See J. G. Riewald, ed., *Max in Verse* (Brattleboro, Vt., 1963), 54.

11. W. Somerset Maugham, *The Vagrant Mood* (New York, 1953), 225.

12. Maurois, *Prophets and Poets,* 92.

13. See Haynes, *H. G. Wells,* 42.

14. Antonina Vallentin, *H. G. Wells: Prophet of Our Day* (New York, 1950), 236.

15. Wagar, *H. G. Wells,* 252.

16. *Men Like Gods* (New York, 1923), 323; hereafter cited in the text as *M.*

17. West, "H. G. Wells," 73.

18. *World Brain* (Garden City, 1938), 134.

19. Carl Becker, "Mr. Wells and the New History," in *Everyman His Own Historian* (New York, 1930), 190.

20. *The World of William Clissold* (New York, 1926), 1:80–81; hereafter cited in the text as *C.*

21. Becker, "Mr. Wells," 171.

22. Wagar, *H. G. Wells,* 146.

23. Quoted in ibid., 146.

24. Wagar, *H. G. Wells,* 147.

25. *The Outline of History,* 3 vols. (New York, 1940), 3:1195–97.

26. Maugham, *The Vagrant Mood,* 223. Maugham himself repeated this story when I interviewed him at his villa at St. Jean-Cap Ferrat, France, on 9 September 1959, when he was eighty-five. See Costa, *Nimrod,* Fall–Winter 1976, 117.

27. Arthur Salter, "H. G. Wells, Apostle of a World Society," in *Personality in Politics* (London, 1947), 124.

28. Colin Wilson, *The Strength to Dream* (Boston, 1962), 107.

29. D. H. Lawrence, *Phoenix: The Posthumous Papers of D. H. Lawrence,* ed. Edward D. McDonald (New York, 1936), 349–50.

30. See Shaw, "The Man I Knew," 115.

31. *Apropos of Dolores* (New York, 1938), 1.

32. *Brynhild* (New York, 1937), 1–2.

33. *The Anatomy of Frustration* (New York, 1936), 50.

34. Ibid., 51.

35. West, "H. G. Wells," 53.

36. His chiding of Julian Huxley is in a letter of 3 October 1928; in the Wells Archive.

37. Vallentin, *H. G. Wells,* 308.

38. Anecdote related by novelist Elizabeth Bowen at a lecture at the Art Alliance in Philadelphia, Pennsylvania, 10 November 1958.

39. Colin Wilson, *The Outsider* (Boston, 1956), 18.

40. *Mind at the End of Its Tether* (New York, 1945), 17.
41. Ibid., 2.

Chapter Ten

1. The inference can be drawn from George Orwell's obituary tribute, "The True Pattern." The explicit statement is Odette Keun's "H. G. Wells—The Player."
2. Jessie Chambers, *D. H. Lawrence: A Personal Record* (New York, 1935), 121.
3. Rebecca West, review in *New Republic,* 20 November 1915, 4.
4. E. M. Forster, review in *Athenaeum,* July–November 1920; reprinted in *Critical Heritage,* ed. Parrinder, 254.
5. Forster, *Aspects of the Novel,* 111.
6. T. S. Eliot "Wells as Journalist," in *H. G. Wells,* ed. Parrinder, 320.
7. Ibid., 321.
8. Parrinder, ed., *H. G. Wells,* 24.
9. Quoted in John Batchelor, *The Edwardian Novelists* (New York, 1982), 1.
10. Ibid., 233.
11. Quoted in ibid., 101.
12. Quoted in *H. G. Wells,* ed. Parrinder, 150.
13. Quoted in ibid., 146.
14. Quoted in ibid., 156.
15. Mark Schorer, "Technique as Discovery," in *A Grammar of Literary Criticism,* ed. Lawrence Sargent Hall (New York, 1965), 374–87; first published in the maiden issue of the *Hudson Review,* Spring 1948.
16. Ibid., 375.
17. Ibid., 380.
18. Kenneth B. Newell, "The Structure of H. G. Wells's *Tono-Bungay,*" *English Fiction in Transition* 4, no. 2 (1961):2.
19. Arnold Kettle, *An Introduction to the English Novel,* vol. 2 (London, 1953), 82.
20. Lodge, *"Tono-Bungay,"* 216.
21. Ibid., 215.
22. Bernard Bergonzi, Introduction to *Tono-Bungay* (Boston, 1966), xxvii.
23. Geoffrey Galt Harpham, "Minority Report: *Tono-Bungay* and the Shape of Wells's Career," *Modern Language Quarterly* 39, no. 1 (March 1978), 57.
24. Lucille Herbert, *"Tono-Bungay:* Tradition and Experiment," in *H. G. Wells: A Collection of Critical Essays,* ed. Bernard Bergonzi (Englewood Cliffs, N.J., 1976), 142; my italics.
25. Hillegas, *The Future as Nightmare,* 6.
26. Martin Green, *Science and the Shabby Curate of Poetry* (New York, 1965), 4.

27. Frederick J. Hoffman, *The Twenties* (New York, 1948), 345.

28. See West, in Bergonzi, ed., *H. G. Wells,* 10.

29. Golding draws his epigraph from the following characterization by Wells of Neanderthal Man: "Its thick skull imprisoned its brain, and to the end it was low-browed and brutish" (*Outline of History,* 1:81).

30. Robert D. Evans, "The Inheritors: Some Inversions," in *William Golding: Some Critical Considerations,* ed. Jack I. Biles and Robert O. Evans (New York, 1970), 105.

31. William Golding, "The Meaning of It All," *Books and Bookmen* 5 (October 1959): 9–10.

32. Mark Kinkead-Weekes and Ian Gregor, *William Golding: A Critical Study* (New York, 1967), 71.

33. Ibid., 73.

34. Carlson Yost, "William Golding and *The Inheritors,*" in "The Researched Novel: Definition, Explication of Five Examples, and Theoretical Discussion of Research in Fiction" (Ph.D. diss., Texas A&M University, 1982), 145–46.

35. Huntington, *Logic of Fantasy,* 5.

36. Quoted in *H. G. Wells,* ed. Parrinder, 28.

37. "Jorge Luis Borges on the First Wells," in ibid., 332.

38. Vernier, "Evolution as a Literary Theme," 85–86.

39. Darko Suvin, Introduction to *H. G. Wells and Modern Science Fiction,* 29.

40. Ibid., 23.

41. Ibid., 16–17.

42. Ibid., 28.

43. Patrick Parrinder, *Science Fiction: Its Criticism and Teaching* (London, 1980), 94.

44. Robert M. Philmus, "The Logic of 'Prophecy' in *The Time Machine,*" in *H. G. Wells,* ed. Bergonzi, 67.

45. "Borges and Wells and the Labyrinths of Time," in *H. G. Wells,* ed. Suvin and Philmus, 167.

46. Huntington, *Logic of Fantasy,* 53.

47. Ibid.

48. Ibid.

Chapter Eleven

1. Hammond, ed., *H. G. Wells,* 117–19.

2. George Bowling is the protagonist of *Coming Up for Air* (1939).

Selected Bibliography

PRIMARY SOURCES

The most important collection of Wells papers is now the Wells Archive at the University of Illinois, Urbana. For the purposes of this critical study the materials, while not nearly so valuable as Wells's published writings, often yielded a strikingly valuable letter, or a press clipping, or an entry from an appointment book to buttress an insight. The Archive contains several thousand letters whose range of correspondents is perhaps more impressive than the letters themselves. On vital points the letters contain little that Wells did not say in print.

The following bibliography lists chronologically only the major publications, and only the fiction titles are complete. For a listing of Wells's complete writings, see J. R. Hammond's *Herbert George Wells: An Annotated Bibliography of His Works* (New York: Garland, 1977). The first comprehensive bibliography, *A Bibliography of the Works of H. G. Wells, 1893–1925*, by Geoffrey H. Wells (London, 1925), appeared in 1968 under the imprint of Burt Franklin, New York. The H. G. Wells Society attempted to update G. H. Wells's compilation with *H. G. Wells: A Comprehensive Bibliography* (foreword by Kingsley Martin), with editions in 1966, 1968, and 1972. The most important collected edition of Wells's writings is *The Works of H. G. Wells*, Atlantic Edition (28 vols. [London: Unwin; New York: Scribner's, 1924–27]), prepared by Wells himself. For students of Wells the principal service of the Atlantic edition is the preface Wells wrote for each volume. In 1968–69 Heron Books issued a uniform edition in 24 volumes. Included are two novels, *The World of William Clissold* (1926) and *Brynhild* (1937), not part of the Atlantic edition. *The War of the Worlds* (vol. 1) contains a general introduction by Frank Wells. *Seven Famous Novels by H. G. Wells* (New York: Knopf, 1934), with a revealing preface by Wells, and *The Famous Short Stories of H.G. Wells* (Garden City; Doubleday, 1938) are easily the best among numerous omnibus science-fiction and short-story compilations. Both are used for text references in this book.

The Time Machine. New York: Holt & Company, 1895.

The Stolen Bacillus and Other Incidents. London: Macmillan, 1895.

The Wonderful Visit. New York: Macmillan, 1895.

The Island of Dr. Moreau. New York: Stone & Kimball, 1896.

The Wheels of Chance. New York: Macmillan, 1896.

The Plattner Story and Others. London: Macmillan, 1897.

The Invisible Man. New York: Harper, 1897.

Thirty Strange Stories. New York: Harper, 1897.

The War of the Worlds. London: Heinemann, 1898.

When the Sleeper Wakes. London, Nelson 1899. Republished, 1910 and 1911, by
   Nelson, in a revised and altered edition, entitled *The Sleeper Awakes.*

Tales of Space and Time. New York: Doubleday & McClure, 1899.

Love and Mr. Lewisham. London: Harper, 1900.

*Anticipations of the Reaction of Mechanical and Scientific Progress Upon Human Life and
   Thought. London: Chapman & Hall, 1901.*

The First Men in the Moon. Indianapolis: Bowen-Merrill, 1901.

The Sea Lady. New York: D. Appleton & Company, 1902.

Mankind in the Making. London: Chapman & Hall, 1903.

Twelve Stories and a Dream. London: Macmillan, 1903.

The Food of the Gods. New York: Scribner's, 1904.

A Modern Utopia. New York: Scribner's, 1905.

Kipps. New York: Scribner's, 1905.

In the Days of the Comet. New York: The Century Company, 1906.

First and Last Things. London: Constable, 1908.

New Worlds for Old. New York, Macmillan, 1908.

The War in the Air. New York: Macmillan, 1908.

Tono-Bungay. New York: Duffield, 1909.

Ann Veronica. New York: Harper, 1909.

The History of Mr. Polly. New York: Duffield, 1910.

The New Machiavelli. New York: Duffield, 1910.

The Country of the Blind and Other Stories. London: Nelson, 1911.

The Door in the Wall and Other Stories. New York: Mitchell Kennerley, 1911.

Marriage. New York: Duffield, 1912.

The Passionate Friends. New York: Harper, 1913.

The World Set Free. New York: Dutton, 1914.

The War That Will End War. New York: Duffield, 1914.

The Wife of Sir Isaac Harman. New York: Macmillan, 1914.

Bealby. New York: Macmillan, 1915.

Boon. New York: Doran, 1915.

The Research Magnificent. New York: Macmillan, 1915.

Mr. Britling Sees It Through. New York: Macmillan, 1916.

God the Invisible King. New York: Macmillan, 1917.

The Soul of a Bishop. New York: Macmillan, 1917.

Joan and Peter. New York: Macmillan, 1918.

The Undying Fire. New York: Macmillan, 1919.

The Outline of History. New York: Macmillan, 1920.

Russia in the Shadows. New York: Doran, 1931.

The Salvaging of Civilization. New York: Macmillan, 1921.

The Secret Places of the Heart. New York: Macmillan, 1922.

Men Like Gods. New York: Macmillan, 1923.

The Story of a Great Schoolmaster. New York: Macmillan, 1924.

The Dream. New York: Macmillan, 1924.

Christina Alberta's Father. New York: Macmillan, 1925.

The World of William Clissold. New York: Doran, 1926.

Meanwhile. New York: Doran, 1927.

Mr. Blettsworthy on Rampole Island. New York: Doran, 1928.

The Open Conspiracy: Blue Prints for a World Revolution. New York: Doubleday, Doran, 1928.

The Autocracy of Mr. Parham. New York: Doran, 1930.

The Science of Life (with Julian Huxley and G. P. Wells). New York: Doubleday, Doran, 1931.

The Work, Wealth and Happiness of Mankind. New York: Doubleday, Doran, 1932.

The Shape of Things to Come. New York: Macmillan, 1933.

The Bulpington of Blup. New York: Macmillan, 1933.

Experiment in Autobiography: Discoveries and Conclusions of a Very Ordinary Brain (Since 1866). New York: Macmillan, 1934.

The Anatomy of Frustration. New York: Macmillan, 1936.

The Croquet Player. New York: Macmillan, 1937.

Brynhild. New York: Scribner's, 1937.

Apropos of Dolores. New York: Scribner's, 1938.

World Brain. New York: Doubleday, Doran, 1938.

The Brothers. New York: Viking, 1938.

The Holy Terror. New York: Simon & Schuster, 1939.

The Fate of Man. New York: Alliance, 1939.

Babes in the Darkling Wood. New York: Alliance, 1940.

All Aboard for Ararat. New York: Alliance, 1941.

You Can't Be Too Careful. New York: Alliance, 1942.

Crux Ansata. New York: Penguin, 1943.

'42 to '44. New York: Alliance, 1944.

Mind at the End of Its Tether and *The Happy Turning*. New York: Didier, 1946.

The Wealth of Mr. Waddy. Carbondale: University of Southern Illinois Press, 1969.

SECONDARY SOURCES

1. Biographies and Bibliographical Materials

Brome, Vincent. *H. G. Wells.* London: Longmans, Green and Co., 1951. A highly readable, nonscholarly work whose final chapter is a brilliant exposition of the schizoid tendencies in Wells. The book, however, is too full of evasions and palpable reconstructions of the truth for the air of authenticity necessary to the authoritative biography.

Dickson, Lovat. *H. G. Wells: His Turbulent Life and Times.* New York: Atheneum, 1969. This was the first full-dress biography in nearly twenty years and would be preempted by that of the MacKenzies four years later (see next entry). Dickson's discussions of the unread novels of Wells's middle period are the best things in the book. Dickson, once an editor and director of Macmillan, knew his subject as a client in the 1930s. He finds that Wells failed as man and artist because he lacked moral values.

MacKenzie, Norman, and **MacKenzie, Jeanne.** *H. G. Wells: A Biography.* New York: Simon and Schuster, 1973. A massive (nearly 500 pages) and cooltoned biography, the first to catalog Wells's amours and to name names. What the MacKenzies know of Wells's rampant sexuality becomes grist for the larger story they would tell of Wells's destructive disposition always to excuse individual disorder where exceptional brains or fine spirits were involved.

Ray, Gordon N. *H. G. Wells and Rebecca West.* New Haven: Yale University Press, 1974. Ray has built his narrative largely around more than 800 letters that Wells wrote to Rebecca West. Only five of her letters to Wells during the ten years they were together survive. The reader feels this imbalance, and Gordon Ray expresses honestly the resultant difficulties. The presence of Dame Rebecca looking over Ray's shoulder as he wrote is pervasive.

West, Anthony. *H. G. Wells: Aspects of a Life.* New York: Random House, 1984. Balanced judgments and fairness of comment are usually considered necessary staples of the literary biography. This one draws a kind of venomous strength from its bias. Anthony West has set out to even the score against everyone he deems to have done his father wrong. It is to biographer West's credit that none of critic West's earlier crusade for a reassessment of Wells as literary figure is repeated in this book. But it is instead a devastating pillorying of his mother Rebecca West as woman, mother, writer. This is a stunning yet troubling book that brings to biography the involvement that is missing in those tomes that reproduce in a thousand pages every day of their subjects' lives. A tribute to the man who formed him in love as well as agony.

West, Geoffrey. [Geoffrey H. Wells]. *H. G. Wells: A Sketch for a Portrait.* New York: W. W. Norton & Co., 1930. The author, who knew Wells during his heyday, gives a glowing yet fair estimate of Wells as a creative artist. Its early publication was saved the fading promises of Wells's last two decades.

Hammond, J. R. *Herbert George Wells: An Annotated Bibliography of His Works.* New York: Garland, 1977. Most complete listing of Wells's writings to date.

Scheick, William J. ed. *H. G. Wells: An Annotated Bibliography of Writings about Him.* DeKalb: Northern Illinois University Press, in press. Will be an important tool for scholars.

Wells, Geoffrey H. *The Works of H. G. Wells 1887–1925: A Bibliography, Dictionary and Subject-Index.* London: Routledge & Sons, 1926. Exhaustive, useful. Necessarily incomplete, it is encyclopedic in scope. Indispensable for scholars.

2. Books and Parts of Books

Amis, Kingsley. *New Maps of Hell: A Survey of Science Fiction.* New York: Harcourt Brace & Co., 1960. Notable for its forecast that "Wells will soon get all, instead of part, of the recognition as pioneer of SF he clearly deserves."

Ash, Brian. *Who's Who in H. G. Wells.* London: Hamish Hamilton, 1979. Just what its title indicates—and indispensable.

Batchelor, John. *The Edwardian Novelists.* New York: St. Martin's Press, 1982. Includes Wells among six writers discussed. The others are Conrad, Bennett, Galsworthy, Ford, and Forster.

Bates, H. E. *The Modern Short Story.* Boston: The Writer, Inc., 1941. Accords high rank to Wells in the genre; rebuts charges that Wells's style lacks beauty.

Becker, Carl L. *Everyman His Own Historian.* New York: F. S. Crofts & Co., 1935. "Mr. Wells and the New History" (169–90) critiques Wells as historian and thinker.

Belgion, Montgomery. *H. G. Wells.* London: Longmans, Green & Co., 1953. Brief, fair assessment. That Wells's major characters were all alter egos is seen as main flaw.

Bellamy, William. *The Novels of Wells, Bennett and Galsworthy: 1890–1910.* London: Routledge & Kegan Paul, 1971. Although somewhat too heavily influenced by Philip Rieff, Bellamy sees the Edwardian years as involved in postcultural crisis and their leading novelists, especially Wells, as reflecting that crisis.

Bergonzi, Bernard. *The Early H. G. Wells: A Study of the Scientific Romances.* Toronto: University of Toronto Press, 1961. Perhaps the definitive study of Wells as mythmaker and fin-de-siècle figure.

———, ed. *H. G. Wells: A Collection of Critical Essays.* Englewood Cliffs, N.J.:

Prentice Hall, 1976. Inclusion of Wells, at last, in this prestigious series is a sign of positive reassessment. All previously published.

Bloom, Robert. *Anatomies of Egotism: A Reading of the Last Novels of H. G. Wells.* Lincoln: University of Nebraska Press, 1974. An admirable attempt to demonstrate that Wells remained a remarkable novelist to the end.

Borges, Jorge L. "The First Wells." In *Other Inquisitions, 1937–52.* Austin: University of Texas Press, 1964. This short essay (86–89) lauds Wells's tales as "symbolic of processes somehow inherent in all human destinies."

Brooks, Van Wyck. *The World of H. G. Wells.* New York: Mitchell Kennerley, 1915. Earliest book-length critical study.

Caudwell, Christopher. *Studies in a Dying Culture.* London: Bodley Head, 1938. "H. G. Wells: A Study in Utopianism" (73–95) is an effective Marxist polemic.

Costa, Richard Hauer. *Edmund Wilson: Our Neighbor from Talcottville.* Syracuse, N.Y.: Syracuse University Press, 1980. Contains assessments of Wells's influence unpublished elsewhere.

Delbanco,Nicholas. *Group Portrait: Joseph Conrad, Stephen Crane, Ford Madox Ford, Henry James and H. G. Wells.* New York: Morrow, 1982. James's condescension of Wells and latter's *Boon*-ish reply are among intrigues told in this lively book.

Forster, E. M. *Aspects of the Novel.* New York: Harcourt, Brace & Co., 1927. Notable for its sympathy for Wells in his dispute with James.

Frierson, William C. *The English Novel in Transition.* Norman: University of Oklahoma Press, 1942. An attempt to place Wells in the *Bildungsroman* mainstream.

Hammond, J. R. *An H. G. Wells Companion: A Guide to the Novels, Romances and Short Stories.* London, Macmillan, 1979. A potpourri of Wellsiana.

———, ed. *H. G. Wells: Interviews and Recollections.* London: Macmillan, 1980. Mostly memoirs and all of them well worth reading.

Haynes, Roslynn D. *H. G. Wells: Discoverer of the Future.* London: Macmillan, 1980. Most thorough analysis we have of the influence of science, not only on the romances and utopias but on his style and methods of characterization.

Hillegas, Mark R. *The Future as Nightmare: H. G. Wells and the Anti-Utopians.* New York: Oxford University Press, 1967. For Hillegas none of the major anti-utopians—not Huxley, not Orwell, not Zamyatin—could jump over the long shadow of Wells. An essential book.

Huntington, John. *The Logic of Fantasy: H. G. Wells and Science Fiction.* New York: Columbia University Press, 1982. A substantive and sympathetic theoretical study in which Huntington sees Wells's writings following twin compulsions: nondirectedness and directedness.

Hynes, Samuel. *The Edwardian Turn of Mind.* Princeton: Princeton University Press, 1968. Hynes traces skillfully and concisely, the main currents of Edwardian thought, and locates Wells—among many figures—within those currents.

James, Henry. *Notes on Novelists.* New York: Scribner's, 1914. Contains an essay, "The New Novel, 1914" (314–61) which led to Wells's parody of James in *Boon.*

Kemp, Peter. *H. G. Wells and the Culminating Ape.* New York: St. Martin's Press, 1982. An uneven book, seemingly written from file-cards, with Kemp, who is an alert critic, crowding excerpts from every book Wells wrote under five arbitrary headings.

Lodge, David. *The Language of Fiction: Essays in Criticism and Verbal Analysis of the English Novel.* New York: Columbia University Press, 1966. Contains Lodge's "*Tono-Bungay* and the Condition of England," perhaps *the* seminal essay in the rescue of Wells's best novel into thematic—even poetic— respectability.

McConnell, Frank. *The Science Fiction of H G. Wells.* New York: Oxford University Press, 1979. Introduction to Wells's science fiction by a scholar who writes extremely well.

Maugham, W. Somerset. "Some Novelists I Have Known." In *The Vagrant Mood.* New York: Doubleday, 1953. An affectionate, enlightening memoir of the aging, disappointed Wells.

Maurois, André. *Prophets and Poets.* New York: Harper, 1935. Wells's mistake, Maurois says, was to discount human frailty.

Mencken, H. L. *Prejudices. First Series.* New York: Knopf, 1919. In "The Late Mr. Wells" (22–35) a former admirer decries Wells's messianic complex.

Nicholson, Norman. *H. G. Wells.* Denver: Alan Swallow, 1950. In less than one hundred pages, the author reveals in measured, never-hysterical tones how rich a literary vein Wells mined during his best period.

Orwell, George. *Collected Essays.* London: Secker & Warburg, 1946. "Wells, Hitler and the World State" (160–66) infuriated Wells ("Read my early work, you ———!"). Whether he was right that Wells had misread the dangers of totalitarianism is less important than that Orwell was the ally Wells could least afford to lose.

———. *The Road to Wigan Pier.* London: Secker & Warburg, 1937. This compassionate book contains an early recognition of *When the Sleeper Wakes* and an excoriation of Wells's worship of the Machine.

Parrinder, Patrick. *H. G. Wells.* Edinburgh: Oliver & Boyd, 1970. An informed and articulate study of Wells as novelist.

———, ed. *H. G. Wells: The Critical Heritage.* London: Routledge & Kegan Paul, 1972. Useful collection of reviews and responses by contemporaries.

———. *Science Fiction: Its Criticism and Teaching.* London: Methuen, 1980. Good introduction to SF and to Wells's importance to the popular genre.

———, and Philmus, Robert M., eds. *H. G. Wells's Literary Criticism.* Sussex, England: Harvester Press, 1980. A good antidote to anyone who relegates Wells to philistinism.

Philmus, **Robert M.** *Into the Unknown: The Evolution of Science Fiction from Francis Godwin to H. G. Wells.* Berkeley: University of California, 1970. Philmus, an indefatigable researcher, traces the process by which science fiction emerged from nineteenth-century romantic traditions. Provides setting in time and ideas for Wells.

————, and **Hughes, David Y.** *H. G. Wells: Early Writings in Science and Science Fiction.* Berkeley: University of California, 1975. A number of Wells's very early papers, scientific sketches, and fantasies are collected. Useful for the light these occasional papers cast on the extrapolative mind of Wells.

Pritchett, V. S. *The Living Novel.* New York: Reynal & Hitchcock, 1947. Contains an early essay which, if not the most scholarly, is the most passionate and readable of a growing shelf of criticism which displays the scientific romances as proof of the anarchy at the heart of Wells.

Reed, John R. *The Natural History of H. G. Wells,* Athens, Ohio: Ohio University Press, 1982. Reed pushes effectively Wells's notion that human life inevitably becomes the assertion of human will against chaos; that his own life exemplified this Huxleyan imperative; and that his novels are the recorded assertions of that doctrine.

Salter, Sir Arthur. "H. G. Wells, Apostle of a World Society." In *Personality in Politics.* London: Faber & Faber, 1947. Sympathetic and discriminating critique by a man who knew Wells. This essay bears out the spirit of the *New York Times*'s obituary leader which called him "the greatest public teacher of our times."

Schorer, Mark. "Technique as Discovery." In *Forms of Modern Fiction,* edited by William Van O'Connor, 9–29. Minneapolis: University of Minnesota, 1948. This famous essay holds up Wells's best novel, *Tono-Bungay,* to an arbitrary standard for excellence and finds it deficient.

Wagar, W. Warren. *H. G. Wells and the World State.* New Haven: Yale University, 1961. The best book yet written on the ideas and influence of Wells. Wagar examines all the charges brought against Wells and still concludes that there will always remain indelible traces of Wells.

————, ed. *H. G. Wells: Journalism & Prophecy 1893–1946.* Boston: Houghton, Mifflin, 1965. Wagar's continuing effort to salvage Wells's dying reputation in the sixties was little served by this exhaustive compilation of lesser works. Commentaries are invariably excellent.

West, Anthony. *Principles and Persuasions.* New York: Harcourt Brace & Co., 1957. Contains an essay, as touching as it is revealing, on West's father. He concludes that pessimism, not optimism, was the true grain of Wells's thought. Began one line of rebuttal against the detractors.

Wilson, Colin. *The Strength to Dream: Literature and the Imagination.* Boston: Houghton Mifflin, 1962. Useful for its unorthodox view of Wells as a victim of the denial of the existential aspects in men.

Woolf, Virginia. "Mr. Bennett and Mrs. Brown." In *Reading I've Liked,* edited by Clifton Fadiman. New York: Simon & Schuster, 1941. This famous essay, on its surface almost diffident, ranks with the most effective demolishments of the kind of novel written by Wells, Bennett and Galsworthy.

3. Letters

Edel, Leon, and **Gordon N. Ray,** eds. *Henry James and H. G. Wells.* Champaign: University of Illinois Press, 1958.

Gettmann, Royal A., ed. *George Gissing and H. G. Wells.* Champaign: University of Illinois Press, 1961.

Wilson, Harris, ed. *Arnold Bennett and H. G. Wells.* Champaign: University of Illinois Press, 1960.

Index